Narratives in the Making

NARRATIVES IN THE MAKING

*Writing the East German Past
in the Democratic Present*

Anselma Gallinat

berghahn
NEW YORK · OXFORD
www.berghahnbooks.com

First published in 2017 by
Berghahn Books
www.berghahnbooks.com

©2017, 2021 Anselma Gallinat
First paperback edition published in 2021

Library of Congress Cataloging-in-Publication Data

Names: Gallinat, Anselma, author.
Title: Narratives in the making : writing the East German past in the Democratic
   present / Anselma Gallinat.
Description: First edition. | New York : Berghahn Books, [2017] | Includes biblio-
   graphical references and index.
Identifiers: LCCN 2016024744| ISBN 9781785333026 (hardback : alk. paper) | ISBN
   9781785333033 (ebook)
Subjects: LCSH: Germany (East)--Historiography--Social aspects. | Anthropology
   and history--Germany. | Collective memory--Germany.
Classification: LCC DD281.6 .G35 2017 | DDC 943/.1087--dc23
LC record available at hjps://lccn.loc.gov/2016024744

British Library Cataloguing in Publication Data

A catalogue record for this book is available from the British Library

ISBN 978-1-78533-302-6 (hardback)
ISBN 978-1-80073-008-3 (paperback)
ISBN 978-1-78533-303-3 (ebook)

CONTENTS

ILLUSTRATIONS

Acknowledgments

This book emerged out of three research projects in eastern Germany beginning with my PhD. I am grateful to Durham University for funding the PhD (1999–2002) and to the Economic and Social Research Council (ESRC) for funding the following postdoctoral project and the First Grant project "the social construction of the socialist past" (2007–2009; RES0061-23-0035) on which this book is primarily based. I dearly thank Peter Collins for introducing me to narrative and to the work of Jerome Bruner, and for his supervisory and collegial support. The First Grant would not have come about without the considerable support lent by Peter Phillimore at Newcastle University, whose keen and critical eye also helped shaped most of the chapters in this book. I am grateful to Steph Lawler and Ruth Graham for their feedback and emotional support. Versions of chapters were presented at a number of conferences, meetings of the research network "After the Wall" (2009–2011) to which Anna Saunders and Debbie Pinfold kindly invited me, and the sociology seminar series at Newcastle in October 2014. I thank members of "After the Wall" and colleagues at Newcastle and beyond for their comments, observations, and questions. The research greatly depended on Sabine Kittel, who contributed her hard work, skills as an interviewer, and perspective. I am greatly indebted to her. I also remain indebted to members of the Victim Association in Tillberg who welcomed me back into their group, the Office for Political Education, and the *Daily Paper* for opening their doors to the project and to Sabine and I. I am also grateful to the former Stasi prison memorial museum, the inner German border memorial museum, the Stasi commissioner and the commissioners for Stasi files based in Mittelland, and all other members of the Working Group *Aufarbeitung*, as well as all their staff. Dr. Reinhold Gallinat, my father, carefully enquired and patiently listened to my many stories of successes and setbacks both during fieldwork and when writing, and I thank him also.

INTRODUCTION
Questions of Discourse, Narrative, and Memory
after Fundamental Regime Change

$\Rightarrow \bullet \Leftarrow$

Twenty-five Years On, Does the East German Past Still Matter?

It is the summer of 2013, four years since the research project on "the socialist past today," on which this book is based, finished. The project explored
how two different types of institutions, a group of policymakers/bureaucrats
and a daily newspaper, create representations of the East German[1] past
in the present. I have just returned to my desk at Newcastle University
after visiting my family in Germany. Questions of the East German past
and identity, unification,[2] and East–West German differences were on my
mind during the last week because I knew I would come back to write this
book. These topics usually present themselves swiftly and without much
invitation during fieldwork stints and visits home, but halfway through the
long weekend with my brothers and their partners, I had begun to wonder
whether they had now really moved into the background. Three days in
Berlin and there had been no mention of before and after, of East versus
West, or similar.

It did not take long, however, for these questions to reemerge. As soon
as we—my oldest brother, Clemens, his partner, and I—had set off for a
last bit of sightseeing in Berlin, the East Side Gallery, Steffi asked, "Is this
now East or West? I can't even tell anymore what used to be East or West."
My brother explained, but when the question returned as we parked at
Ostbahnhof (East station), his response got cheeky: "Well, look around:
there is a Lidl, a Mercedes retailer, a DIY store—that can only be the West."

Well, it was not and he knew it, and so did Steffi, judging by the grimace she made at him and the laughter that followed. This side used to be East Berlin, and some may say that this mixture of derelict buildings, deserted spaces, budget shops, and car retailers indicates exactly that—a poor East Germany infiltrated by the shine of Western capitalism, like a scene from *Good Bye, Lenin!* (Becker 2003).

Contentious Pasts in the Present

Later that day we were at my dad's, talking over coffee. My father had explained a certain complex situation to which Clemens remarked how no one would have made such a fuss in the past, "back then." My father agreed, leading Clemens to quip, "See, it wasn't all bad in the GDR." Dad retorted, "I didn't say that!"

There is more in this exchange than the brief sentences might suggest. "Back then" can refer to many different pasts, of long-gone childhoods, previous decades, or wholly different eras. Eastern Germans employ the phrase in the last sense to refer to a shared and fundamentally different past prior to unification that is almost like another world that cannot be returned to. This is certainly what Clemens had meant and what I believe our father agreed with, although with the hindsight of his longer life, he may include an appreciation of the GDR past as also characterized by certain decades and caught up in wider social and technological developments: you might not have had such a fuss in the 1970s more generally. Yet Clemens responded with a version of the popular statement "Not everything was bad (in the GDR)." This phrase, or rather trope, is commonly used in reevaluations of the GDR past that appeared to have been quickly deemed outmoded and just as quickly done away with during unification. For some, however, the phrase also speaks of a problematic attitude toward both the socialist past and unification—an attitude that hangs onto the past of a dictatorial regime that caused much suffering and an attitude that now creates obstacles for unification as it, in turn, rejects important aspects of the free and democratic present. I was surprised my brother had used that phrase in the parental home, even if in a version that suggested a certain caution.

As both our parents were trained pastors in the German Lutheran Church, themselves the offspring of families who had fled from East Prussia (Ostpreussen) into heartland Germany at the end of World War II, our family belonged to a pocket of GDR society (see Thelen 2009). Our parents were critical of the East German state and its authoritative structures. Through the church we had regular contact with befriended families in West Germany, and our father traveled there relatively regularly. He brought back presents, sweets, and political magazines, the inevitable *Der Spiegel* hidden among theological literature.[3] Both our parents, as many eastern Germans, were conscious of the keen eyes of the State Security Police and experienced a number of state and Stasi interferences in their working and family lives.

Given this background, the fall of the Berlin Wall in 1989 and unification were embraced without question by our parents and both my then-adult brothers. The two brothers had grown up within the critical family discourse and made some of their own difficult experiences with socialist authoritarianism, while I, as the youngest daughter, who was to be protected from "too much knowledge," had happily joined the socialist children's organization, the pioneers (the Young Pioneers and later the Thälmann Pioneers), and taken up roles in the school class committee. The troubles many eastern Germans experienced with unification, the rapid changes, and East–West German cultural differences thus largely passed us by. Reevaluating the dictatorial socialist past in conversation is therefore, however, also very much out of the question, at least if our father has anything to do with it. And this marked his quick-fire response that day, "I didn't say that," as well as Clemens's fast retreat as he realized that even his amended version of the popular statement touched a sore spot; my father's quick response also wiped any agreeing grin off my face.

The above episodes reveal that talking about the GDR past is still very much an aspect of everyday life twenty-five years on, at least for eastern Germans. It does not come up every day, but certain situations, events, or problems lead to references to this shared past whether for orientation, jokingly, to reminisce, or to make a point. Inevitably, some of these references have become tropes that suggest very particular kinds of meanings in the present that now go beyond the then-lived reality. Shared as it may be, this past, its interpretation, and the way it is invoked in the present nevertheless differs between individuals even within eastern German society depending on how speakers position themselves toward this past and the present. All of this memory talk, whether it concerns former socialism and one's life directly or whether it concerns rhetorical invocations of the past to comment on situations in the present, is suffused with often political and just as often moral messages. As the above shows, evaluations of personal and collective life achievements "back then," for some a throwaway comment, can function for others as political statements contesting West German judgments of apparently inferior GDR culture, just as it can be seen as an inappropriate reevaluation of an inhumane regime. If this is the case, comments about aspects of GDR culture—the "it" in "it wasn't all bad" can concern anything from kindergartens to road traffic management, from financial benefits for mothers to a piece of fiction one once read—will also apply to individual lives.

Another day that week my father, a supporter of Angela Merkel's chancellorship, gave me his take on recent revelations. Although critical of aspects of her leadership style, he strongly disagreed with a recent attempt to disqualify Merkel on the basis of her East German background. It had emerged that she had carried office within the socialist Free German Youth (FDJ), which, some people argued, indicated that she was trying to set herself up for a political career in the GDR (Kleine 2013; Martin 2013). If this were true, it would cast doubt on her suitability to hold office with the conservative Christian Democratic Party (CDU) today, never mind leading the country. Father felt, however, that that was taking interpretation too far. The "FDJ wasn't that kind of organization," he said. He explained that if you lived in East Germany, you had to come to some kind of accommodation with the state. People had to decide for themselves where their line was in terms of compliance or involvement with the regime, since living in this country and completely withholding yourself from socialist structures was not possible; that got you arrested eventually, he finished. The problem is that the accommodations people made are not always acceptable to others.

What people did in GDR times, what professions they learned, and what roles they exercised continue to matter in post-unification Germany, not just in the political realm where opposing parties or unsympathetic media ask thorny questions about individual biographies but also in everyday interactions. During previous fieldwork with former political prisoners of the State Security Police, whenever a new person appeared in any conversation, the immediate question would be, "What did he used to do?" Individuals' work "back then" gives an indication of not only their closeness to the regime but also their level of political training, or "indoctrination." Some people thus become immediately doubtful and untrustworthy. "Victims" of the former regime are not the only people who engage in this kind of discourse: I had heard those kinds of questions and assumptions before, at home.

The fall of socialism and the "unification by accession" (Glaeser 2000) created a wholesale cultural change in eastern Germany that included the value system—an already ambiguous value system that had previously supported decision-making and life paths. While the demonstrations in the autumn of 1989, with their calls for democratization and freedom, were already defining the GDR leadership as controlling, if not outrightly "totalitarian," few East Germans who joined the thousands of people on the Monday demonstrations or who left the East for the West that summer, had imagined how far into their own biographies this *Wende* (the political "turnaround" from a "dictatorship" to a free democracy) would go on to reach.[4]

In Germany, in contrast to many other postsocialist states (cf. Adler 2012; Borneman 1997), the socialist past was very quickly approached by the new government, which, following the Federal German Republic's "antitotalitarian consensus," defined it as a difficult period in history that required reckoning. This consensus had developed in the aftermath of the Third Reich and the Holocaust and is intrinsically intertwined with a sense of safeguarding the freedom and democracy that Germany had only achieved relatively recently (see chapter 1). The discourse of the *Aufarbeitung der SED-Diktatur*, the "reworking of the SED (Socialist Unity Party) dictatorship," that was then initiated, which encouraged historical research, museumification, and commemoration, was soon challenged by popular nostalgia in the mid-1990s.[5] This *Ostalgie* (nostalgia for the East; a play on words) was prompted by senses of dislocation and loss caused by the fast-paced, wholesale change that followed unification. This nostalgia was moreover bound up with an assertive East German identity that challenged the new all-German narrative that was so clearly a West German one (Berdahl 1999a; Cooke 2005). While often seen as an inevitable aspect of the experience of historical rupture (Berdahl 1999a; T. Richardson 2008: 137), for people who had been victimized during GDR times and for policymakers invested in *Aufarbeitung* and the unification process, *Ostalgie* spelled trouble. It was soon judged to be an unreflective reevaluation of the dictatorship ("it wasn't all bad") put forward by people who were possibly still hanging onto the same socialist ideas that state control and surveillance had been founded on.[6] The East German identity with which *Ostalgie* came to be bound up was seen as creating obstacles for unification as an "inner process," thus reestablishing the wall, now in people's minds (e.g., Veen 2001).

Many years have passed since the mid-1990s, and social memory in eastern Germany continues to change. *Ostalgie* no longer has the character of the collective and public performances that Daphne Berdahl observed (1999a) and I experienced (Gallinat 2010a) in the 1990s. At the grassroots, in personal conversation, references to the past have also lost some of their contentiousness, and eastern German identity is no longer so defensively assertive but rather based on more muted senses of local belonging (Gallinat 2008). Even our father has recently used the tricky phrase "it wasn't all bad," albeit speaking very quietly. Nevertheless, the memory discourses that developed in the early years after socialism's fall gave rise to tropes and master narratives that continue to circulate in German society. The political contestations and moral positionings they are bound up with still give certain metaphors political force, moral currency, and emotive power.

Few eastern Germans like to see themselves as "ostalgic," given the contentiousness of the term, yet few can see themselves as having lived in a dictatorship either, given the term's associations with the Third Reich and the image it casts of a society of victims and perpetrators.

Most people's experiences and memories move between these opposing poles. Many experienced the state's harsh hand—the limitations placed on choices and freedoms—at one point or another in their lives, and almost everyone struggled with the "shortage economy" (Kornai 1980; Verdery 1996).[7] There are thus widely shared understandings of the socialist regime's shortcomings. At the same time, people also remember successes in their professional and private lives that "happened to take place" during or were achieved despite socialism (Gallinat and Kittel 2009). Moreover, socialist ideology purported ideals of equality and peace, the value of which increased (Straughn 2009) with the experience of growing inequalities in the transition to a free market economy. Just as a collective East German identity pushed to the fore after the East German state's dissolution, so did reflections on the value and meaning of some of socialist ideology's key ideas. The narrative frameworks that emerged out of the interaction between the discourses of "reworking" and East German identity ask questions of individual lives in the past, their position in German society today, and their views of the future that continue to emerge in social interactions. Similar questions are asked in turn of stories created for wider public consumption as they go on to provide pointers for individual memory narratives and to govern the interpretation of such narratives.

An Ethnography of Postsocialism

At its heart this book is an ethnography about the production of versions of the socialist past in the democratic, postsocialist present against the backdrop of imagined national futures. Katherine Verdery argues that in the field of postsocialist studies, historical anthropology may well be privileged (Hann et al. 2002). When considering the question of whether the notion of postsocialism still makes sense, some ten years after socialism's fall, Berdahl pins her response almost exclusively on the question of memory, arguing that the category remains useful "as long as the socialist past remains a prime reference point for many people in their own personal histories and memories as they struggle to make sense of the present" (2010b: 131). Questions of memory are of particular import in the postsocialist realm because history writing was central to Marxist–Leninist ideology and was frequently censored and rewritten as a result (Rausing 2004; also Kaneff 2004; Wanner 1998; Watson 1994). Thus "the demise of state socialism and with it its hegemonic hold on memory and history production has allowed and in fact generated an outpouring of counter memories and histories hidden, 'forgotten' and forbidden under the intrusive discipline of the socialist regimes" (Pine et al. 2004: 1). Moreover, as Frances Pine et al. state, institutional bodies but also interest groups now "attempt to legitimate their claims, and to establish their *right*, to power . . . in claiming a particular version of the past as 'true'" (2004: 4). Such attempts to institutionalize new cultures, however, including new memory cultures, always lead to contestations, as Catherine Wanner argues (1998), which in turn means much public and private reflection. For Germany, John Borneman thus notes that an apparent silence on issues of the GDR past in polls in the early and mid-1990s was not an indication of public amnesia but rather an effect of an intense social involvement in postsocialist, or postdictatorial, memory-work (1997: 107).

The relevance of memory and history in postsocialism has been explored in a number of anthropological works. Authors have highlighted how the rewriting of national histories brings to the fore struggles over notions of belonging (Kaneff 2004; Rausing 2004; T. Richardson 2008; Wanner 1998), reconfigurations of local-center relationships (Kaneff 2004), legitimation of power holders (Verdery 1998), boundaries of the national and the state (T. Richardson 2008; Wanner 1998), and how the political is lived and new persons are created (Berdahl 2008; Kaneff 2004; Rausing 2004; Wanner 1998). Exploring the writing of the socialist past thus affords insights into the dynamic relationships between state and nation, government and citizenship, and into the making and unmaking of institutions and persons. Considering these questions of change, the anthropology of postsocialism usually focuses on the arrival of capitalism. Free markets, privatization, and production appear as the main sites of changing values and relationships where new kinds of people are produced: atomistic, individual consumers who are self-actualizing agents apt at making choices (Berdahl 2010a; Buchowski 1997; Creed 1998; Dunn 2004; Kideckel 2008; Humphrey 2002; Verdery 2003). At times democracy is included in these considerations but often as an addendum and as "market democracy" at that (Kideckel 2008: 7). This ethnography in turn focuses on the question of political life by asking what kinds of imagined democracies different actors work toward when producing histories or when using references to the past to make arguments about the present, as well as what this means for the making and unmaking of citizenship attempted by different kinds of institutions.

The fall of socialism and the subsequent transformation was marked in the West with no little amount of "triumphalism" (Berdahl 2010b; Berdahl et al. 2000; Kalb 2002; Verdery 1996). This appeared to be based foremostly on economic and technological superiority, now ultimately proven.

But beyond this there was a moral superiority, a sense that after all, democracy had proved to be the (only) order that (adequately) protected human rights and freedoms. Verdery's observation that evolutionary perspectives underpin the teleological notion of the "transition" that involves "rescue scenarios"—as if eastern European markets were "a person suffering from mental illness" and "our job is to restore their sanity" (1996: 205)—is similarly applicable to both the realm of the political and to personhood. Some ethnographic work has shown that with the aspirational goals of establishing multiparty democracies "like in the West" arose questions of what kinds of lives in the past are legitimate and which actors with what kind of biography are allowed agency in the morally different present (Dunn 2004; Junghans 2001; Klumbyte 2010; Zigon 2010). As Michal Buchowski argues (2006, also 2004) and others show, in many realms eastern Europeans' opinions have been treated as illegitimate or irrelevant due to the taint of their ideological socialization or "eastern" position (also Wanner 1998).[8] Such sentiments are underpinned by senses of the "formerly socialist subjects" as inflexible and preconditioned by the authoritarian state, an issue that seems most notable in sites where "East" and "West" meet directly, such as in a Polish factory taken over by American owners (Dunn 2004), in training for Hungarians in civil society techniques run by Americans (Junghans 2001), in border regions (Rausing 2004), or in eastern German political institutions built up by western Germans (this monograph, also see Berdahl 2010a). As this ethnography shows, it is over these questions of what are legitimate traits in the present vis-à-vis a tainted past that governmental institutions seek to create particular kinds of citizens. However, the explorations here also show that the issue runs deeper than a neat East–West binary, since critics of the lasting effects of socialist "indoctrination" also exist on the eastern side of the former Iron Curtain (Wanner 1998).

These contentions over personhoods and morality are, as my use of terminology above already suggests, bound up with understandings of these past states as dictatorial. An identification of socialist regimes as oppressive of course serves political legitimation of those who condemn it, but human rights abuse in Eastern Europe and the former Soviet Union is a reality that governments, citizens, and scholars of these societies need to face. Anthropology has left this terrain largely to transitional justice and historical sciences, however, so ethnographic explorations of what this difficult character of the socialist past means for belonging, citizenship, and opportunities for agency have remained rare (notable exclusions are Borneman 1997; Skultans 1998, 2001; Verdery 2013). What has in contrast engaged the discipline in recent years is the issue of counter-memories and nostalgia for socialism, which is taken as evidence of the manifold and complex ways people negotiate meaning in the present, deal with senses of loss and despair, or begin to construct alternative visions of desirable futures in criticism of free market capitalism (Bartmanski 2011; Berdahl 2010a, 2010b; Boym 2001; Hann 2012; Haukanes and Trnka 2013; Pine et al. 2004; Todorova and Gille 2010). The issue of memory was, and remains, a pertinent one twenty and twenty-five years after socialism's fall, as a generation that did not experience life in socialism has reached maturity. This generational change will have an inevitable impact on how individuals and groups relate to official memory narratives and how memory is shared and passed on. Simply put, this juncture entails a move from a predominantly social memory that is informed by and related to individual recollections toward a memory that is more cultural, informed by and presented through history teaching, material artifacts, and popular representations of the past in film and print.[9] The investigation this book is based on took place during a time when local policymakers were particularly aware of this change and created narratives that sought to address this new reality, while their attempts are responded to by generations who have their own memories of life in socialism.

This ethnography thus asks how representations of a contentious past are created and maintained, for which present-day reasons and with what futures in mind. To gain insights into why this past continues to matter so much—how it can lead to comforting reminiscing as quickly as to emotionally fought arguments—this book focuses on two very different institutional realms of past production. One of these is a group of governmental institutions, the other a daily, regional newspaper. Each of these groups is differently positioned toward the local population, giving rise to distinct institutional agendas and, from that, specific ideas about present and future, which influence what kinds of stories about the past—the dictatorship, the nation's history, the context of individuals' lives—can be produced.

This question of the production of public memory is a particularly pertinent one in the case of eastern Germany (Arnold-de Simine 2013; Jones 2014; Saunders and Pinfold 2013). Of all the states in the socialist realm, East Germany went through the fastest and most complete transformation. Here, the "transition" based in "linear, teleological thinking in relation to the direction of change: from socialism or dictatorship to liberal democracy, from a plan to a market economy" (Berdahl 2000: 1) could be said to have taken place and, at least on paper, concluded. While German unification meant that eastern Germans might have been spared some of the chaos and violence that unfolded in other former bloc states and Soviet republics, the breathtaking speed of change and sense of cultural devaluation and dispossession brought other challenges. Given the character of unification as accession alone, it hardly seems surprising that eastern Germany was the site of the now infamous *Ostalgie* or that this nostalgia should be bound up with an assertive sense of identity. Moreover, in Germany there is a particularly strong public interest in national history. Pine et al. remind us quite rightly that "it is not only one party [one-party] states which have a vested interest in control and generation of particular forms of commemoration and narratives of remembered pasts" (2004: 3). Rather, scholars of memory agree that modernity's almost utopian future orientation (Huyssen 2003; Keightley and Pickering 2006; also Terdiman 1993) and the growing strength of the state (Antze and Lambek 1996; Olick and Robbins 1998; Pine et al. 2004) in the past two centuries led to an increasing concern with history. This turned into crisis, leading to a shift from history to memory in the aftermath of the fast-paced social and cultural changes modernity initiated and with postmodern thought's attack on grand narratives (Climo and Cattell 2002; also see Arnold-de Simine and Radstone 2013; Huyssen 1995).

Put simply, and following Paul Antze and Michael Lambek (1996), a concern with memory is closely connected to rapid social change and furthermore points to a crisis of identity at national and individual levels. This partly explains why the German "obsession" with history seems to go beyond the European trend (e.g., Assmann and Frevert 1999). Here, a preoccupation with the nation's difficult pasts has become a part of culture and is closely intertwined with notions of national identity. The state has been involved in history writing on both sides of the inner German border not only but particularly so since World War II. The fall of the Berlin Wall added a second difficult past to that of the Third Reich and the Holocaust, creating the "double burden in history" so that democracy, perceived as a lasting form of government that secures the nation's freedom, is now doubly intertwined with memory-work. This moreover so since the postmodern shift to memory also entailed a move to concerns with morality most apparent in the rise of the "memorial museum," which combines aims of the "history museum"—to contextualize and critique—with that of the memorial—to commemorate—in a focus on atrocities to prevent their recurrence (Williams 2007). This coalescing of seemingly contradictory agendas is, according to Paul Williams, indicative of an "increasing (global) desire to add both a moral framework to the narration of terrible historical events and more in-depth contextual explanations to commemorative acts" (2007: 8). In post-unification eastern Germany, a number of memorial museums were quickly established that almost exclusively focused on the State Security Police and its victims (see Jones 2014). Chapter 1 explores these questions of the history of history writing, remembering and reckoning in the two Germanies and the united nation in more detail.

The production of versions of the past and their intertwining with notions of democracy and contestations over citizenship are explored in this book through a focus on narratives and their discourses. On the one hand, this method is apt because much of history writing comes to us in the form of texts (Kaneff 2004; Watson 1994). On the other, a focus on narrative is useful here because it allows the exploration of motivations and intent. Narratives are usually created with certain agendas in mind. They are made to be persuasive. James W. Fernandez (1986, 1991) and more recently Michael Carrithers (2005a, 2005b, 2006, 2012a) and others (Strecker and Tyler 2012a) have argued that culture has a rhetorical edge, as actors continuously try to persuade themselves and others of the truth of their ideas and emotions, the necessity to do or believe certain things, to engender action, to defend themselves, to plea and argue. This view is particularly useful in moments of contestation and open confrontation, some of which are explored in the following pages. But a concern with persuasion and movement is also highly relevant to the two institutional realms explored here. The group of government offices broadly has a remit of political education. It uses events, teacher training, and commemorations to educate the public in *Vergangenheitsaufarbeitung*, the "reworking" of the SED dictatorship. Through all individuals' reconsideration of their own past and memory, this public reworking aims to create both a shared social memory that acknowledges the truth of the socialist regime's dictatorial character and a foundational myth of unified Germany arising from civic struggles for democracy. To reach this double goal that will produce citizens fit to safeguard democracy into the future, the narratives of *Aufarbeitung* need to be highly persuasive.

The newspaper, in turn, depends on its customers' loyalty, which requires stories to appear relevant to readers' concerns, as well as correct and trustworthy in light of wider contexts. News stories thus also need to be persuasive to local readers, particularly so at a regional newspaper that considers a close connection to the readership part of its remit. This positions the newspaper as a fourth democratic power (in addition to the legislative, executive, and judiciary) regionally and at odds with the state government whose policies it critically evaluates while taking the local populations' side. Here the diversity of readership and journalistic staff creates the need for a different rhetorical tactic. While the governmental realm attempts to be persuasive through clarity of its understandings of the past, displaying a certain single-mindedness over what matters, the newspaper does so through multivocality and openness of its categories. While the governmental realm uses rhetoric to cause change in local people to *create* citizens, the paper uses rhetoric to express the concerns of a public that consists of *already existing* citizens to cause change in government. Chapters 3 and 4 explore how these two discourses are distinguished and what kinds of narratives they demand, facilitate, or discourage.

A focus on persuasion moreover highlights the future-directedness of the narratives that are produced within these two realms, while a close eye on narratives as purpose-driven and conclusive renderings of events, as intentionally meaningful fabrics of understandings, shows the considerable concerns that underpin these representations—the worry about the future of democracy—and their unintentional consequences—the creation of certain kinds of citizenship and the denial of others. Chapters 6 and 7 consider how ideas about democracy and the future on the one hand and senses of citizenship and belonging on the other relate to discourses on the socialist past or are engaged through a rhetorical mobilization of the past in the present.

Narrative and Rapid Change

The central arguments of this book are based in a firm belief that narratives are central to meaning-making with regard to the product, the story, and its rhetoric and, just as importantly, with regard to the processes of narrative making, telling, and exchanging (Carrithers 2012a; Collins 2002, 2003, 2010; Ochs and Capps 2001), which are of particular interest when it comes to the memory of socialism. Narratives here are seen as a variety of instances that are not confined to the lingual. They include the large public narratives constituted by newspaper spreads and government position papers, stories long and short that are thrown into arguments or mentioned "just because," story seeds as acted out and embodied in commemorative ceremonies, and life stories constructed during one-on-one interviews.

Although exploring rhetoric and questions of persuasion (Carrithers 2005a, 2005b, 2006, 2012a; Fernandez 1986, 1991; Strecker and Tyler 2012a), where such questions come into play, this monograph's starting position is that storytelling, including figurative speech, is culture in the making and central to meaning-making: to understanding one's life, the world around one, and life's manifold conundrums (Bruner 1987, 1990, 1991; Ochs and Capps 2001). Stories are created by narrators drawing on symbols, scripts, and schemata available to them through culture (Bruner 1987, 1990, 1991, 2002; D'Andrade 1992a, 1992b, 1995; Holstein and Gubrium 2000; Jackson 2002; Ochs and Capps 2001). By relating everyday events to master narratives, describing other individuals through metaphors so they become characters, and comparing unexpected news to previous experiences, individuals interpret what happened and begin relating to it. As Jerome Bruner puts it, "we cannot verbalize experience without taking perspective" (2002: 73).

In doing so, however, tellers moreover creatively engage with the cultural cannon and its discourses to create new story themes and to expand the application of metaphors and tropes to counter new situations and experiences. This culture dependency of narrative taken together with the common expectation that narratives are linear and based in a common moral stance (Ochs and Capps 2001) makes for difficulties in the aftermath of fundamental regime change. The dynamic character of narrative as "culture in the making," however, is exactly what provides the means for managing situations when meanings and values are in flux. Elinor Ochs and Lisa Capps, for example, show that conversations, in which indeterminate and open-ended stories are created, "are a prosaic social arena for developing frameworks for understanding events" (2001: 7; also Bruner 2002), or as Ivo Strecker and Stephen Tyler have put it, "rhetoric flows in times of uncertainty" (2012b: 28).

Furthermore, narratives are treated here as being as central to the self and to self-making (Holstein and Gubrium 2000; Linde 1993; Schiffrin 1984) as they are to educating and informing publics. Whether in the interview situation, conversations with colleagues and friends, or commemorative ceremonies, narratives emerge out of social interaction and present themselves as inherently intersubjective (Jackson 2002). The dynamics of the "dialogual" situation their telling is based in (Collins 2002, 2010), during Working Group meetings or staff conferences—within which, as Strecker and Tyler rightly point out, narrators never have full control over the effects of the figurative speech they employ (2012b: 24)—combine with the dynamics that are inherent to narratives. Stories wield a degree of power of their own that we recognize when speaking of narratives that "ran away" with their teller or of how an interlocutor "got carried away" making those comments. Bruner points this out when arguing that narrative structures influence our perception of the world (1987, 1990, 1991), and Ochs and Capps observe this when discussing everyday conversations:

> The dimension of linearity and moral stance address a central opposition that drives human beings to narrate life experience—the desire to sheathe life experiences with a soothing linearity and moral certainty versus the desire for deeper understanding and authenticity of experience. Imbuing an experience with a linear causal and temporal structure and conventional moral stance is the goal of many narrative interactions. Yet, autobiographically and historically these narrative formats may not resonate with actions, conditions and mindsets of tellers or, more important, those participating in a set of life events. Some tellers resist prevailing versions of events, disagree with one another, or begin to doubt their own memories and sensibilities. (2001: 56)

In telling stories, narrators juggle competing desires or, put differently, competing demands made by the narrative they wish to tell and the still vivid memories of the experiences that narrative addresses. "Good narratives" have a linear structure and a foreshadowed ending. They are clear in their messages, draw on a common cannon, and often relate to wider discourses (Ochs and Capps 2001; also Holstein and Gubrium 2000: 140; Mishler 2006; Schiffrin 1984; Smith 2006).

Yet, in narrative production, as Ochs and Capps highlight, memory may push against these demands of narrative, requiring a telling that is closer to the experience, that conveys the emotional troubles and the struggles of the self to cope with the conundrum. The balance between the powers of narrative and past experience depends, minimally, on the context of the narration and the interlocutors. In written narrative, even more so in texts destined for wider circulation, like newspaper stories or government papers, linearity and clarity are important since they support persuasion. But even here there can be more or less of that. It is thus important to realize moreover that narrative form is both suggestive and seductive, two characteristics that affect not only its interpretation but also the making of narratives (Bruner 1991). Narrative suggestiveness, Bruner argues, lies "in the emblematic nature of its particulars, its relevance to a more inclusive narrative type" (1991: 7). As narrators or authors develop stories that fall under a specific genre or draw on a particular script, certain tropes and symbols suggest themselves as fitting into the story. They are recognized as part of those kinds of stories, like the Stasi file in a story about dissidence in the GDR or the Coca-Cola emblem when expressing East German desire for Western-style consumption (see Becker 2003). Moreover, the more expertly told, the less interpretive work is required to understand narratives. Bruner goes so far as to argue that very well-told narratives "seduce" their audience into certain interpretations (1991: 9), which is also apparent from the way narratives arise out of and intertwine with wider discourses. While both narratives and discourses share many similarities, they differ in their power to guide and delimit understandings. As Sarah Franklin puts it, "the logic of discourse is rather . . . a logic of *enunciation*, defining the terms upon which knowledge is produced and deployed" (1990: 219). While narrative engages listeners who can identify with its subject positions in various ways, discourse ascribes and categorizes. Michel Foucault shows (e.g., 1977, 1981) that discourses more often than not come with claims to truth determining the legitimacy of specific knowledge and views of the world. In Germany, the "reworking of the past" (*Aufarbeitung*) is such a truth discourse that makes powerful suggestions about the past state, society, and lives within it, yet because it is a young discourse that is up against individuals' personal recollections and senses of who they were and are, it is contested and remains fledging; its categories and inscribed subject positions entail a degree of flux.

Nevertheless, the process of *Aufarbeitung*'s establishment has begun, and specific kinds of stories that suit its truths are circulating in this realm. Given the "seductive" powers of narrative, reinforced where they are by a dominant discourse, we can further ask whether communities of narrators and listeners that are used to particular kinds of stories may be seduced more easily into overcome understandings by narrations that follow, or appear to follow, familiar kinds of scripts. This is again particularly important with regard to the realm of *Aufarbeitung* because stories here are created for the purpose of government and underpinned by moral preoccupations based in empathic and ethical relationships to victims. Given the dynamics inherent to narrative, and their intersubjective character, storytelling also works back at the self that it is presenting. Certain stories about oneself come to be told due to the context, the interaction of that moment, and the need for coherence (Holstein and Gubrium 2000, 2001; Linde 1993, 2000). Chapter 5 thus asks how narrative-making in governmental and news realms work back at the stories that come to be told about individual lives.

In the field of *Aufarbeitung*, where stories that transmit a notion of the past as inhumane dictatorship also aim to do right by the regime's victims, the moral underpinnings of narrative (MacIntyre 1981; Ochs and Capps 2001) seem self-evident, even overpowering. Yet in other cases they appear to be more elusive, unless we consider any attempt to come to terms with unexpected events or to solve issues as moral, as Fernandez (2012) and Carrithers (2012b) appear to suggest. Such an inclusive view of morality, however, seems difficult to maintain in postsocialism generally and certainly in the case of the East German past, where different values compete, some narratives claim to be the only right and morally acceptable view of the past, and life stories that do not speak of GDR-time dissidence appear to be called into doubt regarding their morality. While agreeing that storytelling is based in and often motivated by thinking through values, I follow Avishai Margalit (2002) in distinguishing between morality and ethics with regard to memory (also Gallinat 2009a). The author characterizes the "ethics of memory," which he regards as more significant in remembering, as concerning "thick relations" or human "relations to the near and dear" (Margalit 2002: 7). Morality, on the other hand, which concerns higher principles and more abstract concepts, provides guidance for thin relations to "the stranger and the remote" (7). The ethics of memory then concern questions of our intimate relationships in past and present, whom we treated right or wrong, and whose memory we should respect to treat them right, now. The morality of memory speaks, in contrast, to more abstract, discursive questions of what constitutes good, proper memory, as when GDR-trained journalists grapple with the question of whether their professional work sustained a dictatorial regime.

Researching the Writing of the Past

The research project in which this book is based arose out of two previous projects and fieldwork stints in eastern Germany, all of which were facilitated by my status as an anthropologist working at home (Collins and Gallinat 2010; Gallinat 2010a; Narayan 1993).

While growing up as the youngest child in a family critical of the socialist state, I had not always been included in these conversations and therefore participated in many socialist activities, such as joining the socialist children's organization. Living in a particular pocket of East German society that was underpinned by an alternative ideology nevertheless provided a different view on life in socialism. And yet being only twelve years old when the Berlin Wall fell, the reader may rightly ask to what degree those experiences could have shaped later dispositions. My background taken together with the kinds of happenstances in life that influence our work much more than we usually dare to admit (Amit 2010) gave rise to three ethnographic projects in eastern Germany, on one of which this book primarily draws. These projects were fueled by a youthful wish, borne out of my in-between state and family position, to understand better what had allowed the GDR to exist and be so broadly supported for its four decades—an aim that changed with growing expertise and insights into the diversity of East/eastern German experiences and life courses.

The first fieldwork, over twelve months in 2001, was for a PhD and explored continuity and change (and identity and life stories) in the socialist ritual of the *Jugendweihe* ("youth consecration"; Gallinat 2002, 2005). The second project in 2004 investigated the construction of life stories among a group of former political prisoners against the backdrop of a—then—uninviting public (Gallinat 2006a, 2006b, 2009b). Out of these and my reading of the postsocialist literature, this third project developed which sought to explore how discourses about the socialist past that go on to provide narrative frameworks for individual remembering are produced in different institutions (Gallinat 2011, 2012; Gallinat and Kittel 2009).[10] My first interest in that regard was how governmental organizations approach East Germany through *Aufarbeitung*, reworking. As a point of entry, a Landeszentrale für Politische Bildung (Office for Political Education; LpB), which is a part of most federal state governments, was chosen. As a comparative but different institution, a local daily newspaper, referred to here as the *Daily Paper*, in the same federal state appeared to be a good choice, due to its independence from the political sphere and strong relationship to its local readership.

The project was located in the eastern German state Mittelland and its capital Tillberg—both of which are pseudonyms, as are titles of institutions unless these are generic terms. Some minor details of prominent actors have also been changed to protect the identity of our informants who worked in prominent positions in the state's government and one of its very few daily newspapers.[11] Mittelland is characterized by a number of larger towns, like Tillberg, and large rural areas, some of which lie along the former inner German border. The state struggled with high unemployment rates in the 1990s, which started to lift as Germany's economy recovered in the mid-2000s. Apart from agriculture, there are now a number of new medium-sized businesses. Many of the rural areas and their small- and medium-sized towns, which—like many areas in the East—suffered significant population loss in the 1990s, however, remain relatively deprived. There is little to do, especially for young people, and job prospects are dire. In those areas neo-Nazi groups have proved attractive to the local, and mostly male, youth, which is a disconcerting problem for Mittelland, as well as for most of the "new states" (*neue Bundesländer*).

Tillberg itself is a town of more than 200,000 inhabitants and is characterized by nineteenth-century villas and GDR-time and modern-day architecture. The town center features shopping areas, medieval remains like a cloister and parts of the town wall, a cathedral, and parks. Strewn across the city center are restaurants and cafés and, in an area popular with students, pubs and bars. An unobtrusive memorial to unification was built at the cathedral place; other landmarks of East German rule and the transition, like the former Stasi prison memorial museum, are located outside of the center. There is some new economy close to Tillberg, and the city itself includes the state government, a hospital, and a university among its main employers. Over the past two decades, both Mittelland and Tillberg have changed in many ways. Most notable during the most recent fieldwork was growing social disparity. Tillberg's city center has become much more attractive to families and individuals who could be described as middle class in British terms and *Bildungsbürgertum* ("educated bourgeoisie") in German terms than just five or ten years previously. There is also a growing number of events and attractions to satisfy such customers' appetite for culture, history, and education.

At the same time, at the city's periphery, deprivation appears to have become more widespread in recent years. For example, on my way to and from fieldwork at the *Daily Paper*, I usually stopped at a local baker's to pick up the day's newspaper and bread rolls. My query for a specific type of bread was one day answered by a sale's assistant who sounded stressed, even though her day at work had only just started. They do not sell those here, she explained, their clientele are only pensioners (who would not want the whole-wheat, nut-and-seed baguette I was after). "And today the prices went up too!" she continued, revealing how much she dreaded charging her regular customers, who often brought their last change to the bakery, an extra two cents apiece. She had a difficult day ahead, especially in this area of the city that suffered greater deprivation than others, as she reminded me (when enquiring at the local gym's reception about a hairbrush I had lost, I was informed I should not expect it to turn up: "People up here can use anything"). That the city's salespeople had much experience in dealing with customers with tight purse strings was also highlighted another day when I hesitated at the checkout, commiserating about which items I could keep and which I needed to leave behind, having just realized that I did not bring enough cash. The sale's clerk was unimpressed and demanded straightforward information about how much money I had. She then monitored the bill and told me exactly when I had used up my meager budget of 4 euros. It was clear that such practices of managing on tight budgets had become very common.

The project entailed fourteen months of participant observation in Tillberg and Mittelland. For this the two researchers, research associate Sabine Kittel and myself, joined in the working everyday of the two institutional realms. Fieldwork began in earnest in spring 2007 and lasted until the summer of 2008. It started with both of us visiting the LpB and the *Daily Paper* in early 2007. Sabine then moved to Tillberg to conduct fieldwork at the LpB and the Working Group *Aufarbeitung*. I traveled to Tillberg from the United Kingdom every second month, where over repeated periods of five to six, at times eight, weeks, I also conducted participant observation. I spent one month at the LpB and other institutions of *Aufarbeitung* and then focused on the *Daily Paper* for five months, while Sabine continued with the Working Group *Aufarbeitung*. Sabine then followed me to the *Daily Paper* for a concluding three months of research. During this second phase of fieldwork, we maintained connection to the LpB and attendant institutions, met with informants, and attended, often together, relevant events such as commemorative ceremonies or film showings. At the end of the fieldwork period, we ran three workshops to disseminate and discuss preliminary findings in each of the two institutional realms.

We also conducted interviews with employees at different levels of institutional hierarchies. These were life story interviews that began with one open-ended question inviting interviewees to tell us their life "from beginning to end." From there, interviews would unfold conversationally as participants told their story and interviewers asked questions for clarification at appropriate moments. This first part was followed by a semi-structured part consisting of three questions that aimed to explore individuals' perspectives on wider debates about the East German past and the region. We each ran interviews in each realm with differently positioned individuals, with Sabine conducting the majority of the interviews. One interview was conducted jointly. Overall, we recorded hundreds of pages of field notes, which were shared once written, conducted thirty-three interviews, and collected a plethora of textual and visual materials ranging from newspaper cuttings, event programs, and fliers to position and research papers, agendas, and meeting minutes. This joint data collection may raise the question of why this book is single-authored. Sabine and I discussed the question of authorship at various points during and after the project. As the research project was an outcome of my research interests and epistemological preoccupations, Sabine asked to be recognized regarding her contributions to data collection, particularly the interviews where she built on her previous work with Holocaust survivors (Kittel 2006), but she did not wish to appear as co-author. I am greatly indebted to her for her work on this project, her interviewing skills, and her criticism and suggestions during fieldwork.

As is typical in research, neither the field research nor the data we collected were quite what I had in mind when designing the project. While the Office for Political Education provided the focus of the first part of the project, we soon learned that it collaborated with some other governmental, government-funded, and civil society organizations in a formal Working Group on topics that fall under the umbrella term *Aufarbeitung*. Fieldwork widened to include the group and its core member institutions and staff. This included memorial museums,[12] like the former Stasi prison in the capital; government offices concerning the State Security Police, such as the state's Stasi commissioner (LStU); and two local branches of the Federal Commissioner for the Documents of the State Security Police (Bundesbeauftragter für die Stasi-Unterlagen, BStU), which administers the Stasi archives. Since much of the everyday work in this realm is desk based and not all away meetings allow for the presence of a researcher, fieldwork here could be slow going for Sabine and at times awkward, especially at the Office for Political Education, where staff work in individual offices and meet friends and spouses from other government offices at lunchtime.[13] Participant observation here then meant participating in Working Group meetings and discussions, catching up on what had happened in between through informal chats and helping prepare for events—by stuffing folders or sourcing stationery, collecting texts about and produced at these institutions, and attending events together with relevant staff, like teacher training courses as well as the occasional lunch or a beer at the pub. While many of the managerial staff at the LpB were, as Sabine had suspected, originally from West Germany, the move into the Working Group *Aufarbeitung* reestablished an eastern–western German balance. However, during fieldwork it became apparent that eastern–western German differences or contentions played a relatively small role for most individuals in this field, as coming chapters will show. Instead, political affiliation, party membership, and internal hierarchies pushed to the fore.

Less expectedly, due to naïveté on my part, we also found a number of western German staff at the *Daily Paper*, as well as staff who had worked in journalism since GDR times and others who had grown up in East Germany but entered the profession after 1989. Here, ages and backgrounds were more widespread than in the governmental sphere. And fieldwork seemed easier in the open-plan editorial office, where colleagues routinely chat over the shoulder-high screens that separate desks, congregate around printers, and go to lunch together since the office is outside of town. At the *Daily Paper* fieldwork thus involved observing the newsroom, following news agencies, attending staff conferences, and engaging in informal conversations—in short, "deep hanging out" in the newsroom (Geertz 2001). I also provided hands-on help like typing or editing readers' letters and occasionally writing short journalistic pieces (for one reason or another the staff there considered me their local expert on all matters British).

Like my recent holiday in Germany, field research had also begun with concerns over the degree to which contentions about the GDR past were still emerging in and entertaining the public, yet they soon proved unfounded. The years 2007 and 2008 saw a number of éclats and projects that concerned the socialist past and involved the various institutions that we observed, the least of which were the preparations for the anniversary year 2009. To name but a few, there was the revelation that the director of the Chamber for Trade and Commerce had been an unofficial employee (IM; a spy) for the Stasi, leading to his resignation; the finding of an "order to shoot" (to kill; *Schiessbefehl*) at the inner German border at the local BStU office; an éclat over the presence of a GDR-time prosecutor in political cases, now a member of the state parliament, in the advisory committee of the Memorial Foundation; and a public book reading at which GDR backgrounds of local personalities, including the town's mayor, were revealed that was later read as an attempt to interfere with the mayoral election campaign.

As the project progressed, it became increasingly apparent that doing an ethnographic project on the memory of the socialist past and its moral ambiguities was not an easy task. Both researchers found that we would get sucked into the very debates we sought to explore: what can and cannot be said about the past "dictatorship," who is allowed to remember what, who were informants during that period, and what, if anything, did that mean? I have explored these issues more comprehensively elsewhere (Gallinat 2009a). The writing of this book was no easier task. While much anthropology of eastern Germany, for good reason, has focused on the toll that unification and western German hegemony took, my "native" status does not allow me to put aside the dictatorial character of the SED state. How the past is defined is a tense issue "back at home" that I cannot ignore given my family background, previous research, and the relationships that arose from this. At the same time this work has also shown me that memories of the past are much more flexible and multifaceted than the discourse of *Aufarbeitung* seems able to acknowledge, and my training as an anthropologist has taught me to seriously consider the impact of fundamental, dislocating change. This has led me to the present exploration of what the institutional, structural, and humane reasons are for the mobilization of different kinds of memory by different kinds of people in different contexts. And yet it may have left me with the further conundrum that I understand both sides of the argument, for and against the notion of the dictatorship, for and against loose references to the past that could be read as "nostalgic." The writing of this book thus entails a balancing act of my academic understandings and conceptual curiosities, as well as fieldwork and personal allegiances. There may be a point here that in some ways my status as "anthropologist at home" has led to too many sensitivities. However, I believe this work encompasses important insights into a particular aspect of the "postsocialist condition" and the presence of the past in the longer-term aftermath of fundamental regime change.

The Contents of This Book

In order to explore the production of versions of the socialist past, the book begins in chapter 1 with an exploration of the role of history in nation-building in Germany. The chapter considers the development of memory discourses in the two Germanies until and following 1990 in their historical contexts, including the experiences of socialism's fall and unification, which influenced the reception of governmentally driven memory-work at the grassroots of society. The chapter explores the origin of the term *Aufarbeitung* and how it has become connected to the East German past, as well as the main contents and traits of the discourse: its emotive and morally guided character, the intertwining of remembrance with historical research, and the increasingly important goal of education. Exploring the contentions that have arisen around the discourse, the discussion shows up the split in memory culture that appeared to develop in the 1990s (Arnold-de Simine 2013: 160). The chapter concludes with debates about a revised federal memorial concept that unfolded during fieldwork in 2008 and the concept's more recent reconsideration to trace the development of the emerging discourse of *Aufarbeitung* over the past twenty-five years.

Having set out this context, chapter 2 introduces the two realms of field-work, the Working Group *Aufarbeitung* and the *Daily Paper*. An exploration of these institutions' remits and their position vis-à-vis Mittelland's population highlights, on the one hand, the LpB's aim to *shape* citizens fit for the democratic present through education, a purpose that is closely linked to the office's history and the time of its western German staff's arrival in Mittelland shortly after German unification. The *Daily Paper*, on the other hand, tries to *enable* citizenship through information and the expression of opinion on its pages arising from its explicit aim to represent local people's concerns. The chapter concludes by showing how these differential goals relate to the two realms' critical considerations of each other.

Chapters 3 and 4 then explore the distinct discourses that each of these institutional realms produces through ethnographic description and narrative analysis. Chapter 3 focuses on the *Daily Paper*'s approach to creating news stories about the East German past by exploring the news story of the apparent find of a *Schiessbefehl*, an "order to shoot" (to kill), at the inner German border. In this case, the newspaper's goal of presenting local people's concerns and the need to speak to a varied audience led to a narrative production that appears nonlinear and open-ended akin to the "living narratives" of the everyday (Ochs and Capps 2001). This gives rise to a notion of the GDR as the nation's unresolved life event that requires continuous debate for which the *Daily Paper* in turn provides the platform. The story on the order to shoot was published on the anniversary of the building of the Berlin Wall that year, which is commemorated in local events attended by members of the Working Group *Aufarbeitung*.

Chapter 4 begins with a scene from such a ceremony, the ritual and social relations of which remind attendees of the importance of "reworking" to prevent future occurrences of such violence. The chapter then focuses on the development of a teacher training course on East German history by the Working Group *Aufarbeitung* to show how meetings and discussions shape the discourse of *Aufarbeitung* in practice. Notable here is how the group negotiated the potential inclusion of ambiguous content, specifically memories of everyday life in the GDR, which are often considered to lead to "to be countered" nostalgic sentiments. As the group moved from attempts to include the everyday to reinterpret the topic to suit a view of the "GDR as dictatorship," it becomes clear that this discourse requires narratives to be linear, categorically clear, and morally certain. This pressure on narrative production arises from the fact that what is at stake in *Aufarbeitung* is not the past per se but rather the present and future of democracy and freedom.

Given the power of discourse and the subject positions it entails, it needs to be asked how this narrative production works back at the actors in these realms. Chapter 5 thus presents the life stories of two members of the Working Group *Aufarbeitung* and two journalists from the *Daily Paper* to show how narrative making in the governmental and the news realms relates to the stories that come to be told about individual lives. The chapter highlights the particular binding powers of the discourse of *Aufarbeitung* through its impact on the individual narrations of members of the Working Group, which appear as similarly linear and purpose driven as the narratives the group produces for wider audiences. Similarly, the considerably more multivocal and inclusive news discourse creates more space for a telling of personal stories for the journalists. These stories appear more like ongoing reflection on historical events and experiences, some of which seem to remain unresolved in their meaning, that extend beyond 1990. Cutting across the life stories of members of the Working Group are differences in understandings and practices of political agency between eastern and western Germans that impact actors' perceptions and expectations of Mittelland's population.

The question of how memory-work relates to understandings of citizenship and democracy in the present is further explored in chapters 6 and 7. Chapter 6 returns to the Working Group *Aufarbeitung* and its preparations for the twentieth anniversary of the fall of the Berlin Wall, which took place against the backdrop of a large-scale survey that was understood as proving the persistence of nostalgia for state socialism within the population. The survey had been commissioned by Mittelland's government, which also developed the political response to its results. As the survey findings coincided with the approach of the anniversary, the memory-work of *Aufarbeitung* became a tool of party-political problem-solving, as only education about the "SED dictatorship" was believed to help create the civic skills required of local people to bring Mittelland's transition to democracy to conclusion. The chapter explores the kinds of texts that developed in response, showing how, in a process during which *Aufarbeitung* was appropriated for party-political government, particular kinds of citizenship were legitimated while others were delegitimized—this although the meaning of the trope of "democracy," around which actors rallied, was variously interpreted.

Chapter 7 explores the *Daily Paper*'s reaction to the Mittelland survey and the government's response to its findings, the Campaign for Democracy, to show how the newspaper positions itself as local people's advocate vis-à-vis government, both practicing democracy through facilitating debates on its pages and enabling readers to practice their citizenship by raising concerns in published readers' letters. A representation of Mittelland as a "normal," non-transitional state is both an outcome of and a cause for the successful performance of the newspaper's role of narrator/advocate. This presentation is created to avoid any sense of the local population as forever "East German" (Ostdeutsch), an identifier that has become associated with a number of problems such as right-wing violence, a penchant for authoritarianism, and lack of civic courage. In these processes the past emerges as immanent in the present, and shorthand references to the past create memory communities, for example, which bind readers to the *Daily Paper* and facilitate belonging. In these everyday practices at the *Daily Paper*, a citizenship is invoked that extends *from* past *to* present and has always already had legitimacy. The concluding remarks bring together the various strands under exploration, highlighting how the dynamics of narrative and their institutional production impact memory-work after fundamental regime change, which in turn is informed by concerns about the present and future of democracy and citizenship. The conclusion also returns to the question of ethics and morality in memory and narrative that this chapter introduced.

Notes

1. In this book I will use the words "East" and "West" to refer to East and West Germany prior to unification (GDR and FRG, respectively). I will use the terms "eastern" and "western" to refer to the post-1990 regions of former East and West Germany. However, this distinction is not made in the German language, so in some cases the denominators East and West will be used for post-unification times to signal continuations of German division in thinking.
2. I will use the term "unification" to refer to the end of national division in 1990. This is the term most commonly used in academic texts. During fieldwork, articles and reports by the *Daily Paper* used the German version of *Vereinigung* ("unification"). At the Office for Political Education, both *Vereinigung* and *Wiedervereinigung* ("reunification") appear in written texts. In translations from texts collected during fieldwork and when quoting from interviews, I will therefore use the English equivalent of the term used in the original source. Interestingly, in spoken language during fieldwork and in my personal life, the term *Wiedervereinigung* prevails. Either way I am not problematizing this choice of terminology in this book.
3. *Der Spiegel* is one of Germany's leading political magazines. It appears weekly.
4. I discuss the different denotations applied to the GDR and my own terminology in chapter 1. To refer to the fall of the GDR government in 1989 and unification in 1990, I will occasionally use *Wende*, as this is the term most commonly used in popular parlance to describe those two or so years of intense change and upheaval. This usage is not uncontentious (see Simon 2014).

5. *Aufarbeitung*, short for *Vergangenheitsaufarbeitung*, has been translated in various ways. Andrew H. Beattie refers to it as "working through the past" (2008: 9), Sara Jones as "reappraisal" (2014: 11), and Silke Arnold-de Simine and Susanna Radstone as "reworking of the past" (2013: 27). In this book I will use the term "reworking of the past" and in short "reworking."

6. Maria Todorova and Zsuzsa Gille (2010) observe such vilification of postsocialist nostalgia more generally.

7. The term "shortage economy," introduced into the anthropology of postsocialism by Verdery (1996), has been subject to some debate (Thelen 2011, 2012; Dunn and Verdery 2011). My use of the term here should be read not as an endorsement of one position or the other but rather as a shorthand to describe a socioeconomic situation characterized by considerable shortages that people managed through barter, exchange, and hoarding, among other techniques.

8. This issue of a tainted personhood for eastern European personhood has also been raised in the guise of difficult questions over which anthropology and anthropologists get to be heard in an anglophone, Western academic discourse (Buchowski 2004; Kürti 1996, 2000; Lampland 2000).

9. See Assmann (2006) on cultural memory; for a brief critique of Assmann's distinctions between various types of memory, see Arnold-de Simine and Radstone (2013: 25).

10. The project was supported by the Economic and Social Research Council (RES0061-23-0035).

11. For the same reason, I am not providing references to documents produced by these specific institutions. If a reader wishes to obtain more information about data sources, please contact me directly.

12. I use the term "memorial museums" here for places that are maintained as memorials, (*Gedenkstätten*), as they are dictatorial aspects of socialism, but have been developed into larger complexes or museums to engage with the public more actively (Williams 2007).

13. See Lisa Garforth (2012) for difficulties of researching office work ethnographically.

Chapter One

REMEMBERING EAST GERMANY IN THE UNITED NATION

The Second German Dictatorship and Dual History

⋙•⋘

Commenting on German unification, Konrad H. Jarausch remarks that "the debate about the legitimacy and form of unity was saturated with references to the past" as "unification offered a return to and an escape from history" (1994: 182). Although the author concedes that this was inevitable, since "prior experiences offered the only vocabulary in which it could be discussed," he astutely puts his finger on a crucial aspect of German nationhood, that is, as he puts it elsewhere, an "extraordinary public interest in the meaning of history" (1988: 293; also Assmann and Frevert 1999; Carrithers 2012c; Francois and Schulze 2001). Already in the first half of the nineteenth century, historians saw it as their role to educate the nation in values. As Jürgen Kocka notes, their representations of German history were as much a political as a scholarly construct (1982). The role played by history and history education in nation-building and public culture increased considerably after 1945. Both German states integrated the Nazi past into their discourses of national identity albeit in different ways. A similar positioning was required toward national division, which served as a stark reminder of the national socialist past.

With unification in 1990, this situation was resolved, allowing the escape from history that Jarausch alludes to, yet a new past emerged that now needed to be approached which required a return to the immeasurable crimes of the Holocaust. Not just consciously but rather explicitly, unification was thus completed "in knowledge of the continuity of German history and considering the particular responsibility for a democratic development in Germany arising from our history," as noted by the Unification Treaty (Einigungsvertrag 1990). From the start of negotiations, the East German past was thus understood as requiring reckoning at least among politicians, on both sides of the former border, and the eastern German civil rights activists who had helped bring about the fall of the socialist regime. This view and the political will to put measures of retribution and reconciliation into place need to be understood against the backdrop of the two states' relationship to the Third Reich and the national self-understandings arising from this, in addition to the developments of 1989 and 1990 that impacted the public perception of the retribution and memory-work processes that the government soon implemented. This chapter will therefore provide a historical overview of the development of discourses about the East German past. It asks how they are related to political agendas of nation-building, senses of belonging and identity at the grassroots of society, and experiences of the GDR's fall and national unification. This will highlight the contentions that are connected to governmental memory-work, as well as the main shape of the discourse of *Aufarbeitung* in practice: its emotive and morally guided character, the intertwining of remembrance with historical research, and the increasingly important goal of using *Aufarbeitung* for education.

Reckoning with the Past Post-1945

West Germany, with its foundation in 1949, had posited itself as the legal successor to the Third Reich through the assumption of stately continuity since the first unified German Reich of the nineteenth century under Chancellor Otto von Bismarck's reign. This meant the FRG took responsibility for the payment of reparations for wartime destruction and judicial approaches to perpetratorship (Frei 2003; Reichel 2007). This "denazification" focused very much on power holders and individuals in influential positions, leaving most citizens to declare their (non)involvement in a self-completion questionnaire dubbed the *Persilschein* ("Persil certificate," after the laundry detergent). The 1950s have often been described as characterized by widespread silence about this recent past, as, preoccupied with survival and their own losses, many people withdrew into their private lives. However, more recent scholarly work has highlighted that there was collective and individual remembering that focused on Germans' suffering at the hands of a small group of "nasty Nazis" (Niven 2006a). Thus, any amnesia there rather concerned wider German culpability. This changed during the 1960s, which saw a shift in focus toward questions of guilt that gained momentum with time: as the economy recovered, the new republic moved out of a "postwar" mode of life, democracy now institutionalized became more liberal, and further trials of smaller Nazis, as well as historiography, led to increasing knowledge about the crimes of the Third Reich (Wittlinger 2006). The antifascist generation of 1968, often attributed with the breaking of the apparent silence, radicalized this emerging discourse largely to criticize their elders (Niven 2006b; Wittlinger 2006).[1]

Over time, two particular terms came to be routinely associated with a reckoning with this difficult history: *Vergangenheitsbewältigung*, the "management" or "overcoming" of the past, and *Vergangenheitsaufarbeitung*, "reworking" the past. Both terms were coined in the late 1950s. Psychologists Alexander and Margarete Mitscherlich (1967) promoted *Vergangenheitsbewältigung* as the "unmanaged" past of the Third Reich, so their argument, had serious psychological and social consequences. Theodor Adorno ([1959] 1963) in contrast coined *Aufarbeitung* in an essay that highlighted the persistence of national socialist attitudes in society. By the 1980s, when the 1968 generation had come into positions of political power, a national consensus about the Third Reich had developed, which was decidedly anti-Nazi and, in line with international views, saw the Holocaust as an abhorrent crime even if narratives of German victimhood persisted (see Niven 2002, 2006a). The "antitotalitarian consensus," as it is referred to with regard to the political parties of the Bundestag (Beattie 2006, 2008), concerned a rejection of all "totalitarian" rule whether from the right or the left. From the 1960s onward, the East German state was included in this category and treated, at least by some, as broadly similar to the Third Reich (Beattie 2006). Some scholars see a 1985 speech of West Germany's President Richard von Weizsäcker, in which he describes the Holocaust as a "breach in civilization" and refers to German "crimes against humanity" that must remain at the center of public memory discourses, as the height of public acknowledgment of this critical perspective (Moeller 2006: 41).

The holocaust was, however, fiercely debated once again in the *Historikerstreit* ("historians' dispute") of 1986. Seemingly regarding the historical reasons for the genocide of the Jews, the dispute concerned the political meaning of this legacy in relation to national self-understanding, which, some felt, was marked by a "negative patriotism" (Fulbrook 1999) or suffered from an "identity neurosis" (Schwartz, cited in Jarausch 1994: 182) due to the "Nazi stain" (Jarausch 1988). The debate was underpinned by an older historical paradigm: the thesis of German "exceptionalism," the *Sonderweg* (Kocka 1982; also Evans 2005; Kühnl 1997). The notion concerns the degree to which Germany's path into modernity differed from that of the other European states. The tenor of the 1910s, only challenged by defeat in World War II, was that Germany's relatively late development as a nation-state, as well as its strong monarchy and bureaucracy, was appropriate to the nation's political and geographical position and ensured its strength. This view changed significantly after World War II, when discussions of German exceptionalism in the FRG concerned, in a negative manner, the question of what national traits allowed the Nazi Reich to rise to power. Similar arguments emerged then regarding the nation's late move away from monarchy and its preference for a "strong state"—a penchant to follow authoritarian rulers perhaps. Given that, the historical events of the mid-twentieth century had raised the thorny question of whether Germans were actually suited to democracy so that the Bonn Republic, upon its foundation, had a point to prove vis-à-vis the established European democracies. It did this partly through drawing a clear demarcation line both horizontally and vertically, distinguishing itself from the past of the Third Reich on the one hand and the East German regime on the other. The antitotalitarian paradigm thus served the creation of a national myth that legitimized the present state by delegitimizing the Cold War rival on the other side of the inner German border.[2]

Just as the historians' dispute calmed down, a book authored by Holocaust survivor Ralph Giordano (1987) appeared, which accused Germany as not having adequately dealt with the Nazi terrors emphatically described as the nation's "second guilt" (*zweite Schuld*). On the eve of the fall of the East German government, the FRG was thus keenly aware of its historical responsibilities, while, despite all the *Angst* regarding overt nationalism, a confident sense of identity had begun to prosper (Jarausch et al. 1997). This was most of all based on pride in the constitutional patriotism (*Verfassungspatriotismus*) for the Basic Law, which appeared to have proved itself over the past four decades, together with a sense of economic accomplishment and the values of democracy, justice, and human rights it supported (Arnold-de Simine 2013: 48). By the late 1980s, then, "the once provisional Bonn Republic had become a stable, prosperous and self-confident democracy" (Jarausch et al. 1997: 46).

While the Federal German Republic had posited itself as the legal successor to the Third Reich and as anti-totalitarian, the socialist East German republic established itself as the heir to the workers' movement and antifascism (Nothnagle 1999; Reichel 2007). This latter foundation myth emphasized the Nazi prosecution of workers' leaders above and beyond other crimes and cast the arrival of the Soviet Union in eastern Germany as liberation. Nazi perpetrators were persecuted by Soviet forces during the 1940s (160,000 to 180,000 persons were interned) and by the East German administration in the 1950s (Kleßmann 1988; Mironenko et al. 1998). Simultaneously, intense debates were had in the political realm about German guilt and compensation for Jewish victims, but they proved short lived, giving way to the ideological position that all cultural and social bases of the frightful *Sonderweg* had been eradicated by denazification so that the GDR bore no further responsibility for the Nazi past (Monteath 2004). This argument and the antifascist foundation myth, which, despite political exaggeration, carried some merit (Fulbrook 2005), dominated state-sponsored representations of this past until 1990. The Third Reich and World War II thus featured significantly in public discourse, for example, in school teaching and memorial sites (Nothnagle 1999), serving to legitimize socialist rule. Due to this ideological function, observers on the other side of the Iron Curtain have considered East German efforts to approach this past as limited, criticizing most of all an apparent silencing of the Holocaust. While Jewish suffering was not acknowledged much in official memorial sites, narratives about the Holocaust circulated in public culture and were at times recognized by GDR leaders (Monteath 2004). Denazification was extensive in the GDR, but its "Stalinist" character—meaning that persecution extended to political opponents, industrialists, and landlords—has further made it difficult for many to acknowledge East German memory-work as "reckoning" (cf. Reichel 2007).

Meanwhile, the East German state's attempts to foster a socialist consciousness according to ideology and nationhood were only partially successful (Nothnagle 1999; Palmowski 2009). Jan Palmowski (2009) shows how the latter was attempted through facilitating notions and practices of *Heimat*, of feeling "at home" in East Germany (Applegate 1990; Gallinat 2008)—in local festivals, through the encouragement of traditions, with ideological emphasis on the countryside, and similar—at the local and national level. Jarausch et al. (1997) similarly emphasize that senses of identity developed at the grassroots, rather than in relation to politics, and were based in social solidarity and senses of accomplishment, of managing despite the shortage economy—notions that were reinforced during visits to other socialist countries that compared less favorably to "home." This perception was, however, also challenged by the western neighbor (Palmowski 2009). Contacts to West Germany through relatives, the Church, or, for some, work and exposure to West German TV highlighted much of what was missing in East Germany. Here the planned economy created consumptive desires it was unable to fulfill (Borneman 1991). Beyond this, the country of the "class enemy," where, according to socialist propaganda in East German media, crime rates were high and former Nazis continued to live unperturbed, remained a somewhat mysterious place that appeared both desirable and dubious.

By the 1980s, then, history—specifically, representations of the Third Reich—was closely intertwined with identity and political legitimization in both German states (Beattie 2008; Reichel 2007). While the East German efforts may be criticized as too ideologically tainted, the West German "pathos notions" of *Bewältigung* and *Aufarbeitung* (Sabrow 2007; also Frei 2003), which work through a moralizing emotionality that emphasizes commemoration, remembrance, and the voice of victims, similarly reflect political agendas.

From Mass Demonstrations to German Unity: The "Wende Years"

In the late 1980s, oppositional groups in East Germany, which in many places had been meeting under the auspices of the Protestant church, began to gather momentum as news of political relaxation and democratization in other eastern-central European states was proliferating. Protests grew further in response to the resulting arrests and forced exiles (see Jarausch 1994; Miller 1998). The election in May 1988, and its rigged results, catalyzed the growing calls for a democratization of the GDR. As Hungary opened its borders to Western Europe in the summer, a mass exodus of East German citizens intent on making their way to the Federal Republic followed, marking the beginning of an extraordinary autumn for the small republic (Borneman 1991; Childs 2001). Monday prayer meetings at St. Nicholas Church in Leipzig turned into demonstrations, and after joining forces with the growing civic movement, Neues Forum, they spread like wildfire to most East German towns and cities, including Tillberg and Wellau in Mittelland.

When, in early October, more than 100,000 people demonstrated in Leipzig, the overwhelmed police force was left unable to act, so demonstrations proceeded increasingly without arrests (Childs 2001: 71). In Tillberg, around 10,000 met at the cathedral that weekend. Following the activists' lead, demonstrators demanded civil rights such as free elections, free press, and legalization of the new oppositional party, Neues Forum. In the biggest demonstration of all, on Sunday, 4 November, around half a million people met on East Berlin's Alexanderplatz (BpB n.d.). The East German regime was unable to withstand the growing pressure. On 7 November, the government stood down, and on 9 November, the new leadership made its most significant concession by opening the inner German border. Within the first four days, more than four million people crossed the border to visit the neighboring country that had been off-limits for so long (Childs 2001: 88). While civil rights activists hoped for a democratized East German Republic, the euphoria in East and West, the sense of togetherness symbolized most powerfully by the pictures of strangers hugging each other and dancing on the Berlin Wall together that made the rounds in the media, changed public attitude. Slogans demanding German unification soon took over the continuing mass demonstrations. Most poignantly, the earlier motto of "We are *the* people," a demand to be heard by SED leadership, turned into "We are *one* people," the assertion of national unity.

Growing anger was directed at SED leadership and the Ministerium für Staatssicherheit (MfS). One month after the fall of the Berlin Wall, activists occupied Stasi offices in a number of East German cities to safeguard the ominous files. These developments reached their climax in January, when citizen groups stormed the MfS headquarters in Berlin (Jarausch 1994; Miller 1998). During this time of limbo, activists had also begun to work with local power holders, and later with the new East German government under Hans Modrow, for a peaceful changeover, including agreements with the MfS regarding the release of political prisoners and Stasi files, in so-called Round Table meetings (Runde Tische). While in West Germany, CDU Chancellor Helmuth Kohl began considering plans for unification in the winter of 1989, on East German streets, advocates of unification and supporters of independence clashed in continuing demonstrations. With governmental structures crumbling, for a few months the Berlin Republic "teetered on the brink of chaos" (Jarausch 1994: 75).

The Round Tables provided some stability and became the hallmark of the civic revolution, set as they were on cooperation and public dialogue, but it was the course of the Kohl government toward unification that moved the limbo of those winter months to a clearer path. Approaching the first free elections, the East German CDU, resourced by its West German sister party, joined forces with a number of smaller parties and former opposition groups to create the center-right Alliance for Germany (Allianz für Deutschland), whose main goal was unification (Childs 2001). The multiparty conglomerate won the elections, which generated a voter turnout of over 90 percent, sending the conservative CDU into government in a big coalition with the Social Democratic Party (SPD) and the Liberal Democratic Party (FDP). Thus, while many activists continued to hope for a "third way" of an independent, democratic East Germany that would embody the civic movement's core values of direct democracy and social justice (Jarausch 1994; Sabrow 2010), the public vote put the country on a fast-track course to unification. The first democratically elected government's main duty was thus its own dissolution. East Germany officially joined the Federal Republic just four months later on 3 October 1990; the day was soon declared a public holiday.

The negotiations of German unity that then began remained confined to the political elite to the disappointment of the activists who had played a key role in the "democratic awakening" (Jarausch 1994). Since, viewed from Bonn, the West German system appeared to have proved superior, it was agreed that the East would join the Federal Republic by accession, even though the document that led the process was called the Unification Treaty, due to the insistence of East Germany's newly elected and last prime minister, Lothar de Maizière. West German Minister of the Interior Wolfgang Schäuble, however, put it clearly: "This is the accession of the GDR to the FRG and not the reverse. We have a good Basic Law that is proven. We want to do everything for you . . . But this is not the unification of two equal states" (cited in Jarausch 1994: 170). Both constitutional confidence and economic superiority, on which the new eastern *Bundesländer* ("states") quickly became dependent, allowed West Germany to dominate unification, although it was bound by some developments that were already underfoot in the East. Many of these concerned "reckoning": retribution and reconciliation.

Demands for retribution had begun during the mass demonstrations, and the East German government of 1990 had initiated the prosecution of former power holders. East Germans' sense of injustice inflicted by the Stasi moreover supported considerations of vetting individuals with regard to connections to the MfS while West German interest concerned violence at the inner German border. The Unification Treaty included provisions for restitution in these areas and others (see McAdams 2001; Müller 2001), such as property reparation, support, and compensation for victims of the regime. Due to the insistence of civil rights activists, the negotiating governments agreed additionally that the MfS files would be secured and access for the *Betroffene* ("affected," by the regime) enabled, despite some mixed feelings among the political elite (Gauck 1994; Jones 2014).[3] A law passed in November 1991 provided the establishment of the Federal Commission for the Documents of the State Security Police (BStU or Gauck agency; during fieldwork, Birthler agency; and at the time of writing, Jahn agency), and its network of local Stasi archives. The decision to vet individuals who had secretively acted as IMs (unofficial employees) for the Stasi, informing on neighbors or colleagues, was soon criticized by heads of local BStU branches, who felt that vetting should have extended to the SED since the ruling party had governing powers over the MfS.[4]

Joachim Gauck, then head of the BStU, noted that the decision, however, accommodated "people's minimal demand that those who had conspired with the regime, unbeknown to their fellow citizens should be deemed unsuitable for public positions of trust" (1994: 279). By 1997, per James

McAdams's estimate, 50,000 people in both public and private sectors had been dismissed from their posts, although many more had been vetted in the process (2001: 73). The judicial reckoning with the East German regime that many protesters had asked for, however, proved rather more difficult (McAdams 2001; Miller 1998; Quint 2000; Yoder 1999). Some public figures were successfully taken to court, but in many cases the political leaders' advanced age put a stop to their prosecution. Most famously, longtime Head of State Erich Honecker was not tried due to his failing health, much angering the public. This lack of judicial retribution left civil rights activists in particular deeply disappointed. In Bärbel Bohley's oft-quoted words, "We expected justice but we got the *Rechtsstaat* [state based in the rule of law] instead" (cited in McAdams 2001: 7). If measured in convictions, judicial means were somewhat more effective with regard to violence at the inner German border (Ahonen 2006; Quint 2000). Trials began with individual border guards who had killed escapees by using inappropriate force. Prosecution used these trials to begin building cases against those in higher positions. A number of members of the National Defense Council were successfully tried in 1996 and convicted (McAdams 2001; Müller 2001). The public imagination, however, was captured by these first trials. They developed rather quickly after unification while the trials of real power holders, which the public longed for, were drawn out, often ending without result. More than any other measure of reckoning, the prosecution of young men—who, according to public perception, had done their duty and were now suffering for the crimes of their superiors who proved elusive to the *Rechtsstaat*—signaled West German victor's justice to many eastern Germans.

The Wende Years: Living through Transition

For many eastern Germans, the *Wende* years of 1989 and the early 1990s were fraught with tensions. In the winter of 1989 and 1990, the country hung in limbo. Everyday life in the cities was continuously disrupted by mass demonstrations, which, along with government decisions, indecision, changeovers, and negotiations, dominated the news that most people followed closely. Then a twelve-year-old, I remember chats on the street that were ripe with stories of overcrowded train stations and seemingly never-ending traffic jams going west, while some classmates started drawing beards on the pictures of political leaders and youngsters burned their membership cards of the Free German Youth (FDJ)—actions that had been unthinkable just a few days earlier. There was a sense of liminal suspense that was exciting for some, worrying for those who feared for the future, and possibly a mixture of both for many. As unification began to advance, those who favored a democratized East German state resented the fast approach of capitalism, while many others embraced the idea and looked forward to improved services and a greater provision and diversity of consumptive goods. However, the speed of change proved dislocating while West Germany's obvious domination of the process caused resentment.[5]

Unemployment rates, previously an almost unknown phenomenon, shot up as factories and services closed. By the mid-1990s they had risen to 15 percent and a few years later lay at 20 percent in the worst affected "new states" (*neue Länder*), including parts of Mittelland (BpB 2014). Plants that had been heralded as being at the forefront of technological development fell derelict. These changes had a particularly strong impact in a recently socialist society where work had been closely linked to identity (Berdahl 1999a; Jarausch 1994). Not only had the GDR been a "workers and peasant state," according to state ideology, but life had also revolved around work. People had worked in close teams that competed for prizes and socialized during and after work, and East German media emphasized the important contributions that working people and specific brigades were making to society. Moreover, people tended to work for the same business and even in the same job for decades. Due to economic restructuring, within months most had either lost their job or moved to a different one, often in a new business destroying long-stable working teams, while individuals had to get used to a new rhythm of work, new expectations, and new routines (Jarausch 1994: 195). Simultaneously, however, for people who had been denied higher education or careers for political reasons, the changes brought the promise of new opportunities.

Externally, streets, places, and buildings were renamed to rid country- and cityscapes of any traces of socialist ideology. New shops opened, offering unusually large choices of goods at varying prices that easterners found difficult to judge, and a whole host of new processes and practices needed to be internalized, whether they concerned banking, insurances, or school education. Arnold-de Simine posits that in 1990 two-thirds of East Germans' knowledge became obsolete and needed to be replaced with new knowledges and skills (2013: 152). At the same time media were discussing the sell-off of state-owned property and the *Abwicklung*, "unwinding," of East German universities. As many have highlighted (Berdahl 1999a, 1999b, 2010a; Ten Dyke 2001), these changes were uprooting, but they also put a spotlight on West Germany, which provided the blueprint for all matters, from childcare to road traffic signs. Two debates in particular illustrate the extent of the makeover the country experienced and, more importantly, the cultural devaluation this entailed. Applying West German traffic law in the East meant the removal of the "green arrow" at junctions that had allowed cars to join the main road, despite a red light, if it was safe to do so. Easterners considered this a sensible invention that facilitated traffic flow and should have been given serious consideration. Due to fast-growing public pressure, authorities agreed to a longer transitional timeframe and eventually the eastern regulation was adopted nationally. Similarly, pedestrian traffic lights were changed to West German ones, which meant replacing the *Ampelmann*, a small figurine on eastern traffic lights, which was visually more appealing than the rationalized western version. A public campaign saved the *Ampelmann*, which since has become an iconic and heavily commercialized image (Bartmanski 2001).

Unhappiness with the West German government at the seeming disregard of everything eastern was furthered by unpleasant face-to-face encounters with West German entrepreneurs out to make quick money and new managers who had been sent east to reform or build businesses. While many enjoyed meetings with family members, longtime friends, or partnered communities in West Germany, most people experienced at one point or another a sense of difference—in values, demeanor, priorities—between themselves and their western interlocutors. The many encounters of those months thus revealed unexpected cultural differences between the "one people," which was much discussed in media and academia (Erpenbeck and Weinberg 1993; Fessen 1995; Howard 1995; Klein 2001; Koch 1996; Schmidtchen 1997; Schröter 1994; Wagner 1999). These differences found their exaggerated expressions in the stereotypes of the *Ossi*, "Eastie," and the *Wessi*, "Westie" (Fessen 1995). The pejorative term *Ossi*, or *Jammerossi* ("wailing Eastie"), was used by western Germans to describe eastern Germans as lazy and provincial, complaining without changing anything and feeling nostalgic about socialism. Ina Dietzsch (2005; also Arnold-de Simine 2013) describes the situation as one in which German identities became gendered, with the East primarily represented by and through women, a dynamic that entails hierarchies and homogenized society. East Germans in turn dubbed their neighbors *Wessis*, or *Besserwessis* ("better Westies"): superficial and egoistic know-it-alls who failed to value personal relationships.

Disenchantment with unification and resentment over a sense of second-class citizenship led, on the basis of existing senses of solidarity and accomplishment, to a more overt sense of community and identity in the East. Enabled by senses of local belonging, of "being at home" in the East, which had previously been fostered by the socialist state as described above, it turned into an identity with a capital "I" in this context of accelerated change, cultural devaluation, and loss. The term *Ossi* was thus adopted for positive self-ascription marked by local belonging, valuing of social relationships, and awareness of the East German past (Gallinat 2008). These identity politics thus defied the all-German master-narrative from which East German voices appeared to be absent (Berdahl 1999a; Dietzsch 2005; Jones 2014: 11). They went hand in hand with the nostalgic practices of *Ostalgie*.

Amid all this change of the early 1990s, many people began to revalue their very recent past, most visibly through reclaiming East German goods. Items that had been discarded or put into cellars or lofts were dug out again and sold or exhibited at local events. East German "*Ossi*-themed" parties sprang up, where attendees wore uniforms from socialist mass organizations, rooms were adorned with the pictures of GDR officials that used to hang in public halls and schools, music from the 1980s was played, and beer was sold at GDR prices (Berdahl 1999a; Gallinat 2010a). These particular events allowed individuals, as Berdahl (1999a, 1999b) describes, to collectively reestablish a sense of time and place by connecting individual biographies to the passing of an epoch. The practices also served to confirm the troubles of living through the shared uprooting transition and allowed a moment of reflection. They spoke "of a need to establish a community of memory of former GDR citizens that is not divided but united" (Arnold-de Simine 2011: 108). They were not a revival of the GDR as it really existed, as some feared, but in their stylistic overemphasis of socialist signifiers, they rather presented a caricatured picture of the past that simultaneously established the present of unification.

The collective nostalgic practices had their heyday in the 1990s and soon diminished, while *Ostalgie* went commercial (Gallinat 2010a; also Berdahl 2010a). Here it first concerned the reproduction of some East German and local goods, such as the sparkling wine brand Rotkäppchen and later a growing number of products playing on socialist themes: joke compilations, East German recipe books, postcards, T-shirts, and so on. In a number of towns, enterprising individuals opened private GDR museums. These are usually rooms crammed full of stuff—whether toys, medals, uniforms, electrical appliances, household goods, books, or furniture—that local people donated because they no longer had space or use for but which they considered too significant to throw away. The most renowned example of such a museum today is the DDR Museum in Berlin, set up by West German ethnologist and businessman Peter Kenzelmann, who felt that Berlin lacked an exhibition of GDR everyday culture (Arnold-de Simine 2011). These museums were often inspired by a sense of the impending loss of a way of life felt not only at the grassroots of society. Arnold-de Simine observes that both the German Historical Museum (Berlin, founded in the FRG) and the Museum of German History (East Berlin, founded in the GDR) "launched public appeals with the slogan: 'Die DDR ins Museum!' (Put the GDR into a museum!)" (2011: 104). *Ostalgie* museums thus display aspects of everyday East German life, which was often fraught but within which people managed.

Ostalgie has been widely discussed in academic literature, where it is often considered a prime example of socialist nostalgia that is explored in reference to Western colonialism and cultural devaluation, as counter-discourse or critical ironic practice in a fractured present (Bach 2002; Bartmanski 2011; Berdahl 1999a, 1999b, 2010a; Betts 2000; Boyer 2006; Boym 2001; Cooke 2005; Rethmann 2009; for criticism see Gallinat 2008; Hyland 2013; Klumbyte 2009, 2010; Shoshan 2012). The literature shows it is a highly complex phenomenon that incorporates a whole range of different practices but therefore remains ill defined (Jones 2014: 14). Arnold-de Simine concludes:

> *Ostalgie* can also be seen as an attempt to regain agency in the decision of what should be left behind and what should be preserved, but in its favouring of former GDR goods it is not least a veiled critique of a capitalist system that has failed to address the implications of social, economic, and cultural challenges of German unification. (2011: 108)

In German public discourse, *Ostalgie* has been treated as highly contentious (Jones 2014). Through its intertwining with an assertive East German identity and suggestions of critique, however veiled, it has been blamed for the failure of "inner unification" expressed as the persistence of the Berlin "Wall in people's minds" (*die Mauer im Kopf*; e.g.,Veen 2001). Its focus on East German goods moreover continues to link *Ostalgie* to the highly politicized sphere of economic competition between the FRG and GDR, and serves as a reminder that the unrest of 1989 was possibly more motivated by dissatisfaction with economic scarcity than human rights (Arnold-de Simine 2013: 163). Critics thus regard it as a rose-tinted look back at and a revaluation of the past state that denies the reality of state violence, marking such nostalgia as both amoral and historically incorrect. Eastern Germans are attuned to these contestations so that people often explicitly distinguish their senses of feeling at home in the East and of reminiscing about their lives in the GDR from the contentious *Ostalgie* (Gallinat 2008, 2010a; Hyland 2013).

Shortly after unification, however, eastern German civil rights activists, some of whom had joined the main parties, were very concerned by this apparent rise of nostalgia for socialism, which they saw evidenced in growing support for the SED's successor, the Party of Democratic Socialism (PDS), whose very existence was an affront to these actors. In their opinion, revaluations of socialism could only be countered through more aggressive approaches to reckoning and retribution to remind people of what the GDR had really been like (McAdams 2001). Some therefore began to argue for a tribunal or a similar public airing of the many injustices and human rights' abuses of GDR leadership, the socialist party's central committee (*Zentralkomitee*). The new all-German government was receptive to these ideas, and a decision was reached to call for a parliamentary inquiry commission. This solution placed reckoning firmly in the party-political arena, for the first time in German history (Beattie 2006: 157; Steinbach 1999).

Reckoning with the Past Post-1990: The Aufarbeitung of the SED Dictatorship

The parliamentary inquiry commission on the "*Aufarbeitung* of the history and consequences of the SED dictatorship," the first of two such commissions, ran from 1992 to 1994 (Beattie 2008). It took place, like the negotiations about German unification, against the backdrop of a swath of sensationalist media revelations about the Stasi connections of politicians, officeholders, and other persons of public interest (Gauck 1994), which dominated news reporting on the GDR for much of the 1990s. The commission was made up of members of parliament, according to a quota based on the size of each party's fraction, in addition to "experts" comprising of historians and eastern German activists. To avoid giving the impression of victor's justice and to follow requests from easterners that they should be reworking their history, a mixture of eastern and western Germans was appointed, with the former making up 60 percent of the membership. Easterners were represented among the civil rights activists, politicians, and, to a smaller degree, historians. Membership particularly of eastern German politicians fluctuated over time due to the continuous drip of Stasi revelations. Still, eastern German representation never fell below 50 percent, in contrast to public perception of the commission as another instance of West German domination (Beattie 2008).

Observers have regarded the commission's success as limited, which is at least partly because its tasks and goals suffered from a lack of clarity (Beattie 2008; McAdams 2001; Weber 1997; Yoder 1999). Members had differing ideas of what it should be for and different perceptions of what it did. Even the title gives little clue. The term *Aufarbeitung* was chosen over *Bewältigung* due to the realization of recent years that difficult pasts will never be fully overcome, as *Bewältigung* suggests, but require prolonged and potentially changing forms of reckoning. Reckoning, however, is indistinct; it can mean historical exploration as well as remembrance. What is clear, though, is the perception of the past that drove the commission's work, which is that of a difficult period in history and a dictatorial regime, at least in part. This underpinning perception was not only driven by eastern

German activists but shared on the western German side where political will for "reworking" was also an attempt to avoid future accusations of a "third guilt" of silence over this most recent difficult past (Beattie 2008: 31). Or, as Mary Fulbrook puts it:

> [F]or triumphalist West Germans after 1989, who had so successfully shaken off the shackles of their own predemocratic past, the task of energetically "overcoming" the East German dictatorship was in some sense the measure of their own political maturity as seasoned democrats. (1997: 179)

To allow for reckoning while also supporting the fledging founding myth of a unified nation created by eastern Germans' "democratic awakening," the commission was tasked with both documentation and evaluation of the recent past but, unusually for a parliamentary body, not the development of policy recommendations. Beattie summarizes the commission's varied aims as the following:

> "To contribute—in dialogue with the public—to the strengthening of democratic self-confidence and the further development of a common political culture in Germany." The inquiry was to offer the German people, especially those in the eastern states, "assistance in the examination of the past and in the evaluation of personal responsibility," and "to serve an injured sense of justice by laying bare abuses and naming responsibilities." It was also to "contribute to reconciliation in society," although whether this meant East-West or intra-eastern was left open; other references highlighted national reconciliation, expressed as "inner unification." (2008: 47)

In these excerpts *Aufarbeitung* is presented as a collective task for the whole of society that should lead to individuals' reckoning with their lives and moral selves. It is seen as at least contributing, if not essential, to the development of a unified political culture and confident democracy. In turn it would facilitate the "inner unification" that would require a lessening of cultural differences and of senses of East German identity. Finally, reckoning was also to serve retribution for those who had suffered under the regime by identifying those responsible, even if how this would be done was unclear.

With these ideas in mind, a number of voices in the commission argued that a reckoning with the GDR past would also require a critical examination of both states' management of the national socialist past (Beattie 2008; Pearce 2011), which was widely perceived as having been inadequate. This request, however, as well as hopes for the commission to approach the East German past with regard to the manifold life experiences it gave rise to, did not materialize in the commission's final report. According to Beattie (2008; also McAdams 2001; Pearce 2011), for the conservative forces of the Christian Democrats and parts of the SPD, the commission provided an opportunity to delegitimize the socialist regime and reestablish the antitotalitarian consensus of the 1980s, which legitimized the current order. It also allowed the scoring of points against the political left—parts of the SPD, the Green Party—which had long sympathized with the GDR and was now arguing for a softer and more open-ended approach to reckoning. This political game playing was predicated upon the commission's parliamentary character, which came to the fore when the commission coincided with the approach of national elections in 1994.

The Nazi past played a considerable role since the commission approached historical reworking through the means of a *Diktaturvergleich*, a system comparison of dictatorships (e.g., Sabrow 2007). While this signals the gravity of concerns about state violence in the East, it threatened to homogenize these two periods in history. This in turn aided the perception of differences between the now two "totalitarian" regimes versus the democratic and all-German present, in turn proving further that the GDR was "a thoroughly illegitimate state that had never constituted an alternative to the Federal Republic" (Beattie 2008: 36). In this vein, the term SED dictatorship, which had been adopted by the commission to describe their work and which suggests an attempt to focus on the regime of the SED government, was used much more inclusively to mean the "GDR as dictatorship." The Cold War mentalities that underpin these aims of de- and relegitimization were most starkly expressed in views among commission members that, for example, there were no differences between varying types of loyalty in the East, whether they concerned the GDR, the ruling party SED, or socialism (Beattie 2008). The report thus seems to look kindly upon only those who had rejected all of these aspects of GDR life by fleeing the country, even refusing the notion that opposition existed prior to 1989 (145, 150). Such standpoints were contested by various commission members, including eastern German civil rights activists, social democrats, and the opposition parties of the Greens and the PDS. Conservative sentiments nevertheless prevailed so that the commission's report appears to reduce East German history to that of the SED regime and its "sword and shield," as socialist rhetoric described it, the MfS (150). The commission was used by the coalition parties CDU and FDP at least in part to establish the western German political system as the rightful victor over a morally corrupt and repressive regime that was dangerously similar to the Third Reich. It "proclaimed an 'anti-totalitarian consensus' as the political bedrock of unified Germany, implying that alternative views were undemocratic and an unacceptable insult to the victims" (158).

Despite widespread media coverage, the commission's work failed to catch the public imagination, which observers have attributed to a number of factors, including a lack of public participation in its work and a perceived overrepresentation of West Germans within the commission (Beattie 2008: 231–232; Yoder 1999: 78; also Weber 1997). The eastern German dissidents, who at times argued for more nuanced understandings of the GDR, were drowned out by western German politicians, in Jennifer Yoder's view (1999). They also represented only a small percentage of eastern German society that few people could identify with (Yoder 1999). Many eastern Germans thus perceived these early attempts at *Aufarbeitung* very much as western German (Ross 2002: 200), academic efforts to rework a past they did not own and, if that was not offensive enough, through an approach of equation with the much-hated fascist regime. This was difficult to accept for a society that saw itself based in antifascism but which moreover had been crucially aware of the historical importance of the *Wende*. People talked about being a part of history right there in the moment, and, after 1989, many people kept bits of history by holding onto fragments of the Berlin Wall, East German coins and uniforms, and in my own case GDR-time schoolbooks in literature and history. Others handed them over to the private GDR museums mentioned earlier. For people conscious of having "made history" (*Geschichte machen*) with the peaceful revolution, a seeming takeover of the writing of this history was hurtful, and for some it became the most obvious instance of the inequalities embroiled in German unification. The PDS capitalized on this sense of disownership and ran an election campaign that presented party members as eastern Germans sharing a common fate with "the eastern populace's struggle to get out from under the FRG's thumb" (McAdams 2001: 115). From the perspective of longtime critics of the SED regime, however, whether internal or external to East German society, a tough reckoning with the second German dictatorship seemed absolutely necessary given the suffering it had brought and the dangers of forgetting in the context of the *Sonderweg* (Ross 2002: 157). That dangerous nationalist tendencies may be continuing in the East was, in the early 1990s, apart from growing support for the PDS, suggested by the sudden and unexpected rise of neo-Nazi groups in the new *Länder*.

Rather than achieve its aim of leading to societal reckoning and furthering inner unity, the commission thus appears to have unwittingly reinvigorated eastern–western German tensions even if, at least partly, due to misperceptions. The party-political entanglements with reckoning moreover make its historical work questionable from an academic standpoint (Christoph 2013; Faulenbach 1999; Sabrow 2007; Steinbach 1999). Rather, its contributions, just as approaches to the Nazi past previously, need to be seen as concerning the "renegotiation of German identities in the postunification era" (Beattie 2008: 13; Jarausch 1997; Ross 2002) and the use of historical education for nation-building. Even if individuals did not take all of the commission's messages to heart, if *Ostalgie* continued albeit in differing forms over time and continued to trouble *Betroffene* and policymakers, an understanding of dictatorial aspects of the GDR, of the existence of state violence and its victims, began to proliferate in society. This development was furthered by continuing revelations about the Stasi in national and local media.

The commission, moreover, marks the beginning of the discourse of *Aufarbeitung* and its master narrative of the "SED dictatorship." Government-driven and intertwined with Germany's political culture and foundation myth, the discourse has changed little despite much historical research and some hotly contested public debates. In this discourse "the state socialist dictatorship is constructed as 'other,' as the second dictatorship on German soil whose ideology was fundamentally at odds with the current liberal democratic system and national self-understanding" (Jones 2015: 226). Key aspects include the inclusive application of the trope SED dictatorship to mean the "GDR as dictatorship," the attendant focus on state control and violence, signified foremostly by the MfS (Jones 2014; Müller 2001), the comparison with the Third Reich, and the resulting contrast with present-day democracy as securing freedom and prosperity. These pre-concerns have dominated both historical research and public funding since the 1990s together with the intertwined aims of exploration (historical research) and remembrance that arise from the intense, all-German concern with national history.

While the first commission set the tone for *Aufarbeitung*, the second commission (1995–98) was tasked with the development of a national memorial concept that would delineate a landscape of publicly funded memorial sites and potential government funding for research centers or networks. This commission, which began its work under a red–green government, explicitly aimed to include considerations of the complexities of life in East Germany (Beattie 2008; Jones 2014: 11). But although it was acknowledged that many eastern Germans were able to lead "perfectly normal lives and thus have no reason to exclude this period from their own biographies" (materials of the second commission 1999: 195, cited in McAdams 2001: 121), this notion was not further explored. Carola Rudnick notes that in the commission's report "the concept of an 'anti-totalitarian consensus' was retained but 'no longer interpreted in an undifferentiated way based on the theories of totalitarianism'" (2011: 69, cited in Jones 2014: 11). By and large the second commission and the memorial concept of 1999 followed the notions of the emerging discourse of *Aufarbeitung*. For example, many publicly funded sites have a "double history" such as national socialist concentration camps that became Soviet special camps (like Buchenwald) or speak to communist violence such as sites of the former inner German border (Berlin Wall Memorial on Bernauer Strasse) and institutions of the MfS including former prisons—for example, museum "Runde Ecke" in Leipzig) (Deutscher Bundestag 1999; also Pearce 2011).

Historical research has also focused on the structures of the state and the MfS, to such a degree that these aspects of the GDR can be considered over-researched (Sabrow 2007). The field of *Aufarbeitung* is closely intertwined with party-political government not only through public funding but also the remit of public education that almost all institutions carry. This is usually approached through teaching at authentic, historical sites, the memorial museums that fall under national or regional (*Bundesland*) governance, and the involvement of *Zeitzeugen*, historic and moral witnesses who speak of their experiences of trauma and suffering (Arnold-de Simine 2011; Jones 2014). As this shows, not just in the commissions' reports but also in the practice of *Aufarbeitung*, the different goals of remembrance, exploration, and education fall together. This is also evident in the identities and roles of the discourse's key institutions and actors. At the national level, the commission for Stasi files remains highly influential. Its head carries a representative function, and their statements are keenly noted in the media, although the institution's primary task is the, potentially value-neutral, administration of the Stasi archives.

The commission, moreover, has a remit of education and research "to inform the public about Stasi structure and methods of operation" (Gauck 1994: 281). The post with the most public visibility at the level of regional government are the Stasi commissioners of the eastern German states, who primarily support victims, advise in cases of MfS injustice, and contribute to education, in addition to appearing in the media as commentators or observers and advising government. Offices of political education that are part of most state chancelleries also include the East German past in their remit in the new *Länder*, as does the federal office (BpB) in Berlin. Actors from these institutions, in addition to heads of memorial museums and publicly noted commentators, such as vocal former activists, constitute the most influential "opinion makers" from this realm. An organization that enjoys a wider remit and is able to initiate and influence national events is the Foundation for *Aufarbeitung* of the GDR Past (Stiftung zur Aufarbeitung der DDR Vergangenheit) in Berlin. Such a publicly funded institution was first discussed during the second inquiry commission and established in 1998. Its work at times steps outwith the discourse's limited focus on state control and violence, but it appears to have little visibility in local and national media, as well as the grassroots of society, in comparison to the other institutions noted above.

The intertwining of historical and political reckoning is also mirrored in the work of memorial museums to the East German past, whether they are placed within or outwith the national memorial concept. As Jones notes, "it is not unusual for heritage to be linked to contemporary political concerns," especially at sites of "dark tourism," that is, travel associated with death or the suffering of others (2014: 106). At memorial museums, according to Paul Williams (2007), the aims of documentation and education usually converge in the goal to prevent similar future tragedies. Memorial museums thus frequently 'purport to be morally guided' (2007: 131).). Regarding historical exploration, *Aufarbeitung* remains intertwined with research, as many institutions of *Aufarbeitung* employ researchers, and historians also act as policy advisers. This allows the emotive discourse to make claims to historic truth while it gives the historical sciences the public role the nineteenth-century historians had cherished. It also, however, creates difficulties, as a growing number of German historians note (Christoph 2013; Faulenbach 1999; Großbölting 2013; Sabrow 2007).

Questions of Definition: Germany's Second "Totalitarian" "Dictatorship"

The work of historians has been very influential in shaping political and public debates about the East German past, and many of the terms used by historians have made their way into public debates and representations. However, the descriptive and analytical terms used in historiography to refer to the GDR are not always clear, although debates have been "downright acerbic at times" (Ross 2002: 5). Two terms in particular have shaped debates—that of the dictatorship, or SED dictatorship, on the one hand and of totalitarianism on the other. Both terms serve to locate the GDR within a longer German history of repressive political rule, allowing the *Diktaturvergleich* to the Third Reich also used in the inquiry commission.

Views of the history of GDR historiography from abroad largely agree that early interpretations of the East German state were strongly influenced by the Cold War (Jones 2014; Ross 2002). The East German regime was thus interpreted as "totalitarian" following the work of Hannah Arendt (1958) and Carl Friedrich and Zbigniew Brzezinski (1966). While the 1980s saw a mellowing of positions, which Corey Ross (2002) links to West Germany's politics of *Annäherung* ("approach"), German unification meant a renaissance for theories of totalitarianism (also Niven 2006a). Proponents of the "totalitarian stance" viewed attempts of the 1980s to explain the GDR through a "system-immanent" approach as "woolly-headed liberalism" (Ross 2002: 17) that failed to explore repression and state violence. The view of the GDR as totalitarian dictatorship likens the socialist state, as we have seen above, to the, also perceived as totalitarian, Third Reich. Paul Ahonen describes the historical narrative of the totalitarian paradigm or antitotalitarian consensus that arises as one "according to which isolated, fanatical GDR functionaries had terrorized and victimized their own, alienated citizenry" (2006: 144; also Beattie 2006; Fulbrook 1997, 2005, 2007). Ross summarizes the term's analytical application to the GDR as follows: an absence of the "separation of executive, legislative and judicial powers . . . of the rule of law," evident in the fact that the state "systematically infringed basic civil and human rights, and quite obviously because it was not democratically elected" (2002: 20). This approach tends to favor explorations of institutions and mechanisms of rule in order to explain the relative longevity of a repressive system. The totalitarian stance thus views the GDR primarily in terms of a "state of injustice," or *Unrechtsstaat* (171). The term is the antonym to the *Rechtsstaat* as which the FRG describes itself: a state based in the rule of law guaranteed by the independence of the judiciary (Holtmann 2010). For some historians, explorations of the GDR in relation to continuities in German history regarding the authoritarian state and society, illiberal tendencies, but also anti-Western features thus supported the sense of a continuation of the *Sonderweg* (Ross 2002: 157).

A number of historians have criticized this approach primarily for two reasons that also made their way into the discussions of the inquiry commission: for presenting a one-sided view of the GDR and for softening the image of the Third Reich. The approach moreover creates dichotomies in the look back: of state and society, of party and people, and so on (Jones 2014: 3). Critics have thus attempted to create more complex understandings of the GDR and the workings of state power within it. This includes Thomas Lindenberger's revaluation of the notion of *Eigensinn* (loosely translated as "a sense of—or insistence on—one's own interests"), originally used by Alf Luedtke (1993) in relation to resistance on the shop floor, to highlight that "dictatorial rule must not be seen as something wholly separate from social processes and society" (Ross 2002: 50; see also Gallinat 2005). A similar approach has been taken more recently by Fulbrook, who describes the GDR as a "participatory dictatorship" to "emphasize the extent to which 'democratic centralism' as practiced in the GDR, did actually involve very widespread participation of large numbers of people, for a wide variety of reasons" (2005: 12). For her these reasons include commitment to Marxist–Leninist ideals (though not always), coercion (though not always), and *Eigensinn*. Not dissimilar to Gerald Creed's exploration of the "domestication" of socialism in Bulgaria (1998), a process through which inhabitants of one rural area were able to appropriate aspects of collectivization and socialist organization by both adapting *to it* and adapting *it* to their needs, Fulbrook uses the term to highlight that "the people were at one and the same time both constrained and affected by, and yet also actively and often voluntarily carried the . . . social and political system of the GDR" (2005: 12).

These latter historiographic approaches favor social histories that consider micro- and meso-levels in contrast to the exploration of macro-structures that tend to be preferred by scholars of totalitarianism. Another term we will encounter in later chapters, which also stems from this literature, is that of the *durchherrschte Gesellschaft* ("controlled-through society") It was first used by Luedtke (1994) to highlight that authority was an important feature of everyday life in the GDR, not necessarily in relation to the success of authority strategies but more generally in relation to the extent to which such strategies served as reference points (Ross 2002). However, as a descriptor, the term is more commonly understood to show that the power of the party had "far-reaching societal consequences" as it "moulded society all the way into its finest branches" (Kocka 1998, cited in Ross 2002: 49). While Kocka simultaneously insists that "East German society and everyday life [however] cannot be reduced to political steering and control" (49), such fineries of academic arguments appear to have been lost with the term's adoption in the discourse of *Aufarbeitung*, as later chapters will show.

Despite their differing emphases and viewpoints, there is then broad agreement in historiography that the GDR was a "dictatorship." As the above shows, the term opens up a continuum of interpretations that reach from the pole of the "totalitarian system," akin to Nazi Germany, to the "participatory dictatorship." Along this scale lies a range of other terms, such as Kocka's "modern dictatorship" (1994), Stefan Wolle's "loving dictatorship" (1998), Jarausch's "welfare dictatorship" (1999), and the "party dictatorship," which became the SED dictatorship, among others (see Ross 2002 for a detailed analysis). One analytical term that could be seen as stepping outside of this rhetoric is the "authoritarian state" (Müller 2001). This approach does not see power located in one single location but assumes, albeit limited, political pluralism and shows differences in relation to mass mobilization and ideology in comparison to totalitarian states. It is, however, used primarily to make this specific distinction, as historians regard both authoritarian and totalitarian regimes as "dictatorial" (Ross 2002: 24).

With Jan-Werner Müller, I consider the GDR state as a "repressive authoritarian" regime (2001: 250). I choose the term "authoritarian" because, in contrast to the "dictatorship," it is less loaded and as such should keep the arguments presented here from getting tangled up within the morally charged contentions they explore. It is moreover a term frequently mentioned by informants from across the two spheres of fieldwork in reference to their personal experiences of life in the GDR, where they describe the extent of prescriptiveness regarding choices, actions, and behaviors that they experienced and their location within hierarchical settings. Where I wish to highlight dictatorial aspects of this past, I will talk about "repression" and "state violence." I will use the terms "dictatorship" and "SED dictatorship" where these are used in the situations, conversations, and documents under discussion. Where these latter terms appear to be located toward the totalitarian end of this descriptive continuum and to be thought with the Nazi past in mind, I will use "totalitarian." Where the term SED dictatorship is used to refer to the entirety of East German state and society, I will use the "GDR as dictatorship."

Negotiating the Boundaries of Nationally Funded Memory-Work

In the mid-2000s, approximately a decade after the two parliamentary inquiry commissions, a group of academic experts and eastern German civil rights activists were asked by the then-red–green coalition government to develop policy recommendations for a research network on *Aufarbeitung*. The group, led by historian Martin Sabrow, used this task to review institutionalized reworking more generally and argued that the national memory landscape suffered from a number of omissions (Sabrow et al. 2007). According to the group, shortcomings included, among others, an underrepresentation of GDR-time opposition and resistance, of society and state control, and, given that the socialist regime had been if not supported certainly accepted by the majority of the population, of the *Bindungskräfte*, the "ties that bound" people within and to the regime. The later suggests a system-immanent approach.

Although the Sabrow commission anticipated some contention over its suggestions, the fierceness of reactions came as a surprise (2007). A number of influential commentators saw the proposed changes quite simply as "whitewashing" the dictatorial regime (Christoph 2013; Sabrow 2007 et al.). The commission nevertheless had some impact on the rewriting of the national memorial concept, which was under way at the time of fieldwork, then again under a Christian Democratic government (Jones 2014; Pearce 2011). At the parliamentary debate about the latest draft in November 2007, the topic that proved most contentious concerned everyday life in the GDR. Experts arguing for its inclusion regarded it as a matter of social history that allowed exploring how the dictatorship functioned and was reproduced in everyday life. Critics, however, highlighted that including questions of everyday life in reckoning with the Third Reich had never been seen as legitimate and that the prosaic everyday had no place in publicly funded memorial structures that should always forefront the remembrance of victims. In this view, *Aufarbeitung* was to be about a future-oriented, morally guided reckoning that presupposes a difficult past, not "mere" musealization. Most of all, they were concerned that the topic would invite unreflective nostalgia, *Ostalgie*, while others argued that the topic would allow approaching nostalgia, since it offered a way to connect to people through their personal recollections.

The revision that was agreed upon in 2008 paid heed to some of the suggestions made by the Sabrow commission but avoided any changes that could have widened the limited and limiting understanding of the "GDR as dictatorship" (Deutscher Bundestag 2008; cf. Christoph 2013). Jones (2014: 19) cites Rudnick, who sees the rewritten concepts as a return to more conservative memorial politics while also constituting a considerable compromise. The concept's text thus exemplifies the hallmarks of the emotive, nation-building, governmental discourse of *Aufarbeitung* then and now. From the preamble:

> The history of 20th century Germany was lastingly shaped by the regime of national socialism whose crimes against humanity and destructive wars took millions of lives. The politics of national socialism led to the division of Germany. While in West Germany after 1945 the development of a lawful democracy was achieved, a communist dictatorship was established in the Soviet-occupied zone and later the GDR, which could only be overcome in 1989/1990. With the revision of the memorial concept from 1999 . . . the federal government fulfills Germany's historical duty: Its goal is to realize responsibility, strengthen reworking and to deepen commemoration. (Deutscher Bundestag 2008: 1)

Like the inquiry commission, this concept regards a reckoning with the nations' two difficult pasts as a national responsibility. In this endeavor, it continues to roll together practices of exploration and research (here "reworking") and commemoration. The final sentence that sets out these aims is also the concept's motto, which confirms the discourse's aims of a moralizing memory-work in the context of Germany's particular responsibilities: "*realizing responsibility*, strengthening reworking, and deepening commemoration" (emphasis added). The introduction to the concept describes the view of the SED regime that underpins these concerns. The excerpt below follows a long paragraph on the national socialist regime and its rule of terror, from which the East German past needs to be distinguished without, however, being trivialized, as the widely accepted Faulenbach formula has it (Faulenbach 1993).[6]

It is further the duty of state and society to remind of the injustice caused by the SED dictatorship and to safeguard the memory of the victims of communism in Germany in this manner. For decades people suffered behind barbed wire and the wall under lack of freedom, repression and pressure to conform and political opponents faced measures of persecution and dissolution [Zersetzung] by the ever-present State Security Police.[7] The federal government wishes to strengthen the reworking of the dictatorship in the SBZ [Soviet-occupied zone] and the GDR and the remembrance of their victims. (Deutscher Bundestag 2008: 2)

Just as the inquiry commission of the 1990s, the memorial concept from 2008 delineates an appropriate memory of the GDR as of oppression, persecution, and victimhood, which is signified by the inner German border, the MfS, and its victims. In this vein, memorial sites and places of remembrance are categorized under four themes: 1) German division and the border; 2) surveillance and persecution; 3) society and the everyday; 4) resistance and opposition. The latter two are based on recommendations of the Sabrow commission, but the text makes clear that the third, much discussed theme of the everyday and society (*Alltag und Gesellschaft*) is not intended to allow for explorations of social and political structures that reach beyond the controlling measures of a dictatorial state. As the first sentence in this rubric explains, it is included (only) "to counter any trivialization of the SED dictatorship and any *Ostalgie*." Therefore, "everyday life is to be represented within the context of the dictatorship," and "it has to become apparent that people in the GDR were subjugated to extensive state control" (Deutscher Bundestag 2008: 9). The memorial concept and its implementation thus mean that any state-supported museums or memorials "should not be a reflection of the positive memories of social and economic security shared within families, but a counter to [their] perceived dominance . . . in popular discourse" (Jones 2014: 19). The concept considers four sites where the GDR everyday may be represented, and two of these opened new exhibitions in response to the revised concept: one is the Tränenpalast (Palace of Tears) and the other the Kulturbrauerei, both in Berlin. However, while everyday life is represented at both these sites, it is set within a curatorial framework that emphasizes intrusions of the SED and GDR state into private lives (Jones 2015). The narratives presented here are thus of the "controlled-through" society, where life took place "under the dictatorship," leaving no space for potential experiences of any kind of normality.

As the above shows, since the early 1990s, the East German past has been considered by this official discourse as the "second German dictatorship" and thus one part of Germany's "double burden in history" (*doppelte Vergangenheit*).[8] In this vein, the socialist state was also soon characterized as an *Unrechtsstaat*, a state of injustice, as explained above. While the term SED dictatorship is difficult to argue with, since it confines dictatorial rule to the despised SED leadership and since state violence did exist, this latter denotation caused some heated debates in public discourse, where the term was understood in a much wider sense (e.g., Roellecke 2009 and online comments; also Gallinat 2006a). Many people took the term to suggest the GDR had been unjust in every respect, which jarred uncomfortably with their more complex understandings arising from personal experiences and eastern German senses of pride in having managed in the GDR. The debate is symptomatic of contestations about the East German past more generally: its representation as dictatorship and the diametrical opposite of today's democratic and free order, which creates an image of the past GDR as consisting of victims, perpetrators, and bystanders. And many eastern Germans sense disparity between such a black-and-white view and, at least some of, their own recollections (also Jones 2014). Mary Fulbrook puts it thus:

> Faced with accounts of repression, complicity and collusion, former citizens of the GDR claimed that their own memories and experiences told them otherwise. Their own biographies did not seem to fit easily within the bleak picture of oppression and fear. Most East Germans did not feel that they had spent up to four decades of their lives trembling in "inner migration," or conspiratorially plotting against the regime, or making a pact with the Red Devil for private advancement. Life for most people in the GDR was simply not (or not for most people most of the time) the way it was described in black-and-white characterisations of "Germany's second dictatorship." (2005: 2)

Twenty(-five) Years after the Fall of the Berlin Wall

In 2007, when fieldwork began, Germany was preparing for the twentieth anniversary of the fall of the Berlin Wall and unification (2009 and 2010, respectively). At the time of writing, the twenty-fifth anniversary had just passed. During fieldwork, preparations were noticeable in Mittelland, where the Working Group *Aufarbeitung* set up a working party "peaceful revolution 2009" to coordinate anniversary activities in the region and a second one responsible for initiating activities in the city of Tillberg itself; a similar group was active in the state's second largest city, Wellau. At the national level, the discourse of *Aufarbeitung* received renewed impetus with the public discussion of the revised memorial concept in November 2007, which was agreed by parliament in June 2008. In that same session, parliamentary members also debated the development of a "monument to freedom and unity" (*Freiheits- und Einheitsdenkmal*), once again in Berlin, which was agreed upon despite some contentions (such as the monument's location in Berlin instead of Leipzig, where the 1989 demonstrations had begun). According to the parliament's vice president, Wolfgang Thierse—former member of the Neues Forum and now social democrat—the monument was to celebrate the nation's immense "historical luck" and to serve as reminder that "freedom and unity" belonged together ("9. November" 2007).[9]

The debates about the GDR past continue, most recently with the publication of a report on the "current status of *Aufarbeitung*" by Minister of Culture Bernd Neumann in 2013, which was debated in parliament in the same year (Deutscher Bundestag 2013a). In Klaus Christoph's (2013) estimation, both report and debate follow the "well-trodden paths" of *Aufarbeitung*; no change was discussed, and criticism appeared limited to the Left Party. In the debate, the party came under considerable criticism from members of the other parties, who called on the Left to "address its [own] past," which its deputies "insisted the party had done" (Jones 2014: 19–20). One theme that becomes more prominent in this most recent report, however, is education. The document notes that although the federal government spent approximately 100 million euros annually on *Aufarbeitung*, efforts in education needed to be strengthened. Neumann explained this with "disconcerting findings in different studies regarding young people's historical knowledge," which "ought to wake up all those responsible to further strengthen efforts of reworking, especially in schools" (Deutscher Bundestag 2013b; Jones 2014: 19). We will encounter some of these studies and their impact in Mittelland in chapter 6.

In the publicly funded memorial museum landscape, the topic of the GDR everyday, which had proven so contentious in the mid-2000s as we saw above, has become represented in the two new exhibitions at the Tränenpalast and the Kulturbrauerei in Berlin. These joined a number of previously existing sites, including the Documentation Centre of the Culture of the GDR Everyday in Eisenhüttenstadt, which has also long focused on everyday life in the GDR (Arnold-de Simine 2013).[10] As Jones's work shows (2014, 2015), both memorial museums that focus on oppression, particularly sites dedicated to the Stasi, and the exhibitions established recently as an outcome of the 2008 Memorial Concept, use approaches that suggest a narrative of the "GDR as dictatorship" to visitors. The Kulturbrauerei and Tränenpalast achieve this by focusing on the "extraordinary experiences" of repression and state intrusion into the private sphere of "ordinary people." The GDR everyday is then interpreted and represented as the stories of those "normal people," rather than as the experiences of "normal lives" or "in the understanding of the term ['GDR everyday'] as popular material culture" as in nostalgic practices and private GDR museums (Jones 2015: 227).

* * *

The year 2009, the twentieth anniversary of the fall of the Berlin Wall, carried several symbolic meanings that spoke to an emerging foundation myth of unification that sees the GDR as marked by the socialist party's dictatorial regime, overcome by a movement for democratic rights that led to the unification of the long divided nation, which had always been "better together," whereby the FRG's political traditions and practices, which had proved durable and thus legitimate, provided the path forward. The anniversary coincided with the sixtieth anniversary of the FRG's Grundgesetz, the Basic Law that supports western German constitutional patriotism with its attachments to democracy, human rights, and the justice of the Rechtsstaat (Arnold-de Simine 2013: 48). The anniversary moreover brought into sharp relief the maturing of a new generation of Germans who had neither experienced national division nor the GDR and who appeared susceptible to the recruitment efforts of the Far Right, which heightened concerns about a continuation of sentiments that had supported German exceptionalism, the Sonderweg, in the eastern parts of the nation. The view from government is that this was only to be countered through education in history—teaching history and fostering values thus remain closely intertwined.

This chapter has shown that the discourse of Aufarbeitung has developed logics that tie past and present together in categorically clear and morally certain binaries, although this is a relatively young discourse that was also not intended to present such a black-and-white picture of the GDR by some of the actors involved in its production in the early 1990s, such as the former civil rights activists. Moreover, the discourse's master narrative of the "GDR as dictatorship" is contentious in eastern German society and hence not well suited to support senses of belonging in the united nation. The question thus arises how local institutions work within this national framework and how they create narratives about the past GDR that engage and educate the local population while being informed by, or attempting to suit, wider national understandings of German history. This will be the topic of chapter 4. Chapter 3 will ask how the Daily Paper, which sees itself as a democratic institution that rejects totalitarian rule in history, creates news stories about the past while also binding its Mittelland readership.

The perception of divergence between many eastern Germans' recollections and the governmental discourse of Aufarbeitung is furthered by the fact that notions of identity and self-worth in the eastern states remain intertwined with shared experiences of coping in the previous political system, with the shortage economy and likewise with an uprooting transformation during the Wende. The emerging founding myth of unification, however, does not give space to these senses of belonging, which would require an acknowledgment of GDR-time achievements or, at least, the possibility of experiences of "normality." Moreover, although eastern Germans fought for civil rights in 1989, as the above shows, these were not always the same rights as those now guaranteed by the representative, parliamentary democratic state and its Basic Law. Rather, the civic movement that initiated the regime's fall sought direct democracy and social justice, notions that are often in tension with post-*Wende* experiences and present-day political practices. There is then a further disjuncture between the founding myth of Germany as reunited by East Germans' "democratic awakening" in 1989 and these eastern Germans' experiences and hopes for the future. As head of the BStU (and current German president) Joachim Gauck put it in his address to parliament at the first decennial of the fall of the Berlin Wall: "many [of the activists] 'had dreamed of paradise . . . and woke up in North Rhine-Westfalia,' the western Land where Bonn [capital of the FRG] was located" (McAdams 2001: 157). Just as "unification offered a return to and an escape from history" (Jarausch 1994: 182), reckoning with the past thus seems to offer and require an appraisal of the nation's present and future. Such is the case also because eastern Germans have made a unique contribution to German history, which is easily forgotten: "the 'historical gift' of having made a revolution in the name of freedom *on their own*" (Gauck, cited in McAdams 2001: 158; emphasis added). We will return to this question of how the production of memory discourses intertwines with notions of democracy and citizenship in chapters 6 and 7. First we will turn to the local actors who create representations of the East German past in Mittelland today.

Notes

1. For the different phases of memory-work regarding the Third Reich in the FRG, see Fulbrook (1999) and Ruth Wittlinger (2006).
2. It further drew from the notion of *Stunde Null* ("zero hour"), which posits that Nazi Germany's fall in 1945 was complete, leading not to a rebuilding of state and society but an entirely new beginning (Falser 2008). This notion was already widely criticized in the 1980s (see Hüppauf 1981; Wende 2000).
3. This was a significant victory for the civic movement, which wanted to safeguard the files from use by other security services (Miller 1998). Famously, Helmuth Kohl worried that the files would poison the positive atmosphere of unification (McAdams 2001: 84).
4. The BStU estimates that in the late 1980s, around 180,000 individuals (just under 1 percent of the population) were registered IMs (BStU 2014; the figure refers to

IMs registered with the MfS and active in the late 1980s). The ruling SED had achieved a membership of just over two million in May 1989 (Schubert and Klein 2011), around 12 percent of the population. Scrutinizing this category thus was not feasible. Moreover, membership of the SED had been a public aspect of life in the GDR that distinguishes it qualitatively from the secretive collaboration with the MfS.

5. Sentiments about unification differed between generations, as well as between parts of society. These are details I do not have the space to discuss here.

6. The agreed principle regarding comparisons between the two dictatorships is to "compare without equalizing" (*vergleichen ohne gleichzusetzen*), which aims to protect the singularity of the Holocaust (Sühl 1994).

7. *Zersetzung* is a key method of the MfS that aimed to disrupt the social networks of targets so that individuals would find themselves isolated (Behnke and Fuchs 1995; Miller 1998).

8. Various scholars have commented on the problems and values associated with the underpinning approach of *Diktaturvergleich* (Evans 2005; Fulbrook 1997; Sabrow 2007; Sühl 1994).

9. In April 2016 the government decided to stop building the long planned monument. A similar monument may be erected at a later date and different place (Schönball 2016).

10. The DKZ opened in 1993 and exhibits primarily aspects of material culture in order to "represent the diversity of societies rather than giving a distinct narrative of history" (Ludwig 2007, cited in Arnold-de Simine 2011: 101, also 2013). This curatorial approach distinguished the DKZ from other publicly funded sites until its inclusion in the Memorial Concept required the development of a new exhibition (opened in 2012) to show how everyday life in the GDR had been "controlled through" (see Arnold-de Simine 2013).

Chapter Two

INSTITUTIONS THAT WRITE MEMORY
The Working Group *Aufarbeitung*
and the *Daily Paper* Introduced

≥•≤

This chapter provides an introduction to the two institutional realms under exploration in this book, the Working Group *Aufarbeitung* and the newspaper *Daily Paper*. Through ethnographic description, it details the makeup of each realm in terms of relevant structures, institutional histories and remits, and working practices; it explores how these pertain to the question of national history and the institutions' positions vis-à-vis democratic governance structures and the local population. The chapter will highlight how the aim of the Working Group, and, at its center, the Office for Political Education (LpB)—to shape citizens fit for the democratic present through education—is motivated in part by a perception of Mittelland as a project of the transition that needs to be brought to completion. This contrasts with the *Daily Paper*'s goal to enable citizenship through information and the expression of opinion on its pages—a process through which the newspaper simultaneously establishes itself as a fourth democratic power within the region. To provide a flavor of fieldwork relations and realities, descriptions will follow the terms of address used then by the fieldworkers. As the below will show, this was the family name and the polite third-person plural (*Sie*) within the Working Group *Aufarbeitung*, while the *Daily Paper* staff were on first-name terms with each other—a practice that was immediately extended to the two researchers with the explanation that this was "an East German habit." The practice excluded management and some senior staff for whom the polite form of address remained reserved. First, however, we will turn to the Working Group and the institution at its center, the LpB.

Aufarbeitung and Political Education

On a bright, early summer morning, just ten days after the start of fieldwork at the Office for Political Education, Sabine found herself in a car with the office's director, Herr Bohlmann, as always elegantly and officially attired in suit and tie, on the way to a meeting of the Working Group *Aufarbeitung*. As the car moved along Mittelland's newly improved and still in-need-of-repair roads, Bohlmann, who was driving, and his secretary, Frau George, filled Sabine in on who would attend this meeting and what would be discussed, pointing out landmarks as they passed. The meeting was to take place in a small rural estate near Tillberg, which is owned by the Konrad Adenauer Foundation (KAS), the political education institute of the conservative CDU. The quiet estate lies in nice surroundings, offers a venue for weddings or parties, and has poor mobile network coverage, the latter of which was seen as advantageous for this kind of meeting.

On the estate, members of the group had already congregated in a boardroom with an oval table and meeting setup. Chairs for thirteen people were set out, and all participants appeared, like Bohlmann, in smart, professional dress. Sabine was soon greeted by the director of the former Stasi prison memorial museum, Jochen Franke, whom we had met a few weeks ago when setting the project up in Tillberg. At the very start of the meeting, which was chaired and minuted by the LpB through Bohlmann and his secretary, Sabine had a chance to introduce the research project, since, Bohlmann explained, "everyone relevant to the project" was gathered here. There were the usual questions about the research topic, methods, links to local universities, and why this East German topic was of interest to British academia, but everyone seemed generally interested and happy to help out. Mittelland's Stasi commissioner, Herr Schumacher, passed his card to Sabine with a knowing smile. It did not take long either until he formally introduced his role, his office, and then himself, as an "East German." The head of one of two regional branches of the Federal Commissioner for the Documents of the State Security Police (BStU) announced her support across the large wooden table; her colleague, Herr Fuhr, head of the second local BStU office, later had some queries, while the director of Mittelland's border checkpoint memorial museum wanted to know what kind of interviews we planned to undertake. The questions and answers took almost forty-five minutes but signaled participants' keen interest in our interest in their work.

The remainder of the meeting was taken up by a variety of topics, including a recently concluded program on democratic values and a framework on working with teachers and schools written by Franke. Here a discussion followed, where all agreed that the GDR past in particular received too little attention in school curricula. The final point of the meeting concerned the organization of a sub-team to begin coordinating activities for the twentieth anniversary of the fall of the Berlin Wall in 2009. When the meeting ended, participants made their way to the dining room for lunch, where interested colleagues tried to catch Sabine's attention and vice versa. There were representatives of the Friedrich Ebert Foundation (FES)—a political education institute affiliated with the SPD—and the head of a local special camp (*Speziallager*, a branch of a concentration camp), the only representative of an institution that deals explicitly with the Third Reich although, according to Bohlmann, both the Working Group and his LpB of course included the "first German dictatorship" under *Aufarbeitung*. The representative of the KAS and Herr Koehler from the border checkpoint memorial museum also joined the group, which was engaged in a discussion about the difficulties memorial museums face in accessing funding. When energy for the heavy topic was exhausted, conversation turned to the fish that had been served for lunch and individuals' culinary preferences. Meanwhile, at another table Bohlmann was joined first by one, then another, then yet another participant of the previous meeting, as if he was running a drop-in session over his salmon. The Office for Political Education is close to Mittelland's administration, and one of its main remits is to allocate funding for political education work. The office thus has considerable monetary power, and both within and outside of Working Group business, the institutions gathered here need and want to work with the LpB.

The Working Group: From Sharing Experiences to a Meeting of Managers

The Working Group meets approximately every two months to discuss current topics and to coordinate events relating to the "reworking of the past." While the group's remit includes both German dictatorships, the GDR takes a clear priority both in the group's composition and its activities. In fact, the group itself is the outcome of concerns over managing the legacies of socialism in the early 1990s.

During the turbulent *Wende* years, a number of institutions developed in Mittelland and sought to create ways of commemorating dictatorial aspects of the socialist regime. This included the Citizen Initiative, an oppositional group that had been instrumental during the autumn of 1989 and spring of 1990, and the former Stasi prison turned memorial museum, located just next door to the Citizen Initiative, which, in those early years, served both as a port of call for many victims of the MfS and as the target of former Stasi officers' backhanded interferences. The Association of Victims of Stalinism (Victim Association hereafter) soon took residence in the office building attached to the memorial museum. In a similar position were the former Stasi and Third Reich prison in Mittelland's second largest town, Wellau, and the newly elected Stasi commissioner of Mittelland's own state government, who was to support victims with requests for financial support and restitution, write appraisals of individuals' engagement with the Stasi, and liaise with victim associations. The individuals running these and similar institutions knew each other personally through attending relevant events and soon realized they were fighting similar battles, trying to establish roles for their organizations, engage with a seemingly disinterested public (Gallinat 2006a), counter the aggression of former elites, gain funding, and support the *Betroffene* (those "affected" by the regime). Leaders of these institutions therefore began meeting relatively regularly to discuss common problems and support each other as Mittelland's memory landscape and its administration was still very much in flux. At the end of the 1990s, under the lead of the then Stasi commissioner, it was agreed to give these conversations a more formal framework, and the Working Group *Aufarbeitung* was established.

The Working Group extended its membership to the Ministry of Culture and the political education institutions of the main political parties among others. The Office for Political Education had already been part of the group and took over chairmanship a few years later. A part of the State Chancellery, with a well-endowed budget and the sole remit of "political education" under which *Aufarbeitung* is considered to be falling here, the office appeared a logical choice for the role. While discussions at meetings are often critical—sometimes controversial—and remain flavored by participants' work and private experiences, they are clearly business meetings with agendas, minutes, and coffee or lunch. Directors or heads of the represented institutions usually attend to allow for on-the-spot decision-making. Nevertheless, many issues go through more than one meeting and are tweaked and trimmed in between through phone calls and private conversations of individual directors who liaise outside of the formal setting of group meetings. The Working Group today is a meeting of managers who seek to promote topics relating to their remit and the East German past and contribute based on their institutions' needs for impact and financing.

While some meetings of the Working Group, like the one described above, attract many members, it became clear during fieldwork that a

Illustration 2.1. The courtyard of the former Stasi prison memorial museum.
To the right is the former guard barrack (see the tower in the top right), which now hosts the memorial museum's offices. The Victim Association met in the building out of sight to the left. The back wall features a quote from Milan Kundera as the memorial museum's motto: "Man's struggle against power is the struggle of memory against forgetting" (author's translation).

smaller number of institutions collaborates more frequently. Those active in this "inner circle" made themselves known to Sabine and me rather soon during fieldwork, starting with the Stasi commissioner passing on his card in that first meeting Sabine attended. This group of course includes the Office for Political Education and said Stasi commissioner (Stasi-Beauftragter; LStU), Schumacher, a trim man in his fifties who often introduces himself as one of the few East Germans in this group despite there being at least two others of East German and local origin. Additionally, there are the heads of the two local offices of the Birthler agency, Herr Fuhr and Frau Herzog; Jochen Franke, the thirty-something historian who directs the former Stasi prison memorial museum; and the border checkpoint memorial museum and its dynamic director, Koehler. Halfway through fieldwork, the newly elected head of the Memorial Foundation, Schneider, also joined. While each of these institutions has its own remit, all of them also have the task of education, or more broadly, engagement work, conferred to them by their relevant authority. In most cases this is Mittelland's Ministry of the Interior, and in the case of the local branches of the BStU, it is the federal office in Berlin, which during fieldwork was referred to as the Birthler agency.

In this group, Bohlmann, Franke, and Schneider are originally from the FRG, while Fuhr—a confident man in his early forties—Herzog, and Schumacher are East German. Both Schumacher and Herzog were active in the opposition in the late 1980s and helped see through the changes of the *Wende* years. In meetings, however, East or West German origin play little role; even in informal chats it is something these directors and managers raise infrequently, apart from Schumacher's insistence that he can contribute much from his own experiences of dissidence. But it is this that he raises, instead of a concern that engineering and hegemonic West Germans have taken over the management of the East German past, as one might expect given public sentiments in the 1990s (see chapter 1) and as I at times queried during fieldwork. Why East–West German contentions move into the background or are downplayed among this group of individuals will become more apparent in chapter 4.

The brief summary of a Working Group meeting above already indicates the topics that shaped the group's work during the time of fieldwork. This was for several months the issue of teaching GDR history in schools and the training of Mittelland's history teachers, a topic in which the LpB had much stake and which will be explored in chapter 4. Furthermore, the work included preparations for the anniversary of 2009—as well as the question of which, and even how many, anniversaries should be celebrated then—and, finally, democracy education, both topics of chapter 6.

Educating the Educators: The Administrative Center, the LpB

The Office for Political Education is an administrative department that figures primarily in the background, but there rather prominently, of educational and political matters. Founded in the FRG in the 1960s, this office exists in most German states and relates to the Federal Office for Political Education in Berlin (BpB). In Mittelland, as in many other states, it is part of the government's State Chancellery, which at the time was a CDU-majority administration. According to the LpB's constitution, however, the office is "independent" and "beyond parties." Political parties represented in the state parliament can request posts in the office relative to the number of seats they command, and during fieldwork most managerial staff were indeed party members covering the CDU, SPD, and FDP. The advisory committee that oversees the LpB's work (yet cannot determine topics or content) is also made up of parliamentary members on a pro rata basis. Decisions about which topics are to be pursued and what events organized are guided foremostly by topicality and the calendar. In short, they depend on current events or incidents in the region, annual holidays, and anniversaries.

The office in Tillberg is located on a side street to the prestigious, cobbled Government Lane, where most government departments are housed in beautifully restored nineteenth-century villas. The office's building is less historic but still imposing with marble effect flooring in the corridors and glass panel doors. The only publicly accessible part of the LpB is its book repository, which provides current literature, mostly on political institutions and German history, for a small fee to interested citizens. LpBs also have a modest budget for publishing. The main part of the office is located on the building's second floor, however, and clearly designed as less rather than more outward facing, in contrast to many other institutions in the Working Group. The memorial museums, for example, have receptions and meeting rooms; the former Stasi prison also has a library. At the Stasi commissioner's, open doors and a comfy sofa welcome visitors who may be attending the weekly drop-in/advice session. The local offices of the Federal Commissioner for the Stasi Files only recently started doing more engagement work but now regularly offer tours through the archives, which are taken up well. At the LpB, visitors are required to ring the bell at the top of the stairs, which prompts whichever member of staff happens to be closest to open the door, revealing a long corridor of offices and at its end an infrequently used meeting room with a large oval table.

Work at the Office for Political Education consists primarily of writing, printing, and reading documents; coordinating the distribution of paperwork; sending emails; making phone calls to liaise with other institutions; and processing and signing forms. Heads of departments often leave the office for meetings elsewhere, to then reappear and disappear into their individual offices from which they liaise with their clerical support and the director. This routine of mostly quiet office work changes only ahead of bigger events, when clerical staff from different departments come together to organize mailings and pack brochures, info materials, pens, paper, and anything else that may be required for workshops, talks, or exhibitions.

This working everyday is supported by a structure that divides roles and responsibilities between distinct "departments." When research began, there were five departments each led by a head and supported by one or two clerical staff. In addition, there is the directorate with the main office. Department one is finances and manages the office's funding of political education projects run by governmental and nongovernmental organizations (schools, religious organizations, charities, etc.), such as school trips to former concentration camps, events for tolerance and fairness or against extremism, and citizen initiatives. Departments two, three, and four constitute the office's substantive work while department five is the book repository. Department two, which became the main focus of fieldwork, signs responsible for political education in schools and higher education, which primarily meant teacher training and often concerned the East German past. As priorities shifted for the LpB in 2008, this department focused more explicitly on democracy education (*Demokratieausbildung*) and became key to the office's restructuring. Department three deals with "current topics" in general and youth education and was mostly taken up with initiatives against right-wing extremism through collaboration with grassroots organizations. Department four holds responsibility for the topical areas of state, federal, and European politics.

The Working Group's concerns about school history teaching are replicated at the Office for Political Education, where working with the "educators" takes a priority. While the office does some work directly in schools, its primary concern for efficient government, as per the foundational decree from 1991, is training those who do the educating, the "multipliers" (*Multiplikatoren*), which means school teachers and, moreover, subject specialists.[1] Teacher training events developed by department two—under the lead of Frau Wolf, an organized woman with a background in media work—in 2007 included, for example, a training event for history teachers on the GDR past, workshops such as "Changes of Values in East Germany after 1989" and "Cultural Diversity, Approaching Foreign Investors," and one-day projects at or with Mittelland's memorial museums to demonstrate opportunities for teaching "on site." Frau Wolf's counterpart in department three, the resolute Frau Buesing, organized workshops that aimed to spread knowledge about and skills in dealing with extremism, such as learning about right-wing rock music and developing civic engagement. Since neo-Nazi violence proliferated locally in terms of extremism, the Nazi past was considered to fall into this area. At events the LpB both supports the development of content and provides staff and financial support. What exactly is provided, however, depends on agreements with other collaborators.

While teachers are required to take on-the-job training for further development, what they attend is their choice. At the time of fieldwork, both members at the Working Group and LpB staff shared a frustrated concern that GDR history was rarely taught in schools. The subject dropped off the end of a chronologically organized curriculum rather quickly when teachers were ill or when project weeks disrupted teaching. The reason for this was seen as lying with both the curriculum and teachers, who seemed reluctant to broach a topic that remained so close to their personal biographies. For Frau Wolf, this was one reason why this recent past took precedence over the Third Reich, which seemed to be covered well enough in local schools.

In both departments there is a sense of not just working but also struggling with local teachers and other target groups whose East German upbringing seem to create obstacles for the office's aim of political education. From the office's perspective, it is important not just to transmit knowledge about politics but also to instill the values and skills necessary for life in a democratic and plural society. Experiences at workshops, however, showed that, never mind the next generation, even the teachers were trying to bypass the processes that would allow them to accept the new values and knowledges, according to Wolf and Buesing. For example, many teachers seemed to expect to take away fully formed teaching materials, while Buesing and Wolf looked for rich discussions in their workshops to enable teachers to develop their own locally relevant materials. According to Wolf, this was because many teachers were trained during GDR times, as she explained to Sabine. They had learned in those schools and were continuing what had been tried and tested: "The content has changed, but the didactics remain the same because they are rooted in people's minds." She also observes this in the materials her children bring home from school, much of which much is almost identical to GDR-time texts. This perception of the GDR-time legacies in teacherhood is furthered by the continued presence of former citizenship studies (*Staatsbürgerkunde*) teachers, the heavily ideological East German counterpart to general or social studies at secondary schools, which also concerns the two department leads. And during fieldwork, the State Chancellery urged the LpB to address these teachers' apparent lack of training in democratic politics. The proliferation of right-wing radicalism in East Germany, according to Buesing, is also, at least partly, a hangover of GDR socialization and the white majority population that is still prevalent in "the East" ("*im* Osten"). While xenophobia has lessened in western Germany since the 1960s and 1970s, it remains problematic "here," as a member of staff commented. Similarly, staff feel that when confronted with problems, many local audiences tend to expect governments or authorities to step in rather than seeing a need to act themselves. As Buesing and Wolf put it: "The teachers are very focused on authorities. They are very quick to blame 'those up there' and relinquish their own responsibility," which these two colleagues consider problematic in a "democratic and plural society where everyone has responsibility."

Instances of such behavior were, however, rare during fieldwork, potentially because we only visited a small number of teacher training events. And both Buesing and Wolf also highlighted the "good work" going on at some schools and vocational training centers. However, at an event concerning right-wing extremism—how to counter the threat of neo-Nazi groups and racism at schools—one such "typical comment" was made. During the question and answer session following two long presentations that made suggestions for teaching methods and local approaches to the problem, a teacher commented that many young people slipped into the extremist milieu because they lacked opportunities. More jobs were needed, she explicated, and this was the state's responsibility. In field notes this is noted as "one of those comments that tend to simply blame the state and place demands there," which echoes Wolf and Buesing's sense that their audiences focus too much on authorities when it comes to addressing local problems.

The Pioneers of the German East

In conversation with some staff at the LpB, a vision emerges, where Mittelland appears not as a specific region or state but most of all as part of eastern Germany with a local population that is GDR socialized: Buesing, for example, invited us to one event with the comment that there she could "show us some of those proper GDR teachers." This sense is often expressed with the phrase that people were "*geprägt*" by life in the GDR, suggesting that external structures molded or shaped their personhoods. Socialist *Prägung*—which is counterposed to *Bildung*, education in the wider sense of self-development (Boyer 2005)—is often related to a preference for authoritarian leadership, reluctance to engage in politics, and a lack of initiative. In this view, eastern Germans *were shaped to be* subjects under the dictatorial regime that created passive persons and are now asked *to make themselves* citizens through education: adopting an enthusiastic and agentive democratic civility by leaving behind old habits. Elizabeth C. Dunn (2004) and Trenholme Junghans (2001) observe similar processes and attitudes in particular contexts in Poland and Hungary, respectively. In eastern Germany, such notions have become part of public discourse through the unification by accession, which created a sense that the new *Länder* are in need of development to "catch up" with FRG standards. With regard to the GDR past, LpB staff also feels that much needs to be "clarified" for the local population. The Wellau memorial museum, for example, is a memorial both to the Nazi past and the SED dictatorship (or rather Stalinism), as it had been used by both regimes. Few history teachers, however, realize that the prison's use by the Soviet forces in the 1940s and the atrocities committed then had been silenced during GDR times, while its use by the Nazi regime had been highlighted. There is therefore a need to "elucidate" local people by putting perceptions right, Wolf explained.

While eastern–western German differences were less often raised at the Working Group, they appeared to move center stage at the LpB. This was the case not only in chats about difficult audiences but also with regard to the managerial staff members' own experiences and origin. Four of the six department leads are from the former FRG. The "West German" staff arrived in Tillberg in the early and mid-1990s. Almost without exclusion they were university educated and worked in the political sphere. They decided to join a group of West German professionals who went east to build the new political and economic structures shortly after unification; Tillberg's LpB, for example, was founded in 1991. These years of pioneering work in the desolate East are remembered with the fondness that such mammoth efforts and extraordinary living situations can create. At the same time, these experiences mean that the "East" became associated with the image of a "project" that needs to be brought to its conclusion, to finalize the transition. During those years, these individuals, who often came with their partners, also active in government administration, developed friendships among each other, which became stronger due to some of the hardship the easily recognizable *Wessis* experienced in the 1990s, at the height of the defensive, and occasionally aggressive, East German identity and East–West German tensions. Buesing, for example, remembers vividly how a colleague complained in her presence about "the unacceptable fact that West Germans were given posts which could be filled by many a well-trained local" or raised the nasty question of whether she "cashed in on a West German wage."[2] Meanwhile, these pioneers of the *Wende* have lived in Mittelland for more than fifteen years and have extended their social circles. They have settled and become locals; their children are growing up here. Thus, certainly for some, concerns about school education exist because of their roles not only at work but also as discerning parents.

What education, and political education in particular, was meant to be moved in and out of focus during fieldwork at the LpB. A closer look at some staff's concerns and the LpB's events highlights the wide rage that is targeted. It includes addressing knowledge concerning political processes in a pluralist democracy and East German history, values such as tolerance, and skills like independent thinking and civil engagement. The LpB therefore aims to "govern" local personhood in order to create political and engaged citizens who proactively take initiative and who also, crucially, vote. The vision of personhood that some staff at the LpB hold dear is, however, derived from the West German tradition and not always supported by everyone. Certainly one department lead, one of two eastern Germans in this position, had a thing or two to say about his colleagues' underlying perception of Mittelland's population and the GDR. "*Ostalgie* does not exist," he insisted in a conversation with me, sharing his upset about a comment on this issue at a recent staff meeting. Yet political and social structures have changed in Mittelland over the past twenty years, requiring new values and knowledges of the local population. Why certain issues become legitimate topics of education or are contested, and what kinds of education become acceptable goals or are rejected as patronizing, depends both on specific present contexts and visions of the future, as the following chapters will show.

The Past as News, at the Daily Paper

One morning during fieldwork at the Office for Political Education, Sabine chatted with Lang, a young colleague from department one who usually opened the door for her. When Sabine suggested that for the project to get going, ideally, some local persona would be revealed as a former Stasi spy so fieldwork could follow the reactions, his response was dismissive: "All of that Stasi background of important people has been dealt with by now, hasn't it?" Lang could not imagine that there was much left to reveal. Yet, the next morning the *Daily Paper* announced that the local director of the Chamber for Trade and Commerce was an IM. The story soon led to his resignation. And this did not remain the only revelation related to the GDR past the *Daily Paper* made during fieldwork. When I had arrived for the first day of participant observation, I was greeted by the editor-in-chief for my induction talk with the words, "Well, you have actually just missed it, haven't you?" Herr Arnold, an erudite man in his mid-fifties, another trained historian who has worked at the *Daily Paper* with just one brief interruption since the early 1990s, was referring to the most recent scoop of finding an "order to shoot" for guards at the inner German border. The story had received considerable attention, though not all of it was welcome by the *Daily Paper* (see chapter 3). Yet such big events were not the only occasions when the GDR past pushed into news writing.

Of note is a Tuesday morning during my first week at the *Daily Paper*. In a conversation with Arnold and the vice editor-in-chief, Schäfer, we had agreed that, although being a researcher conducting participant observation that was clear to all staff, I would be treated similarly to an intern. This position allowed me to take a desk (whichever was free), learn about the *Daily Paper* by actively participating in its production, and access its digital archive and the "ticker," the news agencies' continuous drip of articles and reports. Interns at the *Daily Paper* are integrated into day-to-day work very quickly, being given research and writing tasks and at times carrying responsibility for entire pages. It did not take long either until I was asked to write the occasional commentary or news piece.

On this Tuesday, however, I used my time to search online papers and news agencies for relevant topics and helped out by typing some readers' letters onto electronic page layouts while also observing and participating in office conversations. The open-plan office, with its rows of doubled desks separated by shoulder-high screens, is divided into sections that sign responsible for particular pages. This includes the Mittelland section, which takes overall priority; politics, where I found a desk that day; business; culture; news from around the world; readers' letters; and the sports section, which has its own office with a television to follow sporting events.

As always, the atmosphere in the editorial office was busy yet chatty. Colleagues talked over the screens and across desks; at times small groups formed around a computer or in the coffee room, where smoking is allowed. While most of these conversations related to news work, there was also a good amount of joking and tongue-in-cheek commenting. Occasionally, the editor-in-chief or vice editor-in-chief, who have their offices just off the reception area, separated from the open-plan office by glass doors, moved through the room for quick chats with certain editors or to bring along newly received information.

This open environment made it relatively easy for both short-term staff and researchers to access the *Daily Paper*. Catching up with the day's edition, for example, I spotted a piece about young people lacking historical knowledge with regard to the GDR past especially. I ventured across to the politics lead editor, who also edits the opinion and debate page where the piece had appeared, to find out what or who was behind the story. Markus, a fifty-something longtime journalist, filled me in. Collecting copies from the shared printer later on, I overheard a conversation about the Federal Commissioner for the Stasi Files from another corner of the room. Werner Otto, a senior editor in his late fifties responsible for topics concerning, among others, the SED dictatorship, talked with a colleague about recent revelations in some of the national press about former Stasi officers' continued employment at the Birthler agency, which soon led to reflections on

Illustration 2.2. The working everyday at the *Daily Paper*.

the order to shoot. Then it was lunchtime and staff began moving, either into the small restaurant downstairs or, if there was enough time, to an alternative venue nearby that offered more choice. Lunch is followed by the daily 1 PM conference that all journalistic staff attends. During this meeting, the day's edition of the *Daily Paper* is reviewed, for criticism and praise, and the next day's issue is planned. Each section provides a summary of the main topics it will cover. At times this meeting is also used to discuss how to approach certain new topics or to share important information. The conference is an open forum where all staff are asked to contribute, whether on the printed paper or on colleagues' plans for their pages, which most do based on their professional and personal opinions.

On this Tuesday, planning opened with an update from the politics section: they would be running something on minimum wage and a Middle Eastern topic but could do with something else. The business and culture sections were in hand; the news from around the world section was also OK for topics. They would run the hurricane in a US state as top story but only if there were good pictures to go with it. Lower down on the page the editor wanted to use a piece on the fortieth anniversary of the arrival of color TV, which aroused other editors' interest. The vice editor-in-chief, who chaired the conference that day, then summarized the day's hot topics. For the final page, which featured readers' letters, there were contributions to the law on dangerous dogs, the order to shoot, and child poverty. All of these were recent topics of the main pages, which had motivated readers to voice their opinion. Following this run-through, the three editorials that appear on the opinion and debate page were shared out. It was the quiet summertime, so finding topics to discuss was harder than usual, but when one of the reporters began joking about East–West German differences in the introduction of color TV—"the West was given the go-ahead, while we were kept in black and white"—at least one editorial was settled.

The afternoon gave way to focused busy-ness as reporters and editors finalized their stories and began putting pages together, which started to take shape by around 4 PM. I was approached by Klaus, one of the newspaper's senior reporters for hot topics, who had finished his tongue-in-cheek editorial on color TV and dropped the printout on my desk: "It [the project] is about the GDR past, right? Well, that fits then."

A Local Paper with History

The editorial office, located in a small industrial area a few miles outside of Tillberg, is responsible for the *Daily Paper*'s main outer pages. These are supplemented by local editions prepared in eighteen local offices, including one in Tillberg. The *Daily Paper* covers the northern half of Mittelland, where approximately 570,000 households hold a subscription. Like most former East German papers, the *Daily Paper* thus maintains a hegemonic position within its GDR-time distribution area (Wuschig 2005).

The *Daily Paper* can be traced back to the late nineteenth century, when it first appeared as a small local paper of the SPD. After World War II, it, along with all other East German presses, was brought under SED control. The paper became one of the ruling party's "organs" (*Organ*) and combined closely monitored ideological content and regional news. Like all East German papers, excluding church publications, it stood under party owner-ship. All GDR journalists underwent heavy ideological training and were required to be party members.[3] In 1990, following unification, the *Daily Paper* was sold to a western German publishing house by the Treuhand, which administered SED funds and privatized state-owned enterprises. Unlike other GDR-time papers, the new management decided to continue using the newspaper's existing name, as it had a longer history.[4] For sev-eral months in 1991, GDR-time staff at the *Daily Paper* worked alongside a number of West German journalists while management decided who would be kept on. A few of the East German editors and reporters stayed, as did some of the new West German colleagues. The personnel were joined by new eastern German recruits who had worked elsewhere or had entered journalism after 1989. So just as in Mittelland's sphere of government, there were also West German "pioneers" at the *Daily Paper*, including its editor-in-chief, Arnold. However, while the LpB staff's pioneering years in the 1990s remain vivid in their memory and seem integral to their current personas, their counterparts at the *Daily Paper* do not seem to problematize their move East and the accompanying *Wende* experiences much if at all.

Today, the editorial office is mixed with regard to East or West German origin, pre- or post-*Wende* training, age, and gender. Markus, Klaus, and the vice editor, in addition to three other staff, are eastern German and worked as journalists in GDR times, but only two had been employed at the *Daily Paper* then. Four of their colleagues are western German, including the editor-in-chief; two are eastern German but changed into the profession after 1990, and another four trained since then. While there are a good number of women on staff, men are overall in the majority and dominate at the senior level. Just as mixed as the staff were responses to the question of whether East or West German origin makes a difference to individu-als' news writing. While some think so, there is more generally a sense that political affiliations and age, or rather position within an informal hierarchy, play a more considerable role.[5] Overall, the line of the *Daily Paper*, or its program, depends on the editor-in-chief, who stands between the publishing house and the diverse staff of the newspaper's offices. And while some think the editor-in-chief is too conservative and will not allow

critical pieces to run due to concerns over the publishing house's preferences, others find that the *Daily Paper*'s political line lacked definition and
that too radically left or apolitical writing should be more strongly policed.[6]
Some of this apparent lack of a specific line, however, is founded in the
Daily Paper's conscious and conscientious focus on its readers.

The newspaper tries to inform and entertain a diverse readership ranging
from the educated middle class of Tillberg to the older generations living
in Mittelland's rural areas. This is attempted at least partly through the
explicit aim to serve the "local and regional concerns of the people in its
area of distribution," as the *Daily Paper*'s journalistic guidelines state. This
is posited as the company's "central aim" that all employees are bound by.
Like the LpB, the *Daily Paper* is "independent" and "beyond parties," which
here means that no single party or interest group can exert singular influence on the reporting. The guidelines furthermore express the newspaper's
loyalty to the *Rechtsstaat*—the free, democratic, and constitutional state of
the German Federal Republic within the European Union—and support
for social market economy and private property rights. Thus embracing the
current politico-economic order, the *Daily Paper* also sees itself as a crucial
part thereof, as it enables local people to "develop their opinions" through
the information provided on its pages. The "free development of opinion"
(*freie Meinungsbildung*) is a key task of German media (Meyn 1996). In
this vein media are seen as helping to develop public opinion (*öffentliche
Meinung*), which in turn links to the freedom of speech (*Meinungsfreiheit*)
guaranteed in the Basic Law (Grundgesetz). In German, the phrases for
free speech, public opinion, and development of opinion all share the same
central term, *Meinung* (opinion). Through this, together with the task of
information and critique, the media are part of the "fourth estate," which
critically observes the other three of executive, legislature, and judiciary
(Meyn 1996; cf. Habermas 2010). As a medium that helps shape public
opinion, the *Daily Paper* thus positions itself as a legitimate and necessary tool of democracy that serves both Mittelland's population and its
government.

The guidelines also detail the *Daily Paper*'s position to the difficult
German pasts:

> Considering the historic experiences with totalitarian political systems the
> *Daily Paper* rejects determinedly any form of extremism whether from the
> right or the left. It strives for elucidation through objective representation
> and evaluation of the recent German past in order to facilitate the political
> shaping of the future in freedom.

Like talk at the LpB, the guidelines make a connection between past and
present in that they distance the *Daily Paper*'s journalism from any form of

extremism. They use the phrase to "elucidate" audiences, but in contrast to discourses at the LpB, which center on why such elucidation is necessary, the guidelines evolve around how it will be achieved. In doing so, they leave agency to the individual reader, who will form their own opinions based on the "objective" news the newspaper provides. Interestingly, the guidelines make a direct connection between reporting on the "totalitarian" past and a future in freedom, so there is also an assumption here that understanding the past is required for a path into the future. Although this path is seen as being prepared in the political realm, it is only described as free; furthermore, denotations of "democratic," "lawful," or similar terms that circulate in the political realm of *Aufarbeitung* are notable in their absence.

That local and regional concerns drive content at the *Daily Paper* also means that readers are carefully considered when it comes to choosing topics and deciding how to broach them. This concern goes beyond the guidelines, of course, since the press is a commercial enterprise that depends on its ability to sell within its area. This is the same region where the newspaper was read during GDR times and largely by the same audiences, many of whom, according to the editor-in-chief, "vote PDS" (the Left Party). The *Daily Paper* has certainly changed its content selection and visual appearance since the 1980s, but changes can only be introduced slowly, Arnold warned, or otherwise readers will protest or simply walk away. This also concerns coverage of the GDR past, which the newspaper has taken on often in spite of its readers, according to the editor-in-chief. What he refers to here are articles in the vein of *Aufarbeitung* that focus on dictatorial aspects of the GDR past, like the order to shoot. These were also the kinds of news that he considered relevant to the research project. However, the *Daily Paper* ran many more stories, opinion pieces, and commentaries that related to or drew on Mittelland's socialist past concerning smaller, more mundane or even quirky everyday news, like the differential introduction of color TV forty years ago. Those kinds of news stories, where the past appears as a part of Mittelland's character and biography, were more prevalent than the big scoops mentioned earlier, although of course those add more to the *Daily Paper*'s esteem. This mixture—of lighthearted references to the GDR past bordering on reminiscing, of hard news stories that seek to add to historical knowledge or question the current elite's credentials, and of much in between—is at the heart of the *Daily Paper*'s discourse. The paper's take on past and present situations is thus highly varied, just like its staff, which becomes clear in the "colorful diversity," as one reporter put it, of its editorials. This can be refreshing and may well satisfy a diverse readership, or at least keep readers on their toes, but it also makes for ambiguity if not inconsistency, as there is no clear approach to issues like the East German past.

Responses and reactions to news stories are largely gauged through readers' letters, while their selective publication allows the *Daily Paper* to present and reinforce its relationship to the local population. Readers' letters are screened by one of two vice editors-in-chief, who makes a pre-selection of publishable comments. He hands these on to the editor of the readers' page to decide with her which letters would be published in the current issue. Letters thus selected then receive careful editing. They are often shortened, offensive language is removed—even if a reader is listed as author, the newspaper remains liable for the text it has chosen to publish—and grammar or phrasing are polished if necessary.[7] While topicality is of prime importance, letters need to relate to a recently run story. Space on the page and balance of opinions vis-à-vis opinions received overall are also highly influential, as are the letters' authorship. It would not look good to repeatedly publish letters from one specific reader, for example. Arnold strongly recommended that Sabine and I follow letters of readers. Similarly to troubles experienced by the region's memorial museums in the early 1990s, the *Daily Paper* seemed to be the target of letter writing by an "old guard" then that in this way attempted to claim a platform for publicity. Like some department leads at the LpB, the editor-in-chief also looked toward the newspaper's readership for hangovers and traces of GDR values and opinions, yet a sense of struggling against, instead of working with, the audience was much less pronounced.

Regarding Each Other: Government and Press

The governmental environment of the Office for Political Education and of the more diverse Working Group and the editorial office of the *Daily Paper* may seem rather removed from each other. The formal atmosphere of the Working Group meeting with its scenic setting, agenda and formally dressed participants contrasts starkly with the newspaper's 1 PM conference in the "glass box" meeting room where jokes disrupt serious conversation, arguments break out, additional chairs are wheeled in for guests, and participants, many of them in jeans, stretch their legs under the table. The differences in address between the two realms explained at the start of this chapter further emphasizes this contrast.

Approaches to creating narratives also differ in crucial ways between the two realms. The Office for Political Education designs workshops and selects publications through a focus on its governmental aim of shaping citizens suited to life in democracy. With regard to the East German past, this is an *Aufarbeitung* that prioritizes stories on dictatorial aspects of the regime, on the ways state control suffused GDR life to dispel myths that may encourage nostalgic reminiscing. Moreover, the Working Group *Aufarbeitung* brings together institutions that follow this approach, which not only provides accurate narratives of the past but also constitutes the one legitimate discourse there is on the topic. This understanding becomes clear already in the way the directors of these institutions responded to the research project. Like Bohlmann said at the Working Group meeting, "everyone relevant" to research on "the socialist past today" was there. Despite its much wider remit, this sense of self-evident importance extended into the Office for Political Education, where department leads would criticize Sabine and me for spending too much time in other parts of the office and not with them, "when their work was also clearly of importance."

While it seems logical that the newspaper, with its very different role and remit, would not follow this example, Working Group members expressed considerable skepticism about the *Daily Paper*'s approach to East German history. Some conveyed muted interest in our observations of that other institution but politely withstood from commenting, which we encountered in a similar way at the *Daily Paper* when mentioning our first site of fieldwork—a result, no doubt, of our being positioned in both institutional realms. Others were, however, rather vocal in their criticism of the newspaper. And at other times opinion shifted to more positive evaluations. Criticism usually concerned three areas: mistakes and omissions when announcing events organized by members of the Working Group, apolitical or uncritical news coverage, and a lack of a clear political line in the reporting. Local papers in Germany are a prime source of information on local and regional events from public lectures, exhibitions, and religious services to out-of-hours surgery times. The *Daily Paper* thus represents an instrument to raise awareness and mobilize audiences for institutions of *Aufarbeitung*, and being overlooked by the newspaper is doubly hurtful.

The issue of lacking political line was raised when one member of the Working Group explained that the *Daily Paper* was nowadays covering issues of the East German past quite well, referring to a time four or five years ago when that had not been the case, but at another time felt flummoxed that a recent event of his had not been covered, while a similar event some weeks ago had led to considerable debate in the *Daily Paper*.[8] This seeming lack of program was at times perceived as biased reporting: with regard to a couple of controversies involving governmental institutions, some readers felt that only viewpoints of a certain kind were published—usually the kind that was critical of the government, potentially left-leaning, and that kept the debate going. So while there was a recognition that the *Daily Paper* now reported with some regularity on issues that concerned dictatorial aspects of the past, it was felt that more could be done. In one case, however, criticism linked directly to the press's own socialist past, which was what I had expected to hear more frequently given that similar sentiments prevailed at times in my parental home. Just before starting fieldwork at the *Daily Paper*, Stasi commissioner Schumacher warned Sabine and me that there would still be many "reds" working there, in a nod to the continuation in personnel from GDR times. There were a number of pretty tough "old comrades," he added, naming one of the lead editors. While this highlights that some readers feel that the newspaper's GDR past taints its reputation in the present, it also shows that there is no easy equating of opinion, derived from a reporter's writings, with the author's background. The editor thus named was from the Rhine region and one of the *Daily Paper's* "West German pioneers."

The editors at the *Daily Paper*, in contrast, had relatively little to say about their institutional counterparts in the project, although many were interested in what we had observed. With time a sense emerged that the Office for Political Education remained rather invisible to editorial staff, even if its book repository was much valued by younger and less affluent journalists. One reporter who covered education, for example, was surprised to hear that the LpB engaged in teacher training. From his perspective, Mittelland's Institute for Standards in Education and Teacher Training solely covered this area. While some reporters thought this withdrawing of the LpB from public view was regrettable, others took a more critical line. Markus thus commented, "They are not doing anything," indicating that a lack of political visibility was synonymous with a lack of valuable (i.e., reportable) action. Just as some members of the Working Group found the *Daily Paper's* reporting partial, either too left or too apolitical, staff at the *Daily Paper* queried the LpB's apparent independence. If the office was a part of the State Chancellery, surely it could not avoid government influence, it was commented. Overall, however, reporters were more aware of and in turn interested in the politicians who hogged the limelight, happily evaluating, for example, the policymaking and speeches of Mittelland's Minister President. For that reason, they knew more of some of the individual institutions of the Working Group *Aufarbeitung*, like the Stasi commission and its director, Schumacher, but had been unaware that the group existed.[9] Moreover, some of our informants from the political sphere, most obviously with regard to the editor-in-chief, Arnold, refrained from opinion. Most likely they recognized the sacrosanct character of relationships to sources, which here cut both ways—toward the *Daily Paper* and the research team. The institutions and individuals we had visited had become our informants and it was accepted—at least by some—that we could reveal little about them, but they also had relationships to the *Daily Paper*, which we in turn needed to honor.

Both these spheres of government and of media relate to each other through newsworthy events that take place in Mittelland. Members of the Working Group read newspaper reports on the order to shoot, IM revelations, and others and used them to form opinions, including opinions on the newspaper's narratives. Moreover, the Office for Political Education offered workshops on dealing with the media, which instructed politicians on having their voices heard and controlling what is published. The *Daily Paper* in turn worked with these institutions whenever they were pushed into the limelight by creating stories with and about them. The order to shoot, for example, was found during research at Tillberg's commission for Stasi files, which had been requested by the *Daily Paper*. When the story broke, the *Daily Paper* included a statement on the document's importance by the head of the commission, Fuhr, on its front page. When the tide turned later, as news in the national press revealed that this document was not all that relevant and questions were raised about the commission's role in what was now becoming an éclat, the *Daily Paper* published an editorial reevaluating the piece and explaining the circumstances of its publication, thus defending Tillberg's commissioner against allegations of sensationalism or incompetence. Other institutions' managers and staff closely followed the story both within the *Daily Paper* and with regard to other media reactions, as did the newspaper's editors and reporters. Whatever Working Group members' concerns about the *Daily Paper* and reporters' sense of not knowing the Working Group, both spheres thus interlink in their creation of narratives about the past. Not only do they interlink, but they also read and narrate each other.

Notes

1. Similarly, in the 1990s the office had engaged in training local politicians and administrators in democratic processes and values, as was seen necessary at the time. Some of this work continues.
2. Since living costs were considerably lower in eastern Germany following unification, differentials in wages and pensions were introduced in the new *Länder*. These have remained in place. Whether individuals receive eastern or western pay depends on their registered home address, not their place of work.
3. Most journalists were members of the SED. This was a requirement at papers owned by the party, which constituted the largest dailies. Journalists working at the smaller papers of the bloc parties, which were governed by the SED through membership in the National Front (an umbrella organization that included all political parties and mass organizations chaired by the ruling party), were often members of the according bloc party.

4. Other newspapers adopted new names. For example, a paper in the region where my mother lived in the early 1990s ran a reader contest for a new title.

5. Although some will argue that affiliation with the political left is often, though not always, linked to an East German background.

6. I have discussed questions of the control of work at the editorial office elsewhere (Gallinat 2010b).

7. See Dietzsch (2014) for details regarding a similar process of treating readers' letters at a weekly magazine.

8. Unbeknown to this informant, it was in fact the debacle that unfolded around this other event that prompted the *Daily Paper* to refrain from covering similar ones in the near future.

9. Near the end of fieldwork, the Working Group considered taking on a more public appearance through the development of a logo and embossed stationary.

Chapter Three

DEBATING THE PAST AT THE *DAILY* PAPER
The East German Border Regime

➤•◄

Fieldwork at the *Daily Paper* began five days after the newspaper broke the news of the *Schiessbefehl*, or the "order to shoot" (to kill). The order was a set of instructions that advised members of an MfS taskforce at the inner German border to shoot anyone, including women and children, who attempted to cross. Following this story, which soon proved contentious, this chapter explores what kinds of images of the GDR emerge in the *Daily Paper*'s reporting, how these are related, or not, to the notion of the SED dictatorship, and indeed whether they suggest any specific understandings of state and society. Whereas the previous chapter explored how the *Daily Paper* positions itself within the *Bundesland* and vis-à-vis Mittelland's population, this chapter now asks what kind of a discourse the newspaper creates about the East German past given its aim to represent local people's concerns, its diverse readership, and its staffing. Through a combination of different types of texts, a privileging of personal memory narratives, and the facilitation of a mediated debate through the publication of readers' letters, the newspaper's discourse appears like the "living narratives" that occur in everyday life and end without conclusion (Ochs and Capps 2001). Accordingly, the GDR past emerges in the *Daily Paper*'s reporting as the nation's "unresolved life event" that requires continuous debate to facilitate meaning-making after fundamental change, positioning the *Daily Paper* as a significant regional player that provides the necessary platform.

On a Tuesday morning, ten days after the news of the order to shoot first published, I overheard that conversation about problems at and controversies around the Birthler agency (chapter 2) and ventured over to join the two reporters. One of them, Herr Otto, one of the senior staff and the *Daily Paper*'s designated reporter on topics falling under *Aufarbeitung*, wrote the breaking story. Informants from the political sphere and members of the Victim Association had mentioned him as the main reason behind the *Daily Paper*'s improved coverage of dictatorial aspects of the East German past. The Victim Association members very much valued their relationship to Otto, which they felt gave them a direct line of communication to the local paper. Now in his early sixties, Otto studied journalism during GDR times and was employed by a paper of the National Democratic Party (NDPD). The NDPD was one of several bloc parties in East Germany, which were part of the National Front directed by the ruling party SED. Otto's biography is marked by his father's escape to West Germany; he had become a target of the MfS. His mother had planned to follow with the child, but circumstances prevented it so the family remained divided. Against this background Otto describes himself as having been critical of the East German state, which impacted his reporting in 1989 when he was one of the first reporters to cover the autumn demonstrations in Tillberg. He began working at the *Daily Paper* in 1990, where he eventually took responsibility for stories that concern dictatorial aspects and victims of the socialist regime. He feels strong ownership over such topics but most of all over his relationships with the people he works with in that capacity.

On this Tuesday another senior editor, Ralf, had approached Otto to talk about a recent controversy involving the Birthler agency in Berlin. The conversation soon turned to the "new debate": the discussion of lacking efficiency at the Birthler agency rekindled by the controversy around the order to shoot. The two men agreed that the national press' and news agencies' description of the story as the "*apparent* order to shoot" (emphasis added) was highly problematic, as the terminology immediately cast doubt on the find's relevance. Feeling aggravated Otto took hold of the book where a similar document had first been published in 1997 but without attracting any attention at the time (Judt 1997). The document is reproduced in the appendix as just one among many. It should have gone to the press there and then, he exclaimed, using almost the same words Arnold had when explaining the problem to me the previous week.

Breaking News, or Broken News?

The *Daily Paper* had revealed the discovery of a *Schiessbefehl* the weekend of the annual anniversary of the building of the Berlin Wall at which victims of border violence are commemorated. The news was given considerable space in the newspaper with a news piece on the front page, an in-depth report on page 3, and an editorial—all three pieces written by Otto. The find had been made during research on the deaths of young people and children at the inner German border, which the newspaper—with a view to the anniversary—had commissioned at Tillberg's branch of the Birthler agency in June. The discovery was a typewritten document found among other materials in the file of a local man who was part of a secret taskforce of the MfS that aimed to reduce the number of border violations by border personnel. The find was taken as evidence of the existence of an order to shoot long denied by the GDR leadership. The document, which had no author, letterhead, or similar official insignia, detailed a range of instructions for members of the taskforce, including a section on the "prevention of border violations," where the contentious passage was found:

> It is your duty to use your . . . capabilities to betray the border violator's ruse, to capture or liquidate him to prevent the border violation he has planned. Do not hesitate to use your firearm, not even if border violations are conducted with women and children, something the traitors have previously used to their advantage.[1]

The publication caused a national stir. And for a few days the *Daily Paper* was unusually busy with requests from other media, some even from overseas, and comments from readers, as was the local BStU office, which faced an endless stream of visitors, as one employee described it. The Victim Association also received a number of enquiries from individuals affected by border violence.

However, soon after the news was out, the tide turned. On Monday a leading political magazine reported that a similar document had been published by the Birthler agency in Berlin ten years earlier already, in the edited volume Otto had waved at us. Even worse, it was revealed that that document hung framed in one of the Birthler agency's corridors. And within days a third such document emerged at another local office of the agency. Meanwhile, a historian had explained that this was not an "order," as it lacked the official signifiers that distinguish such documents. At best it could be described as a set of instructions, it was explained. The inclusion of women and children in the instructions remained distinctive about the Tillberg find, giving it a particularly cruel tone, but in national news and at news agencies, the "sensational find" immediately turned into the "*apparent* order to shoot" or the "find *previously* described as sensational" (emphasis added). With this turn of events, attention moved to the institution that had located and evaluated the document in the first place, the Birthler agency and its branch in Tillberg. This was timely, as a commission, installed by the federal government and working on a new national memorial concept, was considering the agency's future.[2] Critics of the large network of BStU offices found welcome fuel for their fire, and calls for the Stasi files to be moved into the national archives so, for example, researchers would gain access more easily, became louder. Some went so far as to suspect the Birthler agency of having released the strongly worded document so close to the anniversary in a publicity stunt. This had certainly not been the case: when the document was found in June, the Tillberg branch had informed both the *Daily Paper* and the Birthler agency's headquarters in Berlin. Berlin had not responded. The *Daily Paper* had held the news back until the anniversary in August for maximum impact.

This turn of events also meant a change of fortune for the *Daily Paper*, which moved from having landed a media scoop to having printed incorrect or, even worse, nonnews. Yet, its editors did not accept this view, and they seemed to be proved right by some strongly worded readers' letters. Otto and the editor-in-chief both argued that the document should have been placed more prominently in the 1997 volume and, more importantly, released to the press at the time. That this had not been done was the problem, according to them, not the belated find in Tillberg. Both justified this view by the attention the news was now receiving. For Otto, the reader response was determining: "It should have been handed to the press then," he insisted, the 1997 volume in hand. "Because the readers' reaction now shows that this is an important topic. There is a felt need for discussion. Well, then we'll have to have that discussion now!" And this is how the *Daily Paper* repositioned itself vis-à-vis the turning tide.

Reporting the Order to Shoot

According to J. Christopher Crocker, persuasion in rhetoric first of all concerns the truth-value of the argument thus made (1977: 42). Similarly, the main concern of media rhetoric is to persuade readers of any item's news value, which in extension supports senses of the paper's trustworthiness: that it presents correct information, researches stories well, reveals new knowledge, and so on (Fairclough 1995: 93). In arguing how the order to shoot furthers understandings of the socialist past or of how this past should be dealt with in the present, the news pieces also tell a particular story about East Germany. In this way the *Daily Paper* fulfills another goal of journalism, according to John E. Richardson, which is to help readers to "understand the world and their positions within it" (2007: 8), in this case a past world that has significant implications for selves in the present. Norman Fairclough (1995) observes moreover that the emergent and processual (Kitch 2008: 318) discourse of news is curiously located in both the public and the private realm. The media inform public discourse but are consumed in private and aim to influence the opinions of individuals who collectively constitute the public. The *Daily Paper*'s goal in its journalistic guidelines to "dedicate its work in particular to the local and regional concerns of the people in its area" exacerbates this position. It makes for a rhetoric that continuously tries to resolve tensions between the duty to provide objective information and the aim of being locally relevant and engaging. These tensions are further enhanced in the case of the order to shoot, where the *Daily Paper* also aimed to bridge the national relevance of the find, which aided its prestige, with its local origin, which served to bind readership.

To achieve these various goals, the *Daily Paper* used three types of journalistic texts—articles, reports, and editorial and readers' letters—that allowed for a mixing of rhetorics. A style of "objective" news reporting, which employs a rhetoric of factuality that values "facts, truth and reality" (Zelizer 2008: 82) to create senses of objectivity and authority, was combined with conversationalized sections and opinion pieces that help draw readers in and lend persuasion to seemingly objective reporting (de Burgh 2005; Fairclough 1995; also see Friedland 2003; Kitch 2008). This mixture of journalistic forms allowed the newspaper to straddle the different spheres it relates to and positioned the story from the beginning as a topic worth discussing or at least reflecting on. Historical topics are not the *Daily Paper*'s usual staple and even less so when it concerns the unappetizing topic of the socialist dictatorship. As Arnold had explained, they often reported on this issue "in spite" of a readership that voted "PDS."[3] Placing the order to shoot on the first page, and giving a full page to the in-depth report, thus entailed a certain risk but also seemed necessary given the understanding that the find was national news.

The page 1 headline reads, "Women and children were to be shot without hesitation: Spectacular find of a document regarding an order to shoot at the inner German border." The article is very short, taking just about a fifth of the full page, and focuses on providing key information to point readers to the detailed report on page 3. The piece is accompanied by a facsimile of the document that reinforces the text's factual and informative character. As most articles, it begins with a summary in bold:

> Monday will see the commemoration of the day on which the Berlin Wall was built, 13 August 1961. The former GDR leadership always claimed that there was no order to shoot. But now the Tillberg branch of the Birthler agency discovered a document that proves how ruthlessly shooting had been ordered.

This short summary makes three rhetorical moves. First, it links the news piece to the soon-to-be held anniversary, which makes the publication timely. Second, it presents local relevance by stating that the find was made in Tillberg itself. Third, it explains that GDR leaders had long disputed the existence of any such order, which emphasizes the item's newsworthiness. In this third point, the use of metaphors to guide particular interpretations becomes more prominent, for example, in the term "GDR leadership" (DDR *Führung*). Rather than referring to specific persons or using official terminology, like the Central Committee of the SED, post holders of the GDR government are lumped together in this colloquial phrase that is not normally applied to governments of recognized powers. The phrasing thus denies the East German political leaders recognition as legitimate power holders. These potentially illegitimate leaders are further implicated by the term "claimed," which suggests they made assertions potentially without proof or foundation. This view is reinforced by the final sentence, which announces the find of the document that now disproves their claims. In contrast to the socialist government, the location of the find is described by more official terminology ("Tillberg branch of the Birthler agency"), signaling the institution's legitimacy and trustworthiness as a source.[4] The introduction also includes the emotive term that describes the document in all three news pieces: "ruthless" (*rücksichtslos*). This German phrase can be read as a technical term, in the sense of "without pardon," or morally as referring to inhumane actions. The latter meaning seems to be the one intended here, which becomes clearer when the term appears as an adverb in the final sentence: "how ruthlessly shootings had been ordered." Altogether, the summary positions the find as undoubtedly newsworthy because this "discovery" allows for new knowledge about the GDR.

The article's main text proceeds in three parts. The first three paragraphs, which make up just over half the news piece, provide key information about the document. This begins with a quotation of the contentious passage (above), details about the text's location in a Stasi file, the relation of the file and its owner to the MfS taskforce, and background to this force:

> The instructions from Berlin are seven pages long and contained in the files of Sergeant Manfred L., who served as full-time Stasi spy "Matz Löwe" with the GDR's border guards at the inner German border between 1971 and 1974. As a specially trained combatant, the man, who was born in Tillberg in 1952, was meant to spy on his comrades to prevent desertions.

In this more conversationalized section, the protagonist is identified by the term "spy," used as both noun and verb. The term is associated with the morally dubious behavior of IMs—it is used frequently in that sense by members of the Victim Association in Tillberg, for example, whom Otto knows well—and chosen over alternative phrases like "observe" or "gather intelligence" that would maintain a professional image. The term thus serves to discredit the actions of both the East German MfS and, by association, its members.

The second part of the article concerns the importance of the find in the present. It begins with a quote from Fuhr, who, as the local expert, evaluates the document as a "sensational and, for the further *Aufarbeitung* of the Stasi past, immensely important find." He is quoted twice more in the short passage:

> Until now no order to shoot has been found in GDR files that is as clear and that provides for no limitation to the use of firearms. What is frightening, says Fuhr, is the "complete ruthlessness" of the Stasi. GDR border law from 1982 speaks of the use of firearms as "the most extreme means of violence." Previous instructions had usually stated that young people and women should not be shot where possible. "The Stasi as 'shield and sword of the party' was not deterred by that, however," says Fuhr.

This section first restates the newsworthiness of the find and, second, continues to delegitimize GDR powers, now the MfS, which is cast as a "completely ruthless" institution that did not conform to East German law. The final section of the article is a paragraph of two sentences that provides numbers of fatalities at the Berlin Wall and notes that "even today the exact number of deaths at the inner German border is unknown." This further historical detail aids an impression of objectivity while the phrase "even today" again adds rhetorical edge. The phrase is ambiguous. It may decry the poor advancement of research or hint at the secrecy of the East German border regime, or it is borne out of a more general sense of tragedy: not knowing also means not being able to grieve appropriately. In any case, the phrase serves to keep the reader wary about this East German border regime.

While the page 1 article summarizes the story and concentrates its rhetoric on highlighting news value, the page 3 report goes into detail with regard to two key aspects. It provides more information about the "Tillberg man," whose story frames the report on the one hand, and about the legal frameworks of weapon use, which take up the middle part of the text, on the other. This twin focus is already apparent in the headline: "Tillberger served as 'Matz Löwe' in secret taskforce: State Security Police gave ruthless order to shoot." The headline also brings together the rhetorical strategies of factual reporting and human interest, facilitating the bridging of public and private, of national and local domains. The human interest aspect of the report is enhanced by a black-and-white picture at the center of the article, which shows border guards hoisting a dead body over a barbed wire fence. One of them, a young man, looks backward with a tense facial expression. This is a well-known picture of an incident at the Berlin Wall in 1962. A young escapee, Peter Fechter, was shot by East German border guards and died of blood loss after falling into the no man's land inside the border area (see Ahonen 2006). The picture thus serves as a "story seed" (Carrithers 2012c) that speaks of the tragedies that unfolded at this border, while also portraying the youth of many border guards and, with that, the contentious border guard trials of the 1990s. The caption briefly summarizes the incident and adds dryly, "An order to shoot, however, did not officially exist." The picture thus reinforces the emotive evaluation of the find as "ruthless" while positioning border guards as, at least, uncertain executioners of a harsh state's wishes, if not even as potential victims.

The article begins with Manfred L., who becomes more tangible through the bare bones of biographical data: "Manfred L., born in 1952 in Tillberg, registered after completion of his training as a metalworker at the VEB Förderanlagenbau 'Drushba' [construction plant 'drushba' (Russian for friendship)] as full-time soldier."[5] The protagonist's move to the border leads into further information on the MfS taskforce he joined. The second part of the article restates the newsworthiness of the find. It contains Fuhr's evaluation from the page 1 piece and links this again to GDR leaders' denial of such an order. The argument is extended with information on GDR legislation of weapon use, which, it is made clear, was steered by the leading elite. The piece then turns to Manfred L.'s return to Tillberg, where he served as a prison guard and continued to "send his reports to the Stasi" until 1989. The final paragraph of the article considers again the question of numbers of border fatalities that "still remains unresolved"—ending on a similarly suggestive rhetorical note as the news piece.

While the article keeps focus on the document's historical context, the case of Manfred L. provides a local life story. By positioning the narrative's protagonist vis-à-vis Tillberg landmarks, such as the place of his professional training, readers' attention is caught by place names they may recognize from their own or family members' lives. Prior to 1990 the city's economy was dominated by heavy industry, which provided employment for large parts of the local population. Such plants were also linked to local schools, where children learned about them and factory brigades were "guardians" (*Paten*) to school classes, attending end-of-year ceremonies. Older pupils worked there during project weeks. If people were not employed there, they knew someone who had been or who had trained there. While this short reference introduces Manfred L. as "one of us," the "Tillberg man" is quickly marked as "other" as he leaves the region to serve with the border guards and join the Stasi, the agency that has come to epitomize dictatorial state control in public imagination. While Manfred L. later returns to Mittelland, it is highlighted that he remained affiliated with the MfS. This human interest story provides the skeleton of a GDR biography that allows individuals to reflect on their own or friends' and family members' lives in comparison, in turn supporting an "understanding of (this past) world and their place in it" (J. Richardson 2007: 8).

The document is described here again as an "order" (*Befehl*) or "the order to shoot." Additionally, the term *vergattert* is used to describe Manfred L.'s being ordered to shoot. This term, which differs from the German term for "to order" (*befehlen*), is invoked several times in the subsequent debate to describe processes through which soldiers were required to fulfill duties in ways that precluded refusal. The metaphor thus refers responsibility for border violence to higher authorities, most likely GDR leadership. This interpretation is supported by a further discrediting of GDR leadership through use of common language phrases: "SED boss" in one case and "leading SED folks" in another, hardly official denotations. With regard to former GDR leaders' insistence that such an order had never existed, it is said that they "denied" the order, "claimed" otherwise, and tried to present "an image of a 'peaceful border regime.'" These expressions take on a cynical tone, indicated most clearly by the use of inverted commas. The story's protagonist, Manfred L., in contrast receives less rhetorical attention. He is described as a "spy" but is also said "to have been *vergattert*," casting the "Tillberg man" as an ambiguous double character, part perpetrator or wrongdoer and part victim. Overall, evaluative language concerning his personality is sparse since the article's main targets are others.

The editorial, "Despicable: GDR order to shoot," which takes top spot of usually three short and snappy editorials of 100 to 150 words, provides an explicit judgment of the news by Otto. Editorials, which are allocated during the 1 PM conference, often go to headline stories, and are written by the lead reporter. Such big stories are discussed by leading editorial staff as they develop, often over several days. Through these conversations—in the lead editors' 11 AM conference, in the middle of the open-plan office when colleagues enquire, or in the editor-in-chief's office if more difficult decisions are to be taken—a consensus over the *Daily Paper's* take on the story develops, which will be relatively clear to the lead author when it comes to writing the commentary. The editor-in-chief nevertheless views editorials before they are placed on the page to ensure they are suitable and follow the *Daily Paper's* style.

In the "Despicable" editorial, which aims to provide a moral evaluation of the document, Otto focuses on three concerns. Mirroring the two news pieces, one concern is again the fact that previous claims by "GDR functionaries" (DDR-*Funktionäre*) have now been refuted. Second, the editorial concerns the cruel flavor of the text that suggested shooting women and children: "a wickedness that could not be topped." Third, in the final paragraph, Otto, returns to Fuhr's comment in the page 1 article. Invoking the term *Aufarbeitung*, the editorial calls for a reckoning with the past. However, in a departure from the official denotation of *Aufarbeitung* as a "reworking of the SED dictatorship," the call here, as in the quote from Fuhr in the page 1 piece, is for a "reworking of the Stasi past." While Fuhr is clear in the story that this is ongoing, necessarily so since this is his institution's remit, Otto calls for more effort here, with a view toward the future "so that such despicability will not repeat itself."

Together the three news pieces convey an emerging narrative of an East Germany ruled by an untrustworthy elite and policed by the MfS and a ruthless border regime. While the articles also concern the present, their insistence on the news value of the document means the story ought to contribute to the development of a new, or somehow revised, understanding of the past. The MfS and political leadership become the main protagonists in this narrative about the past East Germany. There is some back-and-forth between these two in the different pieces so that it remains unclear which institution is seen as foremostly culpable. While the MfS, which had authored the document, ought to be the primary target, and is in the editorial, the articles call upon GDR leadership as the authority with overall accountability. The connection between the two is only made explicit in Fuhr's quote that, invoking GDR discourse, identifies the MfS as "shield and sword of the SED." This phrase moves attention to the ruling socialist party, a large institution that many East Germans, including the vast majority of GDR-time journalists, were a part of. Otto, however, refrains from picking up on this question of more general party responsibility.

Similar ambiguity surrounds the trope "order to shoot" (*Schiessbefehl*), which becomes associated with this story. Although the articles are clear that the document concerns a special taskforce of the MfS, and any order therefore only applies to this realm, the news continues to be described by this generalized term, a story seed.[6] Michael Carrithers describes story seeds as "minute seeds of story," which, like the "condensed, affecting . . . work of metaphor, unfold to make a movement" (2012c: 60). In this vein, the shorthand expression "order to shoot" speaks of all killings at the inner German border and the authoritarianism of the GDR system. The trope remained in place even after it became clear that this document was no "order" and although editors themselves did not believe a real order to shoot had existed. As Arnold had put it to me at our first meeting, "The order to shoot does not exist and it won't ever be found," and reiterating the *Daily Paper*'s argument he adds, "but this here remains another important find." The term was chosen when the original story was released because it is short and evocative, allowing for attention-demanding headlines. Any change of terminology later on, when the tide of news turned, would have scuppered persuasive power by further questioning the correctness of the story in the first place. Moreover, speaking of an "order" kept focus on the authorities targeted by the *Daily Paper*'s reporting.

Although all these pieces address the question of wider, shared understandings of the GDR, terms that circulate in the official discourse of *Aufarbeitung* and beyond, apart from "reworking" itself, do not appear in any of them. There is no mention of the "SED dictatorship" or the "unjust state" (*Unrechtsstaat*), and the terms "dictatorial" and "totalitarian" are also absent. In avoiding the rhetoric of *Aufarbeitung*, the articles prevent association with the authoritative but contentious discourse, maintaining the *Daily Paper*'s independent voice required by its position in between public and private and its aim to serve local people first of all. Through a rhetoric of factuality that focuses on historical detail in combination with the targeting of very specific agents in this story, the reporting moreover achieves a separation of different spheres of the GDR with and under each other. It is careful to distinguish the state and its former leaders as the perpetrators from the country as a whole, and thereby its population, and to identify the MfS as a further distinct actor within state and society. What thus emerges in this "vernacular narrative" (Collins 2003) is a partial view of a "Stasi-controlled border regime" overseen by an illegitimate SED leadership, which, although acting on society through individuals such as Manfred L., appears to be dissociated from it. This rhetorical strategy allows the presentation of a news item that adds to an understanding of the East German past as characterized by a controlling state, while avoiding judging the population, and thus the *Daily Paper*'s readership and much of its staff, too quickly and too explicitly. In so doing, questions about the relationship between an autocratic leadership and individual responsibilities are left open, and reflecting on them is left to individual readers. This relative interpretive openness in combination with a positioning of the story as both news and opinion empowers readership and allowed the newspaper to reposition itself as the tide of news turned after the weekend.

Reclaiming the News

With questions about the newsworthiness of the order to shoot circulating in national media by the Monday, the *Daily Paper* needed to reposition itself, since "to have value as information, journalism has to be accepted as truth, or at least as an acceptable approximation of the truth" (McNair 2005: 30). The paper needed to save face in front of its readers, at the very least. There was also the *Daily Paper*'s own role to consider in an éclat that had now fallen on the door of the Birthler agency and its local branch, the newspaper's source of information. At the same time, the *Daily Paper* received a good number of reader responses, and the story continued to develop. For example, state prosecutors were now considering bringing charges against the instructions' authors. That this was a crucial moment for the *Daily Paper* was clear when Arnold called me into his office on the first day of fieldwork to discuss, again, how the research could work practically. Instead, however, he started with the order to shoot as soon as the door shut behind us. The story was highly relevant to the project, in Arnold's opinion, and I had just missed it, he added, while we sat down at the meeting table. After recent developments the story was now also contentious, so the editor-in-chief, it seemed to me, needed to ensure that the anthropologist who was also conducting research among a group of governmental institutions, including the Birthler agency, got the right impression. Arnold explained that the *Daily Paper* was morally indebted to Fuhr, who had come under some serious pressure because some people incorrectly assumed he had strategically released the document near the anniversary. The editor-in-chief sounded almost apologetic when explaining to me that it was the newspaper that had held the story back: "That's how it is though, in the media business. You try to link stories to relevant events" (Galtung and Ruge 1965). So now, he added, "I had to make clear that this was not the BStU director's decision," referring to an editorial of his published that very day. The editor-in-chief relatively rarely writes, which marked this editorial as extraordinary, as did the fact that it alone took the space usually shared by three such pieces. In the same issue, a follow-up story from Otto was also published.

The editorial comprises six paragraphs, each of which tackles another aspect of the find and the recent revelations. The introduction reestablishes the story as a scoop: "The entire country is discussing the topic anew." Arnold then turns to the publication of a similar document in 1997 and its lacking publicity, stating clearly that "it is therefore unfair to pretend this had already been known." The piece goes on to defend the head of the Tillberg BStU office, who is described as having been "alert enough" to "realize the meaning of the document." Like Otto, Arnold invokes the reactions of audiences as proof of the find's value: "The enormous public response simply proves him [Fuhr] right." After two paragraphs concerning wider questions this story now raises, the editorial concludes that much research about the GDR is yet to be done:

> Much of this may be painful or politically unpleasant. But truth in the mirror of history can only be achieved with a will to truthfulness. If this discussion contributes to that, it already has value.

The piece's focus is the current debate and provides explicit criticism of some commentators who apparently used the discussion for political maneuvering—referring to the attacks on the Birthler agency during a time when its future was under consideration. Based on this, Arnold calls for an understanding of the news event as a sign of the need for further exploration of the East German past. Here he moves from the focus on the MfS and GDR leadership in Otto's reporting to a concern with East German history more generally. And with some aplomb he requests that such exploration is conducted free of more or less hidden political agendas.

There is considerable overlap between Arnold's editorial and Otto's follow-up article. The news item also reestablishes the find's value, but beyond reference to the "new nationwide debate," it provides quotes from experts and news that prosecution in Berlin is considering the case. Like the editorial, the article argues for a continuation of the discussion. This point is made via indirect speech attributed to Fuhr, who calls on a new group of protagonists: "We owe it to the victims" (*Opfer*). The trope "victims" invokes those affected by violence at the inner German border. While Otto previously referred to deaths at the border—although tragic, a quantifiable and experientially removed issue—the phrase used here relates "victims" to an inclusive "we." Despite making a reference to a generalized group of people—in Alfred Schütz's (1962) phenomenology, "contemporaries" (*Nebenmenschen*) rather than "consociates" (*Mitmenschen*)—the phrase establishes a link between that group of individuals and "us," putting individual fates and tragedies within readers' grasps and thus creating the potential for those generalized victims to become *Mitmenschen*. This then adds to the sense of a moral obligation of giving this topic space in the public realm an ethical dimension that bases this obligation in "thicker" relationships (Margalit 2002). As a story seed, the phrase also points to other East German life stories that contrast with those of Manfred L. and with most readers' calling for an empathetic imagination that recognizes the suffering of others even if oneself did not experience this aspect of socialist rule.

The call for discussion appears to be the article's main purpose, as it was for the *Daily Paper* more generally once the national debate had shifted. It is made twice in the editorial and raised in conversations by both Arnold and Otto: "Then we'll have to have that discussion now." There is a sense here that discussion itself, the airing of views and deliberation of opinions, has immense value beyond the newspaper's commercial interest. It links to the press's implicit goal of allowing for reflection that feeds into understandings of the world, past and present. Like in many other instances, reader interest is invoked when arguing for the importance of this topic, although the editors' relationship to readers is rather more ambiguous than apparent here (more on this in chapter 7; also see Dietzsch 2014). While the *Daily Paper*'s explicit reporting on the issue ended with the combined effort of Arnold's editorial and Otto's news piece on Tuesday, notwithstanding one or two small news items on sideline developments, the story continued through the facilitation of discussion on the readers' and opinion pages.[7]

Mediating Debate: The Order to Shoot, "Discuss"

The *Daily Paper* received approximately fifteen readers' letters on the order to shoot. which was neither the only nor the most popular topic readers wrote in about during that time. Other issues included neo-Nazi violence (as "eastern German" problem; in relation to an incident in a neighboring state), a strike of train drivers for fairer wages (going on for weeks, it inconvenienced the many commuting members of Mittelland's population), a law on dangerous dogs ("how dangerous are 'dangerous dogs'?"),[8] and unemployment benefits (Hartz IV; the troubles of surviving on such meager benefits).[9] The *Daily Paper* gave the *Schiessbefehl* topic considerable space, publishing ten of the fifteen letters over six editions. Publishing readers' letters is another journalistic technique that strengthens links to the locale by including readers quite literally in the newspaper (J. Richardson 2007: 149). The "classic reader's contribution," Arnold explicated during another chat in his office, should be "short and clear," but most importantly it should contribute to or comment on a previously published article. The letter thus adds to an existing topic by looking at it from a different perspective or by contributing a new dimension. Letters that open new topics are therefore rarely published but may occasionally be explored for potential news material. Letters are chosen for publication to show a variety of opinions so that the readers' page comes to represent the diversity of the readership. This is also marked symbolically by including the author's name and place of residence, thus "mapping" the *Daily Paper*'s area of distribution on the page. Since readers' letters are chosen to provide new angles or alternative views, their publication inevitably results in a diversification of the reporting. Beyond publication, all reader contributions are carefully read, often taken to heart, and filed for reference (Dietzsch 2014).

The first letters appeared in the *Daily Paper* on Wednesday, the day after Arnold's editorial. Positioned at the top of the readers' page and with a color picture, another facsimile of the document, they are placed center stage. The letters are linked to the topic by a declaration—"document on the order to shoot at the inner German border." Underneath this, each letter bears a title chosen by the editor—for example, "dark side of the GDR shown"—and a reference to the articles it comments on. The first three letters in this issue welcome the find and hope it will help inform certain others. For two authors, this primarily concerns people who downplay difficult aspects of the past: "There are people who say: 'We used to be well off in the GDR. It was a social state . . . All this about the Stasi, it wasn't that bad. After seventeen years . . . we need to put it behind us.'" Both readers also remind of the victims of Stasi oppression—in one case the reader reveals himself as a former political prisoner—and raise concerns about former power holders who remain in influential positions, in the Left Party, for example. The two letters' twin focus on victims and perpetrators thus suggests a view of the GDR as dictatorship and calls for continued "reworking." The third letter, written from a teacher's perspective, welcomes the find in respect of young people who often have naive views of life in the GDR. In all letters there is a sense that certain parts of the local population, and with that the *Daily Paper*'s readership, need to wake up to more "correct" understandings of the socialist period.

In following editions, letters on the topic appeared as single contributions among others and were no longer positioned at the top or center of the page. As Antje, editor of the readers' page, explained to me after Wednesday: "I opened with the order to shoot yesterday. I don't want to do that again tomorrow." She aims for variety on this page, given that several issues concerned readers at the time. The following day, one letter was published, another two days later, and four more the week after. These additional letters were considerably more varied in opinion than the first three. The letter two days later, for example, queries the find, stating that it suited the current political climate. The reader argues that there had been no difference in the official guidelines on weapon use for armed forces between East and West Germany. Another letter in contrast states again how this find can contribute to teaching young people "how and where a dictatorship begins and what inhumane means it uses to succeed."

The same day as these latter two letters, an opinion piece on the topic, written by the freelance author Willenberg, was placed quite prominently on the opinion and debate page. During a conversation in the office, senior editor Markus explained to me that he likes the originality of Willenberg's contributions. He had listened to an interview with Willenberg on the radio that morning and was still delighted with how it had fit exactly into the drive from the city motorway to the *Daily Paper*'s parking lot. The literary author's arguments are often very subtle but take a perspective or angle that nobody else considered, Markus explained. Unfortunately, his pieces usually require considerable editing because sentence structure can be a little too convoluted for the *Daily Paper*'s succinct writing style, Markus conceded, but he clearly feels that Willenberg's observations are worth the extra labor. He had certainly liked Willenberg's piece on the order to shoot, the editor noted. On that occasion, Markus's colleague, Michael, had been in charge of editing the opinion and debate page.

At the 1 PM conference about a week after the story broke discussion first touched this news only tangentially. Arnold mentioned the issue of the *Daily Paper*'s online appearance, a relatively recent development that is, however, important for the future, criticizing the website's algorithm for choosing which articles to display. With regard to the order to shoot, the page 3 report had appeared online, he noted, when in fact the key piece was the page 1 article. The editor-in-chief is clearly unhappy about this missed opportunity.

The conference moved on and my ears pricked up when I heard "order to shoot" again during planning. Michael mentioned almost by the by that he had "got something else on the order to shoot, from Willenberg," for his page tomorrow. In the afternoon I stopped by the thirty-something-year-old editor's desk to enquire about this piece. Clearly preoccupied with his editorial on the liberal party's announcement that it wished to abolish military service, Michael merely explained that Willenberg is someone who occasionally writes for them. Complaining that the current piece was too long and he would need to cut it down, he sent the text to the printer for me. I left him to his work sauntering off to collect the text. A little later, however, seemingly once he had looked more closely at the piece, Michael came over to my desk, opposite Markus's, commenting enthusiastically that the author had served at the inner German border. He wanted to add this information to the article. Announcing that it was worth finding out a little more, he left us again. Markus, who knows Willenberg quite well, looked at me and then handed me one of the author's literary publications, a picture textbook about Berlin before and after the wall's fall.

The opinion piece itself, however, does not refer to Willenberg's personal experience but rather reads like the contribution of a historically learned author. In broad strokes, the author lays out the ideology and worldview behind the fortification of the Berlin Wall. The piece attributes will to power to a group of individuals described vaguely as "those who saw themselves as executioners of the 'dictatorship of the proletariat,'" as Marxist–Leninist ideology described socialism. It comments that the current discussion is bewildering because it concerns something that could never exist, an order to shoot, because the East German regime's power holders could have never admitted their own cruelty. Instead, soldiers needed to be trained to be "willing to kill out of anxiety." The document therefore evidenced "hidden responsibilities." Willenberg does not comment on the document's origin in an MfS taskforce but focuses entirely on the subtle coercion and arbitrary violence of the GDR system and the responsibility of vaguely defined authorities. In so doing, he paints a complex picture of power in the GDR. But he also, like the report and news piece, shields wider society, the target of such measures, from judgment.

This narrative is reinforced by an unusual biographic byline below the article, added by Michael: "Willenberg is a freelance author and lives in Berlin. In 1972/73 he served as a border guard in Thuringia. His latest book is entitled . . ." This detail positions Willenberg as both intellectual expert and *Zeitzeuge*. Although the term *Zeitzeuge* generally means "historical witness," it more commonly refers to what Avishai Margalit calls "moral witnesses," people who endured suffering "inflicted by an . . . evil regime" (2002: 148), attributing these individuals with the authority that comes from experience (Gallinat 2011; Skultans 2001) and a moral currency derived from their suffering. Willenberg cannot quite claim that position, but he remains a historical witness of sorts through his experience as a former border guard. In previous pieces, border guards appeared as part perpetrators, part victims of the authorities, and Willenberg's identity is referred to that same gray area. He was one of those exposed to the pressure from above to become "willing to kill," and he was someone who may have shot at fellow countrymen. His identity is thus tainted to a degree in the same way many other East Germans' identities could be considered morally tainted. This, in turn, makes his story easier to identify with for many readers, as he is a little bit more like they are: someone who struggled with and through the authoritative system.

This opinion piece marked a shift in the discussion away from the find's historic value to more specific questions about the workings of this border regime. Two letters on the following Wednesday, for example, take issue with the discussion given that weapons are commonly used at international borders. Another letter a few days later that was given much space directs attention back to the question of responsibility at this border of the Cold War. Its argument that culpability lay in Moscow, not with the East German government, is substantiated with reference to a relative who had worked at the border and through personal experiences of visiting a Soviet garrison. In its published form, this letter takes seven paragraphs over two columns. Originally, however, it was three pages long. Sections that the vice editor-in-chief marked for deletion are long paragraphs about the faults of current politicians and institutions, which staff at the newspaper tend to view as unpublishable "nothing but complaining." Sections considered publishable are those that explain in more moderate tones the reader's view of governance at the inner German border and refer to the author's personal experiences in GDR times, not all of which seem entirely relevant. The letter thus edited speaks to the snappy headline created for it, "Moscow ruled at the border," and to the author's memory.

Almost two weeks after the breaking news, one more letter was given considerable space on the readers' page, stretching over four columns under the header "No soldier went to the border against their will." While previous correspondence referred back to the original articles, this letter is instead signposted as a response "to [the] reader's letter 'Moscow ruled at the border.'" The letter returns to the question of responsibility but, in contrast to previous letters and Willenberg's opinion piece, with regard to individual border guards. The author explains that the process of selecting border guards from among young men drafted for compulsory army service allowed for ways out: "There were ways and means to withdraw from this madness without harming yourself. It was down to each individual." He suggests that individuals could present themselves as unsuitable for these duties during the profiling process (not committed enough, emotionally instable). While the author recognizes the influence of Moscow at the border, in response to the previous letter, he argues that it was nevertheless East Germans who carried ultimate responsibility. He concludes, "An unjust state cannot retrospectively be legitimized by downplaying or whitewashing its inhumanity." Using the trope *Unrechtsstaat* ("unjust state"), the author clearly signals his view of the past state as dictatorship, in which individuals were implicated, and simultaneously accuses the other reader of protecting the inhumane regime. Through biographical revelation, the reader identifies as a *Betroffener*: he attempted to flee the GDR several times, which landed him in prison from where he was released to West Germany. He only recently returned to Mittelland. The author can therefore speak of border violence from personal experience. He claims further "authority of experience" (Skultans 2001) by commenting that he never served in the army even though he had not refused service either—he had found ways to avoid it.

While later letters explored what this document means for an understanding of the past, and specifically for violence at the border, earlier ones focused more on what it says about how the past is approached in the present. All letters therefore take position toward the *Daily Paper*'s reporting, which, despite some interpretive openness, constitutes an emerging discourse about the past state and society. As such it has the potential to mark certain views and knowledges about the past as legitimate and "truthful," delegitimizing others. Notions of the SED dictatorship or the "Stasi-controlled border regime" thus guide and restrict what can be legitimately told of selves if individuals wish to appear as socially proper persons worth listening to (Holstein and Gubrium 2000; Linde 1993). Perceiving such a developing discourse, or "canonic narrative" (Collins 2003), some readers set out to shape the debate in a fashion that does justice to their memories and self-perceptions. Those who welcome the find see narratives of a GDR characterized by state control as fitting their own view, as well as their experiences in the present, where they feel not enough people recognize or admit these darker aspects. Through signaling approval, their letters aim to give the emerging discourse further impetus. Other readers find that aspects of the reporting grind with their own memories or knowledge and write in to question some of its certainty and readjust story lines: Yes, there was violence and that is terrible, but should responsibility not lie elsewhere? Yet others question the discussion as a whole, seeing it as either humbug or nonnews, because this is after all what borders are all about.

In this debate, as in many others, the use of personal memory narrative is heavily facilitated by the *Daily Paper*. As the example above shows, the editor cut substantial sections of a letter but left in any references to experiences in the GDR. Where readers do not include this information in their text, it may be added, as in Willenberg's case. Readers themselves employ memory narrative to claim authority on a topic, through the construction of authenticity, and thus rhetorically strengthen their argument. Sometimes sentences even begin with "I know this because . . ." In many cases, nods toward personal experiences are construed as self-revelations—the revelation of personal information that positions authors as particular kinds of people, most commonly as victims or *Betroffene*. Scholars of memory have noted an ethical turn in memory that privileges victim memories of trauma and suffering (Assmann 2006; Jones 2014), which we can see reproduced in the *Daily Paper*. For memory narratives to become persuasive, they need to be considered authentic. In this regard, the testimony of moral witnesses has particular power "by having been there, and importantly, by having suffered there" (Jones 2014: 192). In other contexts, however, people may contrastingly describe themselves as "not resistance fighters," which means they were ordinary East German citizens, who cannot claim the morality of someone who had opposed the state, but at least they are honest about that. Self-revelation of someone as someone specific in relation to a certain topic is part ordinary rhetoric—Kenneth Burke's identification (1969: xiii–xvi, in Rumsey 2012: 129; also Burke 1973)—but it gains specific meaning in postsocialism, where regime change turned terms like "communist" and "dissident" into loaded language that facilitated claims to moral superiority or challenges that of others (Verdery 1998: 38). In eastern Germany, self-revelation emerges against the backdrop of the authoritative discourse of *Aufarbeitung* and its clearly delineated master narrative of the "GDR as dictatorship" that suggests specific person types, entailing "non-negotiable" subject positions (Franklin 1990: 217), for life in socialism that put moral questions to individual selves.[10]

In this vein, three readers position themselves as former political prisoners. They therefore not only claim authority of voice due to having been quite literally the "targets" of orders to shoot, but their accounts also become the testimony of "moral witnesses," entailing considerable moral currency. This self-revelation furthermore adds an ethical dimension to the moral concern of negotiating a view of the past that does right by its—generalized—victims. Revealing intimate experiences or sharing difficult memories with others—here, both editors and readers—even if in a mediated context, is a way of establishing relationships and putting oneself "nearer" the listening/reading other (Margalit 2002). This rhetorical strategy is not without risks, however, as it bears the danger of rejection: not all readers will necessarily be persuaded by such appeals to empathy, moreover so since the life stories of victims can be difficult to identify with (Gallinat 2006a; also Arnold-de Simine 2013: 45).

Whichever self-revelation is employed, letters that include such statements also provide readers with scripts of possible East German life stories. For the *Daily Paper*, this adds the attractive human interest aspect that reinforces its relationship to the local. For the readership, it is a way of sharing recollections and developing a social memory of the GDR past. In Peter Collins's terms, then, the newspaper's reporting provided a "vernacular narrative," "circumscribed in space and time," which combines with others in a fledging discourse on the past iterated by authoritative experts, the journalists. This was in turn challenged by individual's "prototypical" stories (2003: 243). Usually the more "popular language of the storyteller" (Franklin 1990: 217) is not considered powerful enough to change discourses that entail truth claims and, by definition, function as "epistemological enforcers" (Said 1988: 10; also Lawler 2008: 124). However, like the increasing use of victim testimonies in memorial museums (Jones 2014), prototypical narratives at the *Daily Paper* that invite readers to engage in "exchange for the pleasures of recognition and identification" (Franklin 1990: 217) become a part of the medium's discourse through editing and publication. Through this alternate enforcement, they contribute to the creation of "canonic" understandings, "which are imagined to be shared by all" (Collins 2003: 243) and have the potential to challenge some of the much more linear and morally certain portrayals of the past that exclusive views of the dictatorship entail.

Open-Ended Narrative:
The Border Regime as Unresolved Life Event

The publishing of readers' letters not only reinforced the newsworthiness of the find but also enabled the public discussion that both Otto and Arnold had called for. The *Daily Paper* thus became the platform that realized the needed, according to the editors, and wanted, so it seems from the published readers' letters, debate. Through the inclusion of differing views and arguments, the newspaper created a reflective, emergent, and seemingly nonlinear discourse about the "Stasi-controlled border regime" that is not dissimilar to the work-in-progress narratives of everyday conversations. In contrast to written stories, such "living narratives" move to and fro as varying aspects of an "unresolved life event" are raised, explored, questioned, and dropped in the interaction of interlocutors (Ochs and Capps 2001). The discussion of the order to shoot on the *Daily Paper*'s back pages took on the look of such a living narrative that in its incompletion seemed to mirror discussions in the newsroom.

Just over two weeks after the revelation of the order to shoot the *Daily Paper*'s staff was gathered around the large oval table, editor-in-chief and vice editor-in-chief at the head for the 1 PM conference to look through the day's issue for critique and praise and plan the pages for the following day. As discussion of a particular article faded, one reporter, Matthias, who had just returned from holiday, remarked how much he liked the reader's letter published that day, the one that raised the issue of border guards' responsibility: "You know, as a reader's letter it is well written and very calm even though that reader served a prison sentence for attempting to escape." The editor of the readers' page agreed but quickly added, "But we have one today that contradicts that, because that reader argued that you could wiggle your way out of serving on the border, and this new letter says it wasn't as simple as that." Another colleague could relate to that: "I had mates at school who had wanted to go to uni . . ." But somebody else jumped in: "Well, you had to serve, whether that was with the NVA [East German army] or at the border." Another colleague replied that he had to serve at the border and that indeed, you had no choice: "You were ordered [*vergattert*]." Someone else: "Of course, you provoked suspicion the minute you raised the slightest objection to serving your three years."[11] The journalist speaking earlier finished her story by saying that those friends who had served at the border in order to secure a place at university had changed as people; they had been deeply affected by it.

While Matthias began by making stylistic comments on one letter, the reader editor's reference to the letter's contentious argument countered now by another reader set off an exchange of opinion. Colleagues began contributing, talking over and past each other. Like many discussions in the *Daily Paper*'s boardroom, the exchange was fast paced and driven by relatively short but strongly put interjections. Just as in the discussion on the readers' page, the points made all related to the topic but highlighted different aspects drawn from editors' personal experiences or professional knowledge. Matthias could only look on as the discussion drifted away from him while most staff were actually looking at Thorsten. The forty-something-year-old reporter for regional matters had served with the border guards, even at the Berlin Wall, for a (difficult) period of time. He could thus speak with the most authority but was also the one whose reputation was most threatened by the discussion. Thorsten eventually spoke up but kept it brief: "You had to; you were ordered to." He avoided becoming too involved, and he did not need to either. The most relevant points had already been made. The discussion slowed down then, allowing one embattled interlocutor to finish her narrative about her university friends. The discussion stopped when the editor-in-chief turned attention to the planning of the current issue.

A number of factors may explain why this discussion erupted as and when it did. One is that editors, at least the more senior among the staff, have strong opinions and like to have their say when it concerns an issue that matters to them. The question of border guards' personal culpability concerns those who know Thorsten not only as a colleague but also as a friend, which prompts them to dispute a view that would implicate the likeable reporter. Moreover, if border guards are seen to be culpable because they followed orders, similar questions can be asked of other GDR citizens, including the GDR-time journalists sitting here whose writing was reined in by the party orders they followed. This ambiguous complexity of individuals' relations to the authoritarian system is captured by Vaclav Havel's argument that "[socialist] society is not sharply polarized on the level of actual political power, but . . . the fundamental lines of conflict run right through each person" (1987: 91, cited in Skultans 2001: 334). It is therefore also unsurprising that the editors who engage in this fast-paced and emotive conversation are all eastern German—primarily those who were journalists during GDR times—and that the tenor of discussion settles on one position: things were not that simple when individual lives are concerned. This is also in keeping with the wider discourse in eastern German society that challenges sharp, black-and-white views of life in the GDR. As one eastern German member of staff at the LpB put it, "They [LpB colleagues] forget the gray." Similarly, many interviewees insisted that much "differentiation" was required when "evaluating" individual biographies. Putting it differently, Creed talks about "the binary discourse of 'good' and 'bad'" that ought to be challenged by showing how people "domesticated the revolution" in rural Bulgaria (1998), how they "painted socialism," as Michael Burawoy and János Lukács (1992) call it, or "were willing to 'live within a lie,' as Havel (1985: 31) characterizes socialist complicity" (Creed 1998: 4).

* * *

Considering the ambiguity of life in socialism, it is unsurprising that the order to shoot turned into a debate, a contested work-in-progress narrative that time and again called individuals to contribute their recollections. Both in the newspaper and at the 1 PM conference, the GDR emerges as an unresolved life event that needs to be pondered. Certainly the quick exchange among editors signals the attempt to establish or confirm shared understandings of the East German past that have the potential to provide narrative frameworks that are more compromising and allow individuals to find "habitable identities" (Skultans 1998; also Gallinat 2006a), for themselves and for each other. Vieda Skultans uses this notion in relation to individuals' struggles to tell of their traumatic experiences of persecution in Latvia in a semantic environment characterized by an absence of discourses, and thus scripts, about this past violence. While the problem for many eastern Germans is not the need to verbalize suffering and pain, a similar situation arises when an overbearing discourse about the dictatorship threatens to force ambiguous and complex lives into "inhabitable" subject positions.

After the staff conference I asked the reader's editor whether she would publish the most recent reader's letter she had mentioned. Motioning down the aisle of the open-plan office toward the offices of the editors-in-chief, she said she was unsure: "We will have to see what the people down there want in the paper." She added, "It's just that one letter leads to a reaction from someone else, and it can be an endless process." As the news moves on, the readers' page has to follow, and the new letter did not make it into the *Daily Paper*. Just like the discussion at the staff conference that ended when the editor-in-chief moved on to the next agenda point, and just as Ochs and Capps's "living narratives" (2001) that come to halt when another aspect of life intervenes in the conversation, the debate about the order to shoot stopped without conclusion. The *Daily Paper* had raised aspects of the GDR past as the nation's "unresolved life event," putting them through the mill of a living narrative in the arena of mediated public debate.

Such debate is crucial to developing understandings of the world, a key mission of the media (J. Richardson 2007). The debate moreover contributes to the "free development of opinion" (*freie Meinungsbildung*) that positions the medium within the fourth estate, making it an integral part of democratic government. Through a combination of newswriting and opinion, the *Daily Paper* creates a discourse about past and present that is critical while characterized by considerable interpretive openness, ambiguity in short, that safeguards the all-important relationship to readers. It avoids putting people off with images of the past state and society that are too clear-cut, and, leaving interpretation to readers, it empowers its audience—even if not everyone appreciates this. The locale, memory, and, in their combination, local belonging emerge as key issues the *Daily Paper* engages in order to achieve its journalistic goal of serving "the local and regional concerns of the people" and to straddle its position in both public and private realms. This strategy has an inevitable effect on understandings of citizenship and democracy had and employed at the newspaper, to which we will return in chapter 7.

Notes

1. To protect the identities of informants, I am not able to provide references to the original newspaper articles. See the introduction for details. All translations are the author's.
2. In the summer of 2016 the German parliament requested that the Stasi-files be moved into the national archive by 2021.
3. The PDS was the SED's successor party formed in 1990. Arnold uses the term to refer to the Left Party, which formed in 2007 through a merger of the PDS and a western German left-wing group. At the *Daily Paper* and in popular parlance, the term PDS still prevails in reference to the Left, suggesting a sense of continuity from GDR leaders' to the current party.
4. While the term "Birthler agency" is not the BStU's official denotation, this shortening that refers to the head of the institution during the period of fieldwork is commonly used in public discourse (also see chapter 1).
5. More specifically, "VEB" translates as 'publicly owned operation' and applied to the vast majority of factories in the GDR. "Förderanlagenbau" means the construction of conveyer systems and/or wells.
6. Some may consider this discussion similar to the longstanding dispute about the existence of a Führer order for the Holocaust (*Führerbefehl*) (e.g., Longerich 2001).
7. One such development was that the *Junge Welt*, a Marxist paper, announced that a solicitor intended to bring criminal charges against Fuhr and Birthler. After initial confusion, this announcement left the usually very energetic 1 PM conference speechless.
8. "Dangerous dogs" (*Kampfhunde*) here include bull terriers and pit bull terriers of various breeds.
9. For comparison, during the last ten days of August, the *Daily Paper* received approximately forty-five letters from readers, and out of these, six concerned the order to shoot.
10. In the introduction to this book, I also felt compelled to employ a form of self-revelation, although my generation is not usually called to account.
11. The requirement was to serve eighteen months; three years' service was voluntary but sometimes recommended to individuals with particular career aspirations, as we will see in chapter 5.

Chapter Four

ORDERING MEMORY FOR GOVERNMENT
Everyday Life in East Germany

➤●⬥

Having explored the discourse of the *Daily Paper*, this chapter now focuses on how the Working Group *Aufarbeitung* creates representations of the past. As chapter 1 highlights, the notion of *Aufarbeitung* is inextricably intertwined with a perception of the past state as "dictatorship" within what, however, remains a young, emergent discourse. Chapter 2 shows further that the Working Group works in the realm of government. Both of these contexts create certain pressures on the group's work, including a moral obligation to victims and a need to be persuasive so as to have an effect on audiences, while the East German past itself, however, remains a complex issue, and the narratives that can be created about it are no foregone conclusion. Considering the Working Group's development of a teacher training course, this chapter explores how the discourse of *Aufarbeitung* is produced in local contexts in practice. This highlights that in this realm certain factors create a strong urge to tidy narrative order ensuring linearity and moral certainty in events and texts that become about the "GDR as dictatorship". These factors include the discourse's location within the field of political government, the need to compromise in institutional collaboration, and actors" ethical embeddedness in this realm.

Commemorating the Border Regime

While Monday, 13 August, the anniversary of the building of the Berlin Wall in 1961, is taken up by discussions and article writing in the aftermath of the revelation of the order to shoot at the *Daily Paper*, it is spent in a rather solemn and festive way by members of the Working Group *Aufarbeitung*. In their capacity as heads or members of institutions that deal with the dictatorial aspects of the East German state, Bohlmann, Schumacher, Franke, Fuhr, and their colleagues also attend various festive activities across the year, many of which are commemorations, such as this particular day.

On a bright and sunny summer day, the commemorative ceremony takes place at Mittelland's border memorial, part of the larger border checkpoint memorial museum in the state's rural heartland. Sabine and I stop at the public car park, a graveled area to the side of a bumpy road that leads out of the village, and walk across to the memorial space. Groups of people congregate on a green meadow in front of the former wall, which is preceded by a two-meter stretch of brown soil that allowed the spotting of footprints of potential escapees (both Sabine and I first assumed it was a minefield) and a line of metal structures designed to stop approaching vehicles. Planks have been put across the bed of soil to allow speakers and musicians to move to the wall where microphones and music equipment are being set up. Opposite, where the meadow borders on the village, another wall runs parallel to the main one. The latter prevented local residents' sight and

Illustration 4.1. A border memorial.

movement into the restricted border area. A watchtower is located on a small hill in the distance. Dotted across the area are the inevitable plaques with explanatory text that mark this ground as museum space. It is clear that we are congregating in the middle of a heavily enforced border, yet standing there in the green grass and sunshine it does not quite feel like it.

Just over a hundred people, the vast majority in their sixties and older, have gathered to participate in the ceremony. While some are dressed smartly, many of the men are in the more typical attire of jeans or trousers and shirts pulled in under the belt. Some middle-aged and younger people busy with pen, paper, or camera appear to be journalists. A van from the MDR, the regional TV station for eastern Germany, is parked in the car park. There are also some local residents who seem to have unexpectedly run into the gathering while going for a walk or running an errand: dog walkers, a family with children, bicyclists on their way to and from the nearby allotments. Some of them have come over to find out what is happening and stay while others walk past to complete their business.

Approaching the memorial complex, Sabine and I are greeted by Schumacher, who has changed his plans of visiting Berlin today to come here, even though, as he put it, "I have been at more than enough commemorative ceremonies, I could miss one." Soon we discover other familiar faces. Jana from the former Stasi prison memorial museum is here, as is the committee of the Victim Association. All the people from Tillberg came together on a coach, we are told as they greet us. Despite the solemn occasion, there is an almost jovial atmosphere. We also spot the director of the border memorial museum, Koehler, who, as one of the organizers, is running around attending to one thing or another. When we manage to speak with him later, we hear about the recent press tumult the memorial was embroiled in over its attempt to acquire a specific type of border enforcement. Administrators saw collecting the weaponry as part of their "duty to educate" (*Lehrauftrag*) and were surprised by the fuss it caused. We discover Frau Herzog from the BStU—"Also here? We'll catch up on Friday"—who explains that Herr Fuhr also wanted to come but could not make it. He was too busy with the aftermath of the order to shoot. As we stand in the crowd of people looking around, a man passes, handing out yellow leaflets that say "Remembrance" in large bold print. The leaflet, from an association of victims of communism, summarizes in stark language the darkest aspects of the socialist regime in relation to border violence and reminds that former decision makers and perpetrators remain unprosecuted. Sabine is approached by an elderly lady, who remarks that once again none of the locals have come. They were avoiding this because "they all have skeletons in the cupboard," suggesting that many had been East German border personnel. She goes on to say that they had opposed the memorial.

Koehler corrects this later, as some locals had attended. He also explains that resistance to the memorial has several grounds, one of which is that many residents hoped to finally enjoy an unhindered view across the countryside from their homes instead of the unsightly wall. The lady adds that she always comes to things like this with the "prison club," referring to the Victim Association from Tillberg. But now heads turn and conversations change as three black estate cars pull up on the road, marking the arrival of the Minister President (MP) of Mittelland who will speak today. We lose our volunteer informant as the ceremony begins.

The ceremony starts with a musical piece. In front of the wall facing the quiet and slightly windswept audience, the musicians stand next to Koehler and the MP; the head of Friends of the Border Memorial completes the group. The atmosphere is somber and festive. When the music finishes, Koehler welcomes everyone. He adds a few words about the "border with a state," as which he sees the GDR, and the recent media tumults but primarily provides the ground for the MP's speech. There is a musical interlude, a folk song this time, and then the Minister President speaks. He reminds everyone of the reason for the fortification of the inner German border in 1961, which was that too many East Germans were leaving the country, "voting with their feet." He comments on the order to shoot, that given the violence at this border, it is clear that such instructions had existed. Any politicians or others who are denying this are hiding their own responsibilities, which is unacceptable. This earns him applause from the audience. As he summarizes aspects of GDR history, he speaks about the state's control of every facet of life, emphasizing again the population's rejection of this control. He leads on to today's political order, which also comes with problems, but explains that "they"[1] want to show how one can deal with these in a democratic society that is not patronized by its government. He concludes by speaking about the many deaths at the border and suggests that we tell coming generations about this. He receives more applause for this, and in an unplanned move, Koehler turns to the microphone and pledges that "they will ensure" this happens.

Accompanied by music, the laying of wreaths follows. Representatives of groups and associations one after another step forward to pay their respects by placing their wreath along the wall. There are about six or seven wreaths in total, from the Minister President, the Victim Association, the Memorial Foundation, the president of Mittelland's parliament, Friends of the Border Memorial, and the FDP's parliamentary faction, when all respects have been paid. This is followed by a minute of silence, noted as "commemoration" in the program, to remember those who died at the border. The minute passes quickly and quietly, only interrupted by the birds and the wind. This concludes this part of the ceremony. A second part is to follow at the village cemetery to commemorate further victims, now without the MP.

There is some milling about as the audience disperses. Journalists approach the various notables. Frau Woband from the Victim Association is filmed walking with the MP along the wall by a team of young film-makers who are preparing a documentary about her thirteen-year imprison-ment. The project is supported by the Stasi commissioner and funded in part by the Office for Political Education. Most, however, are walking back to the car park. Sabine and I meet Schumacher and Jana again, who are standing by the Tillberg coach. Herr Stiehl, secretary of the Victim Asso-ciation, joins us briefly but then speaks with another attendee about poten-tial funding for similar occasions. We are asked several times if we want to come along to the cemetery on the bus, but we decline. We planned to walk across the memorial space, which we do once the coach with the Tillberg group has set off. Later, on our way out of village, we pass the bus, which is parked by the side of the road, hazard lights on constant, and decide to look for them. We find a much reduced gathering of about thirty participants deep inside the leafy cemetery, quietly and solemnly again commemorating victims of violence to the play of a local brass band. As the conclusion of the ceremony is announced, the group breaks up and people chat or are lost in thought as they walk back to the street. Sabine and I catch up with Frau Herzog.

This commemorative event presents the ethical heart of *Aufarbeitung*. It is attended by politicians—who observe a representative function here, showing their party's serious engagement with these issues—and individu-als for whom reckoning is a cause and mission. *Betroffene*, victims of the regime, attend to commemorate lost "comrades" and some also to lobby power holders and decision makers. The Victim Association in Tillberg, for example, is usually represented by a core group of five or so individuals, the group's committee, and friends and family who come along to one thing or another. These men and women in their seventies were imprisoned by the Stasi in horrendous conditions mostly during the 1950s. Through this trauma, their stories of the dictatorship are highly persuasive. They have now also become what Schumacher aptly calls "professional" moral wit-nesses (*Zeitzeugen*), who engage with a variety of audiences, telling their life stories in order to warn of the dangers of political extremism (Gallinat 2006a, 2009b). Even if representatives of institutions or parties are here to "merely" represent, they cannot escape the personal relationships that inevi-tably develop out of this work. The heads and employees of institutions like the memorial museums or the Stasi commissioner meet members of these associations frequently: at occasions like this, events that involve witness testimony, and meetings of the Memorial Foundation where the association sits on the advisory committee. Through their professional work, they moreover have a deep understanding of the kinds of traumatic experiences that the members of this small group went through, and they know of other people who were also persecuted yet will not or no longer can attend such ceremonies but nevertheless appear behind the small group metaphorically as long, dark shadows. The relationships to these *Betroffene* give the moral messages of *Aufarbeitung* an emotionally felt ethical perspective as institutional commemorative work is turned into a promise toward specific individuals—Schütz's *Mitmenschen*, or consociates (1962), Margalit's "near and dear" (2002)—to keep their memories alive.

As a ritual, the commemorative ceremony creates a "performative memory which is bodily" (Connerton 1989: 71) and through that a particular emotional state. Key tropes of the commemorative ceremony are the laying of wreaths and minute of silence, explicitly denoted as "remembrance" (*Gedenken*) on the program. These ritual actions signal that this is an act of solemn remembrance of suffering and lives lost, which commands humble acknowledgment of participants. This sense is reinforced by the quietness of such occasions, participants' dark attire, and the slow movements that are dictated by the ritual's carefully sequenced flow. Against the specific tempo of commemorative events work other aspects, however, in particular the clapping and cheers from the audience at two junctures in the MP's speech, Koehler's cutting to the microphone in response, and the almost jovial meet-and-greet atmosphere at the beginning that felt as if a community of friends was coming together. These breaks in the ritual highlight that beyond the solemn consideration of past injustice, there are also political messages here that concern the present, specifically how the past should be dealt with in the present. It is this that was cheered for: the comment that some politicians are unwilling to face the truth of the GDR dictatorship, that we should carry knowledge of trauma caused by the GDR to coming generations. These cheers were supported by a sense of a coming together of individuals united by an understanding of the past as dictatorial. Together the metaphors of ritual practice and the social encounters create a persuasive power that make the notion of a dictatorial past almost felt, which those working in the sphere of *Aufarbeitung* will carry back to Tillberg on the coach.

Education for Remembrance and a Teacher Training Event on the GDR Everyday

The Minister President's call to teach young people about the East German past at this event was timely. Education was a main concern of the Working

Group *Aufarbeitung* that year, as apparent in the Working Group meeting Sabine had attended (chapter 2). As the last epoch in a chronologically organized curriculum, GDR history often dropped out of school teaching when time was tight. As one teacher at a workshop regretfully put it, "We usually just about make it to 1949." However, under the paradigm of *Aufarbeitung* and the antitotalitarian consensus, the East German past is considered an important part of "historical-political education." All institutions in the Working Group therefore have a *Bildungsauftrag*, a "duty to educate" through the resources their work affords. The former Stasi prison memorial museum developed its framework for education in 2005, when, with the passing of time and a new director, focus moved from supporting victims, whose remembrance nevertheless remains a core task, to passing on knowledge to the next generation. Under this framework the memorial museum works with teachers by providing space and resources for project days that may include a tour of the prison and talks by historic witnesses, with the university on teaching degrees, and with the LpB and other institutions on developing opportunities for teachers. Crucially, its aim is to transmit knowledge about "oppression by the MfS" and the "control" exercised by the SED and to "inform about resistance and civic courage" to "further democratic values." The framework sets these aims within the context of a society where memories of the GDR are primarily transmitted orally in families, which leads to a lack of knowledge and growing *Ostalgie* so that "many young visitors are furnished at home with the sentence that 'not everything was bad in the GDR.'" Similarly, both the Stasi commissioner and the commissioner for Stasi files have developed documents that inform about the support they can offer schools, including materials "on repression, resistance, refusal, and perpetratorship." Teaching materials typically use excerpts from Stasi documents to illustrate individual life stories, examples of surveillance of particular groups (such as youth subcultures), and/or MfS actions around particular events.

The view of the GDR past that these materials convey is clearly focused and allows for the telling of categorically certain stories that fall under a specific genre. As Bruner argues, genre "commit[s] one to use language in a certain way" (1987: 18). In the political field in which this Working Group operates, texts are characterized by a "goal language" committed to "inspire, uplift, persuade . . ., define parameters" (Apthorpe 1997: 44). Putting it more strongly, Pierre Bourdieu suggests that political speeches are "self-fulfilling prophec[ies] through which the spokesperson endows the group with a will, a plan, a hope, or quite simply, a future" (1991: 191), which means they must be highly persuasive. Although not all texts created by the Working Group *Aufarbeitung* fall so clearly under the genre of political speeches, since they do not seek to rally voters, the particularly strong need for persuasion that is common in political texts also applies here. This persuasion seeks to affect real changes in audiences by educating them about the past to transform their personal memories and create a socially shared memory that follows the "parameters" of the *Aufarbeitung* discourse. This goal is clear in purposefully composed education frameworks such as above, just as it is noticeable in concerns of staff at the LpB and other institutions that ways of thinking learned in socialism and nostalgia proliferate in today's society in ways that prevent people from fully engaging with democratic norms (see chapter 2). Historical-political education becomes the means to develop the knowledge and skills required for life in a pluralist society now that structures of democratic governance exist. The discourse of *Aufarbeitung* thus becomes a technique of governmentality, a means to conduct the conduct of others (Gordon 1991). Foucault uses the term to describe a particular form of political rule that took shape at the formation of the modern state (1991). This governmentality is pursued by an "ensemble formed by institutions, procedures, analysis and reflections, tactics that allow the exercise of a complex form of power, which has as its target the population" (Foucault 1991: 102; Inda 2007). Techniques of government can thus be used to very subtly "[make] up" citizens capable of bearing a kind of regulated freedom" (Rose and Miller 1992: 174) through discourses that legitimize and regulate (Foucault 1977, 1981). Because the object of government here is memory, *Aufarbeitung* emerges more particularly as a technique in the "government of souls," which delivers "the true discourse . . . to convince citizens of the need to obey . . . at least in that aspect . . . which is most difficult to obtain, which is precisely the citizens' individual life and the life of their soul" (Foucault 2010: 204–5).

As expressed rather clearly in the memorial museum's education framework, the Working Group is acutely aware that it faces a generational change that brings familial memory to the fore. Members of the group share a sense that many parents are reluctant to broach the topic or limit conversations to somewhat nostalgic and often incorrect comments, which have become commonplaces: that bread rolls were nicer back then and the health system better, or that everyone who wanted it had work. Some members of the group refer to these as popular "GDR myths" that fail to convey the dictatorial regime or economic mismanagement on which these seeming benefits depended (also Großbölting 2009). To counter an apparent increase in such unreflective nostalgic remembering through intergenerational transmission, the group concentrates on working with school history teachers. To overcome the teachers' seeming reluctance to attend events on a period in history they themselves experienced, Frau Wolf at the LpB began developing new approaches that would avoid "serving totalitarianism up front." She was, for example, in discussion with the former Stasi prison memorial museum about an event regarding the prison's history from the late nineteenth century to GDR times as a way of teaching local history. Since many history teachers enjoyed working with Otto von Bismarck, the nineteenth-century chancellor of the German Empire fabled for his diplomatic skill, the workshop would be entitled, "From Bismarck to Marx." However, her plans came to a halt with developments in the Working Group.

For several years the Stasi commissioner had offered training on GDR history, but recently the event failed to attract sufficient numbers, and Schumacher turned to the Working Group for support. In the summer he therefore invited some of the group's members to a discussion at the commission in one of Tillberg's leafy suburbs. The meeting room in the large nineteenth-century villa was set up with agenda and a draft finance plan on the round table. The LpB was represented by Frau Wolf since this topic falls into her remit, Schumacher, and a second colleague from the commission; Herr Franke from the former Stasi prison memorial museum and Sabine made up the quintet. The discussion quickly established that all were interested in collaborating on an annual teacher training event on East German History. A draft program for a two-day event had already been prepared by trained historian Franke and was briefly considered. It included the topics of the "State Security Police," the "dictatorship," and the "everyday," as well as "democracy" and "system comparison." The second day would focus on learning and teaching methods. Although the group seemed generally happy with the suggestions, some of which echoed Schumacher's own ideas to focus on the "State Security Police" and "the everyday" and teaching approaches of "talks, excursions, literature and witness testimonies," discussion focused instead on finances, which were limited if the event were to run this year. Several ideas were considered until the group agreed to approach Mittelland's Institute for Standards in Education and Teacher Training for support despite some concerns about then being obliged to use their venue, which was considered to be less attractive. The meeting closed on this note to reconvene in a few weeks' time.

As this meeting illustrates, at a practical level much "reworking" concerns questions of funding and cooperation. These questions impact other aspects of planned events, where compromises then need to be found. Frau Wolf's plans to package training sessions on the "dictatorship" in a less explicit manner, for example, took a backseat since Schumacher was used to organizing teacher training as flagship events that were very explicitly about a "reworking-like" (*aufarbeiterlichen*) approach to the East German past. Even considerations of content seemed to be secondary, given how quickly suggestions of topics were passed over in favor of discussing funding and collaboration. Content was later developed in informal conversations between just two or three individuals, as the subsequent meeting of the group showed, where the program had moved on significantly although no formal meeting had taken place in the interim.

That the MfS was a focus of early programs seems predictable given the work of the two institution heads, who had made suggestions for content. More surprising is rather that the GDR "everyday" (*Alltag*) was also mentioned by both as a topic for the workshop. This was so noteworthy to Sabine and me that from this meeting onward the event ran as the "the teacher training *on the* GDR *everyday*" (emphasis added) in our conversations. To my mind it certainly appeared that the group had decided to—finally—approach the tricky but socially proliferating memories of everyday life in socialism.

Memories of Everyday Life and the Dangers of Pollution

Memories of the everyday have been a concern for institutions of *Aufarbeitung* for some years, as chapter 1 indicates. Though recognized by some as an opportunity to motivate individuals to reflect on the GDR past through their recollections and as a necessary aspect of history writing, many others see it as a treacherous topic. Everyday life is perceived to be a source for reminiscing if not the rose-tinted *Ostalgie* that forgets about political oppression altogether. For many critics, instantiations of such nostalgia for socialism are, for example, the private GDR museums that sprang up in the new *Länder* in the late 1990s and early 2000s.

Mittelland has at least two such museums, and Sabine and I visited one of them in a small village near Tillberg. Since I had called in advance to check opening times, the museum's owner greeted us at the door of the former village school. He welcomed us by asking what other museums we had seen, which led him to comment that he is unimpressed, for example, with the better-known GDR museum (DDR Museum) in Berlin. It is considerably larger than theirs is, and very attractive to tourists, but our guide criticized that it only exhibits a fraction of artifacts. Also, he went on to explain, "you have to be a real *Ossi* to do this." He pointed to the tent and camping gear set up on the landing in front of us, a pair of swimming trunks dangling from a washing line above it. Like many others, the museum had acquired its collections exclusively through private donations from local people (Arnold-de Simine 2011). To create this scene and put it into context, our guide explained, you need to know how important camping was in the GDR: "It was a cheap holiday and therefore very valuable." We were then taken through the museum space, where each room has a theme. Most of them are presented as living spaces, such as a dining room complete with furniture, furnishings, radio, and tableware or a kitchen with utensils, appliances, food packagings, and so on. Or they are based on categories of items from uniforms and medals to electronics. And each room is crammed full with pieces so that the building exhibits a stuffy whiff of old and slightly damp times. I recognized bits and pieces in the kitchen, the bathroom, and of course the "playroom" full of toys, books, and games. In those moments I experienced some of that sudden familiarity and sense of loss, which led to the inevitable shout-outs: "Oh, look at that . . . I had one of those. Goodness, do you remember these?" Without any provision of historical context by the museum, the argument that such collections present apolitical views of the past may have some merit, but they are far from celebrations of the past regime. As our guide confirmed, when people come here, they do not just talk about the "good times." They also recollect the difficulties of managing in a shortage economy—for example, the lengths people went to acquire a highly prized color TV—and any problems with authorities they may have had. Yet again, his demand for an "*Ossi's*" authority points to the assertive East German identity that is usually considered intertwined with rose-tinted reevaluations of the oppressive regime. Such equations, however, overlook the much more ambiguous relationship eastern Germans have to the goods of the former GDR, as Paul Betts has observed (2000; also Arnold-de Simine 2013). If such museums invoke nostalgia, it is Svetlana Boym's reflective nostalgia that "thrives in the longing itself, and delays the homecoming—wistfully, ironically, desperately." It "dwells in the ambivalences of human longing and belonging and does not shy away from . . . contradictions" (2001: xviii). This, however, is a complexity of emotions and attitudes that policy debates and truth discourses can rarely accommodate given their need for linearity and moral certainty.

In committees and working groups charged with writing national history, such as the Sabrow Commission in 2005 (chapter 1; Sabrow et al. 2007), the topic of memories of everyday life has given rise to many heated discussions. As discussed in chapter 1, at the public debate of the revised memorial concept in 2007, the "GDR everyday" proved yet again to be a sticky point. As members of the parliament raised questions about the draft concept with the invited experts, a number of concerns were brought to light. Some experts argued that the everyday had little place in publicly funded structures, which should always forefront the remembrance of victims. If anything it might be justifiable to portray German division and the dictatorship *in* the everyday. Protagonists of the inclusion of the everyday in contrast followed the approach outlined in the draft concept:

[When considering the GDR everyday it] has to become clear that the people in the GDR were subject to an all-pervading state control. The instruments and mechanics used by the SED to ideologically suffuse society and all aspects of people's lives have to be named . . . Simultaneously it is to be documented where and how people in the GDR tried to avoid the grasp of the party. (Deutscher Bundestag 2008)

The understanding of the GDR conveyed in this quote is that of the *durchherrschter Alltag*, the "controlled-through everyday," or "life *in* the dictatorship," which emphasizes state control.[2] At the public debate, historian Sabrow explained that it was necessary to explore life in the GDR through the everyday because many had not experienced the GDR as a dictatorship. Representing this topic through places like the Documentation Centre of Everyday Culture of the GDR (DKZ) in Eisenhüttenstadt or exhibitions at the German Historical Museum in Berlin was necessary to "pick people up from where they are" at this juncture of social memory and history twenty years after socialism's fall. Protagonists of this notion explained moreover that exactly this approach, which met socially prevailing memories of the everyday head on, would help counter *Ostalgie*, while a dichotomy of "bad dictatorship," emphasized in remembrance, and the "lovely everyday," banned from national memory, would support nostalgic sentiments.[3] In the finalized concept from 2008 section C, the "GDR everyday" is entitled "society and the everyday," pointing toward a social history (Deutscher Bundestag 2008), while the detailed text, however, remained largely unchanged. Nationally funded museum sites dedicated to the GDR everyday that developed as an outcome of the revised memorial concept, such as at the Kulturbrauerei, the Tränenpalast, and the new exhibition at the DKZ (Arnold-de Simine 2013; Jones 2014, 2015), thus also create representations of the "GDR as dictatorship" by focusing on the "controlled-through everyday," as chapter 1 highlights. Compare this to the reaction at the *Daily Paper* when I returned from the parliamentary debate. Markus had suggested I could write an opinion piece if anything of interest came up and called me to his desk: "was there anything" worth writing about? As I lay out the various positions in the discussion around including the GDR everyday in the memorial concept, his response came fast and unequivocally: "Of course it has to be a part of it!" There was also something about historians who thought otherwise better handing their degrees back.

The political reworking of the past seeks to govern through a remembrance that is a nationwide (in claim, although practically focused on eastern Germany), self-reflective reckoning in memory that does right by the victims and through its realization supports attachment to democratic values for the nation's future. Memory-work thus becomes a moral and political duty for society. Through an affiliation with academia, this discourse stakes claims to truth, which add persuasive power. Out of this, specific kinds of narratives have developed, including stories of victimhood, civil courage, and resistance, which strive for "narrative seduction" (Bruner 1991: 9); that is a self-evident interpretation of their meaning. In turn, the emerging narratives suggest the use of certain linguistic forms and symbols, according to Bruner (1991). The program ideas for the teacher training event and the former Stasi prison's educational framework above highlight some of these: the MfS is used to conveying aspects of state control in the SED dictatorship and presenting them as the polar opposite to current-day democracy. As Mary Douglas (1966) reminds us, however, any structuring entails the creation of inappropriate matter, or "dirt" in her terms, and in turn the danger of pollution. As Douglas puts it, "Pollution is a type of danger which is not likely to occur except where lines of structure, cosmic or social, are clearly defined" (1966: 114). For the discourse of *Aufarbeitung*, memories of everyday life in socialism muddy the waters of the conceptual and moral clarity it espouses:

> Dirt thus "implies two conditions: a set of ordered relations and a contravention of that order. Where there is dirt [or inappropriate remembering], there is a system [a master-narrative]. Dirt is the by-product of a systematic ordering and classification of matter [memory], in so far as ordering involves rejecting inappropriate elements" (36).

For the categorical system of *Aufarbeitung*, dirt is remembering that does not consider the "GDR as dictatorship," like reminiscing about apolitical aspects of life in socialism.[4] Attempts to manage the ambiguity that the topic threatens to introduce follow Douglas in that actors reach for order: if there "is matter out of place, we must approach it through order" (41). The "dangerous" GDR everyday is thus cast aside or redefined by describing it as "controlled through," for example, or as "life in the dictatorship" to prevent "inappropriately" *ostalgic* interpretations to arise from it.

Memories of the everyday entered discussions among our informants in Mittelland in a number of contexts. At a first meeting Franke had explained to me that the memorial museum's work covered three areas: history and historical research, victims, and the everyday. He wanted to turn the institution's attention more toward the latter and had organized a public talk on the Association for Sport and Technology (GST) as a starting point. The mass organization had overseen a range of sporting and paramilitary clubs and societies in the GDR. The talk was held by a historian who had recently published a monograph on the mass organization (Wagner 2007) and took place in a cultural venue near the memorial

museum on a weekday evening. In contrast to other readings that institutions of *Aufarbeitung* had offered that year (like a monograph on the
medical faculty's connections to the MfS, one on intellectuals in political
imprisonment, a diary of political imprisonment, etc.), the topic of the
GST was much less obviously about the "SED dictatorship." Some of the
audience therefore also differed from the "usual suspects": some elderly
gentlemen were keen hobby pilots who had realized their passion through
the GST; there were also some former PE teachers and a few university
students. These people appeared to be attracted by the topic rather than
an interest in the "reworking of the past" per se that, for example, members
of the Citizen Initiative, which has close links with the former Stasi prison,
had come for.

Wagner's presentation on the day highlighted several aspects of the
sports organization, from its link to military training, to its enabling
hobbies and providing "fun" activities for ordinary people. The presenter
finished, saying he had hoped to present a more correct picture of the
GST rather than simply painting it as a means of recruitment for the East
German army. A discussion followed: some listeners contributed their
memories, in one case at such length that Franke asked the gentleman
in question to contact the historian afterward; another attendee asked
about MfS control of the association, given that activities like flying or
diving constituted security risks; others responded to the presenter's question to the audience of what we thought the difference was between sport
and military exercises. After an active hour, Franke closed the event by
emphasizing how this demonstrated that a paramilitary organization with
its strong connection to the army was unable to find a footing in society.
This interpretively certain conclusion, however, seemed a little simplistic in
relation to this detailed piece of academic work. Although Ringo Wagner
had explained that membership of the GST fluctuated depending on how
pronounced the organization's military aspect was (a closer connection
drove membership down; see Wagner 2007), it is difficult to argue that the
mass organization found *no* footing in society. If the talk is seen within
the realm of a purpose-driven, political *Aufarbeitung* rather than academia,
however, the conclusion appears more fitting. It allows Franke to close the
narrative in a way that frames the topic within this well-ordered discourse.

The historical account of the GST, including its presence in the—mud-
dling and ambiguous—everyday, where the organization provided fun
diving outings and a beer in the pub after, is thus turned into an interpretively explicit moment of societal resistance to a regime's militarization
efforts. Franke's sentences added persuasive force and order to a narrative
that appeared to lack seduction. However, attempts at persuasion are not
always successful, as Carrithers (2012b: 7) and Strecker and Tyler (2012b)

remind us, particularly when approaching matters of memory that concern the ambiguous complexity of complicity or of "making do" in socialism. Halfway through the talk, another visitor had entered the room and taken a place in the back. As Franke began his concluding remarks, "This shows how such a paramilitary organization with its strong connection to the army was unable to—" the late guest stood up, exclaiming, "You don't understand, we *had to*" and left the room enraged. None of us in the audience were quite certain what had caused his upset or what he was trying to say, but it was clear that even the very beginnings of Franke's comments, or what he assumed they would be, had jarred with the man.

If audiences are willing to listen, "a [narrative can] effect[s] a change in the addressee's mind" through rhetoric that "involves the charge of energy, a potential," as Carrithers calls it (2012b: 7; Fernandez 2012). However, powerfully stated narratives can also grind severely with listeners whose memories and experiences tell them that the thus presented linearities are an inappropriate way of viewing this aspect of *their* life in socialism, as the desire for the "authenticity of experience" (Ochs and Capps 2001: 56) pushes against discursive boundaries. When powerful stories fail to convince, they do so with just as much force, especially at this historical moment when a narratively suggested view of the past state as dictatorship has serious implications for personhood. Discourses always entail nonnegotiable subject positions (Franklin 1990), but the identifications provided within the discourse of *Aufarbeitung* are particularly compromising. Writing about trauma memory, Antze and Lambek note that people try to render their lives in meaningful terms through creating "a more or less unified narrative in which they identify with various narrative types—hero survivor, victim, guilty perpetrator." However, this process is not without pitfalls and "an *excessively determined story* in which there is an over-identification with a particular character" (1996: xviii; emphasis added) bears dangers for the self (Gallinat 2006a, 2009a). The well-ordered discourse of *Aufarbeitung* and its master narrative of the "GDR as dictatorship" ask for categorically ordered life stories, of victims, perpetrators, and bystanders, which do not easily provide habitable identities for individuals who have to come to terms with the complex ambiguities of individual–state relations in socialism, as highlighted by the *Daily Paper*'s readers and staff in chapter 3, for example.

During fieldwork, it was apparent that in certain situations, some of our informants were aware of these dangers of an overdetermined discourse. This seemed to be one reason why Franke wanted to approach the everyday, which, he assured Sabine and me when we discussed the public debate of the memorial concept, did not have to lead to reminiscing or nostalgia. It seemed to underpin Frau Wolf's attempt to move away from workshop titles that stood too explicitly for dictatorial aspects of the past. Similarly, when Sabine asked Bohlmann, the head of the Office for Political Education, whether it was really helpful to present East Germany solely as "dictatorship, surveillance, and oppression," given that many people had been able to make their lives relatively unhindered by these, he wondered whether political education's preoccupation with these topics had caused a counterreaction in audiences. However, while such comments were occasionally made in individual meetings or informal chats, when it came to presenting narratives to audiences, any slack in their order, any potential ambiguity in their interpretation, was soon tidied up. It appeared that the demands of governmentality, the embodied moral obligations to victims, and the discourse's inherent power also governed the producers of narratives in this realm.

Finalizing the Teacher Training Course about the GDR Everyday

The second meeting of the group to discuss the teacher training course takes place about one month after the first, again at the Stasi commissioner's offices. The small organizing committee of three institutions has now been joined by the border checkpoint memorial museum, the Federal Commissioner for the Stasi Files (BStU), and the Institute for Standards in Education and Teacher Training, which will provide the majority of funding but whose representative is absent today.

When everyone had gathered in the commissioner's meeting room, some coming directly from a commemorative event of the 1944 putsch against Hitler, the meeting began. Its aim was to discuss once more collaborations, venue, and the draft program and to decide on a cultural event for the first evening of the two-day event. The program had moved on considerably since June. Under the title "Dealing with Central Events of GDR History in School Lessons," the course would center on three events of the East German past: the uprising on 17 June 1953, the building of the Berlin Wall on 13 August 1961, and the autumn of 1989. It would begin with a talk by a professor of history from the local university on current historical knowledge on these three events, followed by a talk on "learning and teaching methods" by a lecturer in education, and then another one by Franke on "teaching outside school: working with memorials," the "authentic sites" (*authentische Orte*) as referred to by our informants (Williams 2007: 80–82). On the evening of the first and the morning of the second day, participants would join workshop groups to develop teaching materials on one of the three historical events, and each workshop would be run by two staff drawn primarily from the Working Group. There was no more mention of the GDR everyday in this program. Instead of tackling the topic head on, the Working Group had decided on an event in line with a history teaching that focuses on incidents and dates. The everyday remained present only implicitly through the use of the experiences of "ordinary people" to explore and illustrate these historical events. This approach is akin to that taken in the exhibitions at the Tränenpalast and Kulturbrauerei, which support a narrative of the dictatorship by focusing on the "extraordinary experiences" of repression and state intrusion into the lives of "ordinary people" (Jones 2015: 227).

The three chosen events thus constructed as significant to East German history serve to support both a view of the "GDR as dictatorship" and of "present democracy as freedom": the popular uprising against the socialist state in June 1953 developed in the wake of postwar deprivation and unfulfilled promises of economic recovery by the GDR government, and it was militarily suppressed; the fortification of the inner German border in 1961 is emblematic of rising state control and suppression of the population, "which had been voting with its feet," as the MP will put it at the commemoration in August; and the Berlin Wall fell due to a mass social movement against the regime and for freedom and democracy. Other important events were not chosen, such as the foundation of the GDR as an independent state in 1949, collectivization in 1952, the last and contested elections of 1989, and the first free elections in 1990. These appear to be less emblematic to the "vernacular narrative" (Collins 2002, 2003) emerging here of an SED dictatorship that controlled a population that strove for democratic rights, succeeding in 1989. Beyond their symbolic import, however, the chosen events draw on existing strength and knowledges of the involved institutions. During the 1953 uprising, Tillberg's Stasi prison was taken over and more than two hundred political prisoners were freed, many of whom were able to make their way to West Germany. The locally significant event has been documented by the former Stasi prison memorial museum, the BStU, and the LStU. The border checkpoint memorial museum has expertise with regard to the border's fortification in 1961. Both the LStU and the BStU offices have accessible materials on the Wende of 1989, and the Citizen Initiative's documentary center affiliated with the former Stasi prison hosts a permanent exhibition on the autumn of 1989, which highlights the—never executed—MfS's contingency plans for Day X in Tillberg.[5] The selection of historical dates is thus also based in the discourse's local historicity, which allows for a judicious use of resources.

It was therefore just details to be settled at this meeting. However, it appeared that some agreements made in the interim did not find expression in the current draft. This led to a degree of confusion and potential upset, which centered on the wish of Frau Herzog, not present today, to be involved in the workshop on the autumn of 1989, which in this version was staffed by a member of the Citizen Initiative and Fuhr from Tillberg's BStU office. Some back-and-forth followed as Matthias Neumann, a member of staff at the Stasi commissioner who was standing in for Schumacher, tried to establish what his manager had agreed with whom and what might now be agreeable to those participants who could not be at this meeting. It was decided to move Herzog (also BStU) into the workshop on 1989 while Fuhr would join Franke in the workshop on 1953, which was to be further supported by one of the academics. Staff from the border memorial museum, including the here present Grabowski, would lead the workshop on 1961.

Much of this staffing makes sense in light of institutional remits and expertise, certainly with regard to the year 1961 and the border checkpoint memorial museum, but the discussion about Herzog's wish to be part of a specific session cannot be explained just with her position at the BStU. Rather, it requires a consideration of personal biography. Now in her fifties, Herzog was an active member of an environmental, and thus oppositional, East German group in the late 1980s. She became involved in the political turnaround of 1989 and 1990 when she participated in Round Table discussions and in the guarding and opening of Stasi offices. Although Herzog has thus combined her personal experiences of the GDR and the *Wende* with her professional career, her wish to be involved in this workshop must be seen as rooted in her status and self-understanding as historical, and to some degree moral, witness. Her work thus entails a personal conviction. In a similar vein, Frau Zarge from the Citizen Initiative contributes to this workshop because the initiative has reworked the local unfolding of the autumn of 1989, but her personal involvement in the group, which has led her to become one of the most visible members of the Citizen Initiative, is based in her experiences of having been a target of an MfS operation in the 1980s. For more reason than one, then, the group was always unlikely to move her from this workshop.

This is not the only time when matters of prototypical narratives or the "popular language of the story-teller" (Franklin 1990: 217) entered and steered discussion at Working Group business meetings, which may seem conspicuous in this administrative and governmental realm. The final agenda point of the meeting concerned the question of a cultural entertainment on the evening of the first day. Such an element had been included in previous installments of this two-day training event, and the group wished to continue this practice. Introducing the question, Neumann made a couple of suggestions: a reading from the novel *Water Colors* (*Wasserfarben*, 1991) by eastern German author Thomas Brussig—a story of a teenager's experiences of life in East Germany, struggles with growing up, and his increasing regime criticism—or a viewing of the documentary *Everyone Keeps Quiet about Something Else* (*Jeder Schweigt von Etwas Anderem*; Bauder and Franke 2006)—a film about three families with experiences of political imprisonment and their struggle to speak about, remember, or forget these painful pasts. Neumann's preference was for the novel, but the group agreed that after a long day of talks, a film might be more suitable. Grabowski from the border memorial suggested another one, to be released that month—*An die Grenze* (*To the Border*; Egger 2007)—about a young East German border guard who struggles with the pressures of service and develops a relationship to a local girl whose brother seeks to flee the country, thus working through a range of conflicts. The group agreed to this and suggested approaching the screenwriter for a post-viewing discussion, and if not, then contacting the author of *Water Colors* about a reading. At this point the meeting was disrupted by a mobile phone and one colleague's departure. Once the group settled down again, a discussion erupted between two colleagues about what kinds of films may or may not be acceptable at such an event.

The disagreement possibly started with an aside comment from Neumann, who had expressed the same concern in conversation with Sabine the previous day, that even though a movie was a good choice for such an evening, there were certain movies he would not want to show. He took particular issue with *Sonnenallee* (Haußmann 1999), a feature-length film that provides a quaint and caricatured picture of life in 1970s East Germany following the trials and tribulations of four adolescent men; the film enjoyed wide popular appeal. The author of *Water Colors*, Brussig, wrote the screenplay, which may be why it was on Neumann's mind. He considered the film to be historically incorrect, plain "awful," and in any case "unsuitable" for their workshop. Fuhr, however, was taken aback by this categorical rejection, which reminded him of GDR-time censorship. He explained that it is was not up to this group to judge what was and was not allowable in fiction or who may be allowed to watch what kinds of films. Neumann defended his position: young people already knew too little about East German history, they did not even know who Erich Mielke was (the infamous head of the MfS), they already encountered the GDR as just a "fun society" (*Spassgesellschaft*), so there was no need to choose a film that reinforced this view. Certainly, he emphasized, "it is not my GDR that is represented in that movie." Using self-revelation to add moral currency to his argument, he noted that he had "experienced repression" and "*that* movie" made light of it. Fuhr countered by commenting that the group could not make choices based on everyone's individual reality. Films were works of fiction that could not be historically correct in every aspect. He mentioned a movie about the Third Reich that had created wide public debate at the time, but that did not justify disallowing it.[6]

Given that the group had already settled the question of entertainment, this seemed an unnecessary conflict. It reveals, however, that the linear certainty of vernacular narratives in *Aufarbeitung* is at times contentious and how such contestations pertain to individual memories and convictions where, at least for eastern Germans, they become pressing concerns. What Fuhr heard in his colleague's arguments was an attempt to predetermine symbolic representations of the past following a narrow perception of what kinds of views this discourse allows. Neumann, however, continued to return to the content of the film and his sense that this movie contravened what he knew about life in the GDR, knowledge derived from personal experience ("the film presents a fun society, as if you could live there just like that"). Neumann and Fuhr are of similar age and both are eastern German. As an adolescent with a Christian background and an interest in astronomy, Neumann had felt increasingly restricted within the socialist state and under the watchful eyes of the MfS. The Stasi had even made an attempt to recruit him as an IM, which he had been able to reject, but the frightening incident has become a watershed memory. Fuhr also had an antiauthoritarian streak that had caused him some trouble, even if he had not been put through direct encounters with the Stasi as a result.

Both men were now making arguments based in their not too dissimilar experiences but in contrasting ways. Like some of the readers of the *Daily Paper,* who used their prototypical life story to engage with an emerging media discourse on the past, Neumann contested the story he felt the movie *Sonnenallee* presents by highlighting his own in a bid that sought to protect the teleological linearity of the teacher training event and beyond that the master narrative of the "GDR as dictatorship," whose moral stance he feels personally invested in. Certainly, showing the lighthearted story of the four East German lager louts would have been out of keeping with a story of an East German past of dictatorial control and civic resistance. It could enter potentially dangerous ambiguity into the program, lessening its narrative seduction and allowing for wider interpretations. Like some of the historians at the public debate of the memorial concept, Fuhr saw less danger in such an opening up of some of the discourse's categorical certainties. His concern was rather with the interpretive predetermination with which representations of the past are treated by some of his colleagues. This he perceived as reproducing the authoritarian, judgmental structures of the socialist state, which he could not accept. While Neumann employed the metaphor "repression" to describe life in the GDR, Fuhr rhetorically invoked an aspect of the socialist dictatorship, "censorship," in order to make an argument about this present moment.

After some back-and-forth, Grabowski intervened. He had recently attended training on the effects and function of films. In agreement with

Fuhr, he explained that film writers move beyond truths and facts, which was problematic for many historians, but film writers concern was with emotive messages rather than authenticity. Important was how such films were embedded in any event. The discussion finally ended after a contribution by Sabine, who explained that this discussion highlighted that issues around representations of the socialist past were close to people's hearts and affected them emotionally, which should be borne in mind. She used the metaphor *Betroffene* (those affected by the past), which rallied participants' moral and ethical sense of obligation for those who suffered under the socialist regime. Since there were now a good number of films available, it should be possible to find an alternative, she added. Whether it was the highly persuasive "victim argument" that calmed the waves, the steer to an ethical recognition of emotionality, or the protagonists' realization that an outsider was present, the comment turned the discussion to attendees' personal film preferences. It became apparent that no one liked *Sonnenallee* all that much, although it was noted as one of the first feature-length films about East Germany. Soon Neumann summarized their choice, the movie about the border guard who falls in love and helps the girl's brother to escape, "a love story that also shows the harsh reality," thus filled with emblems and symbols that suited the event's vernacular narrative of an SED dictatorship that sought to control an unwilling population.

*　　*　　*

Donnan Hastings and Graham MacFarlane remark that bureaucrats are far from oblivious to the fact that policies are abstractions and a far cry from the complexity of lived experience. They "know as well as anthropologists that the world is a complex place, with no single issue reducible to a set of key-variables which may be manipulated to produce 'true' accounts" (1997: 278; also Herzfeld 1992, 2005). Yet the question of whether their events and speeches paint too black-and-white a picture seems to make little sense in the realm of the Working Group *Aufarbeitung*. In contrast to the emergent discourse at the *Daily Paper*, the narratives produced here have a degree of self-evidence, some struggles over specific content notwithstanding. The discourse of *Aufarbeitung* is predicated upon a customary perception of the GDR past as in need of reckoning through memory-work. The very raison d'etre of these institutions is this reckoning, which their staff deal with on a daily basis: the memorialization of Stasi persecution, the administration of the vast archive of MfS files documenting thousands of operations against individuals, support and advice for victims and their families, or the vetting of individuals in public service. The truth of this understanding is confirmed at a meta-level by historical research, and it becomes heartfelt in the relationships to individuals who were affected by the regime. It works back at notions of the self of the actors in this realm, more of which in chapter 5. From the perspective of those working inside this institutional realm, certain types of narratives suggest themselves that illustrate an—as true perceived—understanding of the "GDR as dictatorship." How these develop depends on the specific circumstances of their production, but the narratives' purpose is always clear: against the backdrop of an as unknowing and unwilling perceived audience, these stories are instruments of government. They are meant not only to be the outcome of "reworking," of reconsiderations of the past, but also to serve as persuasive tools that create individual and societal reworking so that the discourse of *Aufarbeitung* begins to govern citizens. In Raymond Apthorpe's words, the texts are to "inspire" listeners to rethink the past and to tell of it, to "define the parameters" of the memory of this period and to "persuade" audiences of this true view of the past (1997: 44). In other words, they are to "govern souls" (Foucault 2010).

The requirement of government creates a strong temptation to make these stories, as good narratives ought to be (Labov and Waletzki 1967; Ochs and Capps 2001), causally linear and clear in their messages so that they are convincing to their audiences and avoid a collapse of the narrative's messages that would risk the dignity of the regime's victims. This order can become overbearing, however, and thus entails dangers, as categorical certainty that seeks to reduce ambiguity increases the potential for "unsuitable" and hence "polluting" memories and interpretations that however may ring truer to many people's experiences. As Tanya Richardson points out for the Ukraine, "the afterlife of socialism (in family memory for example) creates ambiguities and uncertainties that subvert attempts to create new hegemonic understandings" (2008: 103). Here questions arise, albeit rarely, for those who are active in this field about how much certainty and linearity are necessary or useful. Nevertheless, when these narratives are put to their audiences, it seems difficult to withstand the urge to tidy their order and make their "morale" explicit because in this government of memory, not the past but rather the present and future are at stake. The sense that a repetition of history must be prevented by remembering past suffering, which is also the remit of many memorial museums, as Williams argues (2007), is particularly strong among the Victim Associations for whose work this notion provides impetus.[7] Within the Working Group, it is more commonly expressed as a concern for the future of democracy. The government of East German memory is understood to be inexorably intertwined with the government of citizens' attachments to democracy in the present, as expressed in the education framework of the memorial museum, for example, in the Minister President's speech at the beginning of this chapter and the concerns of the Office for Political Education about its audiences' GDR mentalities in chapter 2. This concern with and for the present in this realm is underpinned by the perception of a dichotomic binary between past socialism and present-day democracy, which will be explored in chapter 6. The question of democracy is also where differences in narrative production and interpretation between the realm of *Aufarbeitung* and the *Daily Paper* become particularly apparent, because it is heavily intertwined with the recognition of citizenship in which the newspaper has a great stake. Before turning to this issue, however, the following chapter will consider the question of the degree to which the production of different discourses in the two realms under consideration relates to and impacts individual actors' self-narratives.

Notes

1. In direct speech "they" is expressed as "we" and it is left open who exactly this refers to. The term suggests simultaneously an inclusive "we" of everyone gathered for the ceremony as well as the exclusive "we" of the government and CDU party.
2. See Ross (2002) for a discussion of German historians' attempts to interpret the GDR.
3. Differences in opinion between the experts were also predicated upon difference in approach between social history and a history focused on macrostructures. There is more to be said about theoretical differences and positivist versus postmodern inclinations, which I do not have space for here.
4. Dietzsch shows how a Federal Department for Media Harmful to Young People similarly attempts to create order and avoid pollution. Here the concern is the government of young people as "citizens in the making" (2014: 46–50).
5. Commonly referred to as X+24; see Auerbach and Sailer (2000) regarding the MfS's preparations and the planned isolation camps.
6. *Life Is Beautiful* (Benigni 1997), a comedy set partly in the Auschwitz concentration camp.
7. This sense of remembering atrocities to avoid reoccurrences is evident in many witness testimonies and drives political action in such contexts (Antze and Lambek 1996; Cohen 2001).

Chapter Five

WHAT MAKES AN *AUFARBEITER* AND A JOURNALIST?

Democracy education became an increasing focus for the Office for Political Education during fieldwork. In 2008 the State Chancellery announced a new initiative for democracy, the realization of which largely fell to Frau Wolf. Much of her work already concerned civic skills and understandings of politics, topics that also dominated many of our conversations with her. She frequently commented on people's lacking knowledge about democratic political government, the need to teach skills for life in a free and plural society, and the need to rally for greater political involvement. For her, these issues not only are concerns at work but have also become heartfelt, as her repeated arguments and responses to our interview questions revealed. Like for some of her colleagues, these convictions stem from a life in politics, her reasons for coming to Mittelland, and—resulting from this—her view of her role in political education.

The previous chapter has already indicated the close connection between personal biographies and the day-to-day work for members of the Working Group *Aufarbeitung*. This chapter explores in more depth how the production of representations of the East German past—as well as their characters as categorically certain in *Aufarbeitung* and interpretively relatively open in the *Daily Paper*'s journalism—relates to the presentation of the self in life stories for actors from the two types of institutions. We collected life stories during the project by asking informants to "tell us [their] live[s] and experiences with the state, from beginning to end," without interruption apart from questions for clarification. In the second part of the interview, we asked individuals to respond to three questions on how they felt "the East German past is dealt with today," "whether East German biographies can be judged from today's perspective," and what they thought "the region's greatest challenges are." The analysis in this chapter focuses on the telling of significant events in the life story to ascertain narrative structure and themes in addition to narrators' self-portrayals. This is important since life stories, as Charlotte Linde argues (1993), need to portray individuals as socially and morally proper individuals, which is achieved through the creation of coherence and the acknowledgment of wider discourses that frame the telling. The chapter explores how this is achieved in different ways in the stories of employees in the two institutional realms, explored here in the aftermath of fundamental regime change that challenges narrative coherence, especially in relation to morality. The chapter shows not only how narratives differ—most notably between journalists and actors in *Aufarbeitung*, due to their being based in the tension between wider memory discourses that need to be acknowledged and the reality of lives lived—but also how different notions of political agency emerge in the stories of eastern and western Germans.

Working Lives in Politics: Western German Perspectives

Ulrike Wolf, now in her early forties, developed an interest in politics early on. At the age of sixteen, she joined the CDU youth group, Junge Union. Although she says this was simply the only functioning youth group in her hometown, she also made her decision in the context of the "vote of no confidence" against then SPD Chancellor Helmut Schmidt and the electoral victory of CDU politician Helmut Kohl in 1982, the would-be engineer of German unification. Two years later, Wolf was elected onto the local council. She went on to study German, media sciences, and history, supported by a scholarship from the CDU-affiliated Konrad Adenauer Foundation. As part of the scholarship program and due to a growing interest in the question of German unity, she visited East Germany several times. She also experienced the opening of the inner German border quite consciously as the town near the border, where she was living with her husband, quickly filled with East Germans exploring their newfound freedom to travel. In 1990, during her last year at university, Ulrike's youth group supported East German CDU groups in their first free elections. When an opportunity to help develop governmental structures in eastern Germany presented itself, she took it with both hands. She heard at a party conference that one of Mittelland's ministers was looking for an aide and suggested to her husband that he apply. He moved to Tillberg in early 1991, and Wolf followed some months later to work for the press department of the new State Chancellery. The Chancellery was staffed by both East and West Germans, but the latter dominated in leading positions. This meant on the one hand, so Wolf, that she never experienced many "East–West German animosities" and on the other that the couple socialized primarily with their compatriots—a situation that only slowly changed through their children growing up here. When Wolf returned to work after maternity leave in the late 1990s, she felt ready for a new challenge. So when asked to replace a retiring CDU colleague at the Office for Political Education, she quickly agreed. She enjoys this new role that puts her closer to Mittelland's population.

Frau Wolf's narrative is told in a matter-of-fact style that quickly summarizes major stations in her life. There is little exploration and almost no episodic memory. This is evident from the very beginning of the interview:

> OK, I'll begin then with my interest in politics. That started when I was about sixteen. I learned relatively quickly that it's easier to realize ideas if you're willing to join a party. I then came to the CDU relatively early, and I continued political work, voluntary work, during all my time at school from year 11.
> *In what areas? I didn't want to interrupt.*
> Especially youth education, and traveling, and German unification. The goal of German unification was always present—even before 1989. There were discussions in the youth group but also at training events.

In just five sentences Frau Wolf summarizes her way into politics and the kind of work she got involved in. Descriptions of situations or events are absent. Therefore, when the rather fast-paced narrative style is broken to include detail that brings some of her experiences to life, the described events appear significant both for her life and within the interview situation.

Although often presented as monologues, interviews are dialogical situations (Collins 1998), particularly so when they take place during ethnographic projects in which interlocutors have developed a "talking-relationship" (Collins 2010; Rapport 1987, 1993). The interview becomes a continuation of the conversation—about the East German past, party squabbles, and democracy education—that Frau Wolf and Sabine had established over the previous months. That does not mean that alternative topics are no longer possible but rather that certain themes suggest themselves as fitting that conversation. Within this, events that were experienced emotionally at the time and that may have been recounted on other occasions make their way into the narrative. Some such events might be described as "turning points," moments that lead to a reinterpretation of past, present, and future (Rosenthal 2004). However, such moments do not detract from but rather add to life stories' "startling consistency" because they are emblematic of the genre used in the telling (Bruner 1994: 47). As such, their narration also maintains the coherence of life stories that is crucial for the presentation of a socially proper self (Linde 1993). The unique or unexpected occasions that make for "tellable events," however, require work by the narrator to convince listeners of the event's veracity and to avoid disruption (Halverson 2008; Ochs and Capps 2001). The narrator's telling is therefore usually marked by an engaged style—increased speed, more complex syntax and rhetoric—to capture listeners' attention and to relay the emotions that the recollection stirs. Autobiographical remembering then takes place in a tension between past experiences and the present retelling, which is closely intertwined with portrayals of both the remembered and the remembering self (Neisser and Fivush 1994; Reed 1994).

Given both Wolf's engagement with the project and the interview question for a life story that explains her current work, it is unsurprising that she quickly moves from her path into politics to the question of German unification, which motivates the first longer narration:

In the August of 1989, I went on a four-week tour of the GDR with a group of foundation fellows. We had a preparatory week . . . and studied various topics—cultural topics like German poets who came from the area of the GDR but also the [East German] agricultural program and the housing project. And we tried to explore these topics journalistically, as far as we could, in teams of two. But this proved difficult because each group was overseen by a travel guide and it was almost impossible to move about outside of our touristic program. We could only gather some personal impressions in the evenings. I met some people from Tillberg on that trip. And a young student, who squatted with his girlfriend in a derelict house . . . That was their only chance to live together.[1] . . . We could only meet young East Germans. And I noticed that there was a certain "pack up and go" attitude. It was split: "I stay here, I'll struggle through this." But many also knew of others who had already left.

For Wolf the episode speaks of a generation's desperation, a sense that there was no future for them in the socialist state. While this is her personal perspective on some of the mood, it would also have chimed with the CDU party's view of the GDR. Wolf includes her next longer narrative when speaking about the fall of the Berlin Wall. Among the throes of East German visitors that cold November was a couple whom the Wolfs took in for the night after hearing they had intended to sleep in their car. This episode is clearly "tellable," given the extraordinary circumstances, but Wolf relays the episode after explaining that she and her husband "soon also established personal contacts to East Germans." This comment and her choice of retold events make the theme of her life story explicit: increasing involvement with and closeness to the GDR, beginning with a political interest and journeys across the border, leading to relationships with eastern Germans and her eventual settling there.

The life story then turns to this later phase. Almost bypassing the fact that her husband was already in Tillberg, Wolf stresses her reasons for moving, which, although put concisely, are weighty: "And I came to Tillberg in late 1991, because I saw it as a real challenge to help with the development of a state government here." The phrase "real" gives away the importance that the remembered self attached to this opportunity. The next point of more description concerns those first months in the city:

> We worked there under really basic conditions compared to today's standards: poor phone connection, terrible equipment; even the rooms were inadequate, quite different from what you'd imagine today for a State Chancellery. But then again, you were part of a small team where everyone did everything; everyone had their job and was equal to others, from government speaker to the driver who distributed press announcements by courier, meaning by car or even bicycle since there was no fax or email.

Although those early experiences in eastern Germany clearly matter to Wolf, it is telling that they concern her work environment rather than private life. This supports not only the narrative's genre of career story but moreover the degree to which work is relevant to the self that is portrayed here. While Wolf related some episodes from her private life earlier, these also served a narrative of her professional development. This focus may seem predicated upon the interview question, yet its exclusivity is singular among the interviews. More information on how her move to Mittelland affected her personal life, for example, is only presented in response to Sabine's query of whether moving to Tillberg was ever in doubt. Rather than add private detail, however, this passage reestablishes the narrative theme of political engagement:

> No, it was clear to us that this was a massive chance for us personally—that such an opportunity would not present itself again in our lifetime. You could participate in a historical event, support it, so that for us there was never a question whether we could do it. But once we were here, the first winter, looking out of our concrete tower block flat at 6 AM, we did wonder whether we really wanted this. But in the end we always agreed that we did, and that we enjoyed it.

In this retelling, any difficulties settling in the East are overshadowed by the singular opportunity to actively shape a central event in German history. This is why Wolf had entered party politics as a young girl, studied history, and come to Mittelland, where government for the development of democracy has become a central aspect of her professional self. In this view, Wolf and other West Germans become experts who move to the East to provide aid in the transition, which in turn associates Mittelland with the image of a development project as we see similarly in chapter 2. In Wolf's response to interview questions regarding her opinion on how the past is dealt with today, Mittelland's population thus also appears from a distance through the evaluating eye of the government official. The earlier theme of developing personal relationships to East Germans does not reemerge.

> There are different ways . . . There are also enough people who long for the social benefits. And say that it was all better. But in that sense then they haven't arrived in the democratic state . . . Take engagement. I learned civic engagement from the beginning. That wasn't a virtue you just had, but you had to grow into that society [that asked for this engagement] . . .
>
> *This relates to my final question: what would you say are current social problems?*
>
> Apart from high unemployment, which is seen by many as a real threat, another problem is that too much is asked of the state—that things like conflict ability [*Konfliktfähigkeit*][2] and individual initiative are still not very widespread.

In this typically succinct response, Wolf makes a direct connection between people's attitude toward past socialism and their relation to the current political order, which was also made by other members of the Working Group in informal conversations. However, rather than seeing this as "institutional talk" (Holstein and Gubrium 2000: 154; 2001) carried into the interview situation, I would suggest that Wolf had already internalized this understanding through her political work propounded by her experiences of being a "pioneer" in the new German state. It then met existing concerns at the LpB.

Frau Wolf's story shares several themes with those of her western German colleagues. Buesing, Bohlmann, and Franke from the former Stasi prison memorial museum have all been politically active at least since their university days. Bohlmann, like Wolf, became a CDU member seemingly accidentally. He was able to secure an internship in politics that he had been looking for at an office of the conservative party. Yet, like her, he also notes that this move took place at a historical juncture, in his case Willy Brandt's chancellorship and a period of approach to the Soviet bloc, indicating already existing or reflexively developed political leanings. A different story is told by Frau Buesing, who was politicized in antinuclear energy protests and joined the Green Party very consciously. Franke and Buesing had also had contact with political groups in East Germany during the late 1980s, and Buesing and Bohlmann were, like Wolf, offered positions in Mittelland's government during the 1990s. Their interviews are, however, richer in stories and explication than Wolf's "narrative-poor" narration, whereby the move to Tillberg and the personal transition it signified contain more detail.

Bohlmann, the director of the LpB, came to Tillberg in early 1990 to provide administrative support at the first free local elections in what was then still the GDR. He argues that this early arrival—he was one of the very first West Germans to move across the border—led him to develop a different relationship to the town and its population:

> This time, I think, really made an impression on me in many ways. It also helped me to see many things differently and to cope with much in contrast to other colleagues who arrived 1991, 1992, 1993 and who—I don't want to criticize this—but who don't have many roots here, no friends. But who spent time with each other, because there was no one else, which isn't a bad thing. Our social circle consists of Tillbergers even today. Because when I went to the pub, I went with friends from Tillberg, from work . . . I am sure these friendships also helped me, or us, to cope with the difficulties we encountered in those first years—I don't want to say hostilities or envy, which did exist—so that we stayed and managed.

Bohlmann explores his experiences of life during the GDR's last few months in some detail. Conspicuous consumption, socializing, and house hunting remain vivid in his memory and are highly tellable, certainly from a western German perspective. In all episodes, friends and acquaintances feature, giving rise to a story of Tillberg told through the lens of personal relationships to local people. Against this background of an ethical memory, Bohlmann's responses to the additional interview questions are revealing, particularly the issue of whether East German life stories can be judged from today's perspective:

> I think that you can evaluate . . . But I just said it, I refrain from criticizing. Because it is not appropriate for us, who didn't face those situations, to then judge people who did certain things under pressure. We don't know what we would have done, if we had lived here and had had certain goals, like a university degree . . . But you have to face up to it. And that's my problem . . . I have no sympathy for people who don't want to face a part of their own past. But I keep encountering the same strategy: denying it, crying, "That can't be," "I am not guilty," "I didn't harm anyone." For me, that's a sign that something did happen. . . . This denial is part of the *Tschekist* vow.[3]

Bohlmann's response is first of all diplomatic, like the previous excerpt where he immediately mediates ("which is not a bad thing") self-aggrandizing statements ("it helped to see to see things differently"). Such statements are used by narrators to present themselves in a good light (Labov and Waletzki 1967; Oliveira 1999), but they also have the potential to depreciate others, creating a tension that Bohlmann is trying to manage. When arguing above that a lack of experience of the pressures of GDR life precludes him from criticizing biographies, he appears to call for an empathic imagination, even if he holds, like many of his colleagues and as the discourse of *Aufarbeitung* suggests, that eastern Germans are now required to reckon with their individual pasts. This sense of an ethical memory becomes even clearer later in the interview when he explains that when eastern Germans speak about the socialist past it is "not only about the nice things." In his experience, everyday conversations also often include critical points like "freedom to travel, choice of newspapers." He goes so far as to criticize people who "accuse" eastern Germans summarily of "whitewashing the GDR." This is surprising for someone so deeply involved in a discourse that readily casts nostalgia as morally inappropriate and socially proliferating. Moreover, Bohlmann follows this line of thought to its logical conclusion—the question of democracy—arguing that to his mind democracy is strong enough to cope with current challenges.

Following the Russian formalists, Bruner explains that three key aspects of narrative are intertwined (1987, 1991). *Fabula*, the "particularity of time, place, person, and event is also reflected in the mode of telling . . . the *sjuzet*" (1987: 17). Genre (*forma*), respectively, "commits one to use language in a certain way" (18). When Bohlmann uses the theme of ethical memory to craft a story of a government worker legitimized by his local relationships, he becomes committed to answering the additional questions about East German biographies in an empathic vein. The narrative's drive for stylistic coherence, however, is in tension with the narrator's governmental work and the morally certain discourse of *Aufarbeitung* he helps write. This tension makes its presence felt in some more government-like comments, such as when he notes the importance of exploring different aspects of the GDR and of teaching about "the two dictatorships." Tropes of the governmental discourse, like "democracy" and "nostalgia," also push into the personal narrative but are mediated by the narration's empathic style. Much more so than in fieldwork (chapter 4), there is a sense here that Hastings and McFarlane's (1997) observation that bureaucrats understand more of the real-life complexities than their work may suggest also holds true for the field of governmental *Aufarbeitung*. Nevertheless, this ethical style needs to be seen within the context of the interview in which the life story's main purpose is to reflect a self-portrayal of a manager in government and, for

Bohlmann, one who leads Mittelland through his relations into the state's social fabric. This positioning requires the narrator to mediate messages of the categorically certain discourse of *Aufarbeitung*.

The interviews with western Germans in *Aufarbeitung* yield narratives that construct individual lives in relation to five themes: party-political engagement, an interest in East Germany and/or German history, the arrival in Mittelland, present-day Mittelland, and East–West German animosities. While Frau Wolf did not experience the latter much, Bohlmann acknowledged their existence but passed them over; only Frau Buesing spoke in detail about those challenges. Many of these interviews moreover reveal the discursive environments of government, when interviewees suggest that attitudes and practices from GDR times continue to shape local people's behavior in the present. As the above excerpt shows, even diplomatic Bohlmann employs this thinking in relation to former IMs.

Becoming Political in East Germany

Bohlmann's argument that outsiders could not easily criticize eastern German lives is something rejected by the forty-five-year-old head of Tillberg's branch of the Federal Commission for the Stasi Files, Steffen Fuhr. Sitting opposite me in a small restaurant on the picturesque Government Lane, he speaks with typical Mittelland directness: "I just think then that that person got no spine, no principles." He says this in part because, as he admits, he himself cannot fall back on a "typical" dissident biography. He has to use research to gain understandings of Stasi activities, just like other "outsiders."

Fuhr correctly notes that most eastern Germans in leading positions in the realm of *Aufarbeitung* come from a civil rights background. Both Fuhr's colleague Herzog and Stasi Commissioner Schumacher were involved in oppositional groups in the late 1980s. However, even their lives do not offer clear-cut dissident biographies. For Schumacher opposition developed out of a youthful attraction to the opportunities West Germany offered (in terms of knowledge and goods) combined with a certain outspokenness. Yet he joined the socialist mass organizations, volunteered for leading roles with the local Free German Youth (FDJ) group, and served with the army, like the vast majority of the population.[4] His "inner opposition" grew over time, fueled by discussions with friends and by experiences taking him to a point where he joined civil rights groups that met under the auspices of the church in Tillberg. Frau Herzog speaks of three particular turning points that led her to increasing regime criticism until she joined dissident groups over a local environmental issue.[5] Both Herzog and Schumacher were actively involved in the political developments of 1989 and 1990, taking over MfS offices and participating in Round Table discussions.

Stories of more exclusive lives in opposition are in contrast told by two administrative support staff, both of whom have a Christian family background. Jana from the former Stasi prison memorial museum, for example, did not join any of the socialist children's organizations that enjoyed over 90 percent participation rates and started her professional training at a church rather than state institution. An active member of Tillberg's congregation, she participated in the demonstrations of 1989, which began in the churches, right from the start. Certainly in Mittelland, however, life stories that speak of relatively "normal" East German upbringings where regime criticism, if at all, develops over the course of time and is narrated through particular turning point memories, like that of Steffen Fuhr, are more common.

The first experience Fuhr relates as part of his reflective and episode-rich life story is a school report that noted, "Steffen has trouble fitting into the collective." He explains that this made him realize there were "certain standards" he did not fit. This early turning-point memory sets the tone for the remaining narrative that tells a story of push and pull, of participating in and withdrawing from state structures. Fuhr's parents were both compliant party members. Their credentials meant that he was offered opportunities for political involvement, which the outspoken young man, however, then often found lacking, adding to family conflicts. The resulting seesawing narrative is suffused with moments of discovery in which the behaviors of others reveal to Fuhr that even in the carefully policed East German system, "he and others could always do and be otherwise" (Carrithers 2005a: 433). His profession and present-day attitudes to past socialism then come to be foreshadowed by a carefully considered life story of developing regime criticism.

The next, longer narration, set in his teenage years when he and some friends began to experience authoritarian control, is emblematic of the push-and-pull theme. At fourteen Fuhr was asked to do a speech at the weekly school assembly. Feeling flattered he agreed but then found that his speech had been heavily edited by a member of staff. The youngster refused to hold the speech that was no longer his. Fuhr explains this was one of several "bad experiences" that led him to avoid official roles in the future. He then turns to his professional development where, uncertain about what degree to pursue, he took up vocational training as a locksmith, an unusual step given his good results from the *Erweiterte Oberschule* (extended secondary school; EOS). The next episodic recollection follows when speaking about his time at the army, where he volunteered for the longer three years to gain access to the desired training in engineering. It concerns a situation some months into service when he saw the doctor about digestive trouble:

> And he said, "Well, your stomach is poorly, the digestive acid is imbalanced. If you continue like this, you'll damage the gastric mucous membranes" . . . He asked what I did all day, whether I exercise, if I have anything to balance out the stress. I said, "No, I read a lot and I don't really do any sports." And then he said, "Well, Herr Fuhr, you need to get out sometime, you need to go and have a beer, you need to let off steam, and I'll take you out of service for a week so you don't need to see your superiors." That was very interesting that he did that.

This recollection is distinguished by the use of direct speech and the amount of detail. It is moreover one of several events evaluated by the term "interesting" (Labov and Waletzki 1967). Throughout the interview, Fuhr uses this phrase for situations when unexpected things happened in the authoritarian system, like when an army employee acknowledged that service and army hierarchies may be stressful for soldiers, marking such moments as revelatory. Rather than disturb the narrative's linearity, these stepping-stone-like turning points indicate the life story's genre (Bruner 1994), which is that of a *Bildungsroman* of how a naive yet learning protagonist develops an understanding of the SED dictatorship. In the narratives of Fuhr, Schumacher, and Herzog, turning points almost exclusively concern problems with political control or institutions of the state and are evaluated as moments of growing knowledge about the regime that facilitate increasing criticism and potential dissidence.

The next period that Fuhr explores narratively follows Gorbachev's politics of *glasnost* and *perestroika* in 1986, which gave him a "new perspective for action." He explains how, assuming that political relaxation in the Soviet Union would follow suit in the GDR, he volunteered again for the role of FDJ secretary in an attempt to introduce free speech in member meetings at the military base. After a particularly heated discussion, a senior officer warned Fuhr of potential repercussions: "That was a warning. I found it *interesting* that he'd done that" (emphasis added). Fuhr moves on to discuss his study choice of German and history at Leipzig University, a departure from previous career plans but one that opened the door for an accelerated development of his critical mind, as we will see below. The next narrated episode, however, concerns an encounter with the MfS, which he only learned about after the *Wende*. It was the second time Fuhr noticed the State Security Police: a regular visitor at the army base was a Stasi officer, as he was told eventually. On this second occasion, his study group was asked to write reports on each other for submission to the FDJ secretary. The unwittingly self-authored report—the group had decided to self-write;

the other would simply sign the text as theirs—made it into a Stasi file, where Fuhr discovered it some years later.

Encounters with the Stasi, whether experienced at the time or learned about in the aftermath, are an important feature of eastern German life stories. They have high tellability in a post-unification public discourse that has been heavily focused on IM revelations and high credibility due to the evidence of the file. As epitome of the state's controlling force, the Stasi appears in life stories to symbolize danger, justify caution, or evidence courage and nonconformism. A lack of such encounters is in contrast often used to legitimize biographies that cannot tell of the dictatorship, such as life stories of individuals who may self-reveal as "not resistance fighters" (chapter 3). Fuhr evaluates this moment by noting that the Stasi must have had an interest in him. He adds that he had also been approached to join the SED and had refused. In the stories of many staff in this institutional realm, from managers to clerical support staff, party membership emerged as an important measure of involvement with the socialist system. While almost all had joined the pioneers and FDJ and participated in the socialist coming-of-age ritual *Jugendweihe* (youth consecration) without considering this worthy of commenting, all interviewees bar one signaled their distance to the state by talking about their refusal to join the SED when asked to do so. This is usually a moment of conflict with authorities, which, like the Stasi narratives, speaks in an identity-projecting fashion of danger, courage, and nonconformity.

The next turning point in Fuhr's narrative is placed in the late 1980s. This is the longest single narrated episode and the most vividly told. In his second year of study, he had to decide which subject to specialize in and was approached by a historian:

> We had "Red Week," this political week at the start of the year, when you came together after the holidays, to be updated about what was politically current. We were in a large lecture hall, all three faculties together. And up front someone did a speech, and none of the students there opened their mouth. . . . In one such situation I lost it . . . when the professor had finished his speech, I said that surely he didn't think anyone believed any of what he had just told us. It didn't relate to reality. Lots of murmuring in the hall. Afterward, a lecturer who had sat next to the professor approached me. I thought, goodness, what is she going to say now? And she said, "Herr Fuhr, I would like you to do your thesis with me."

Fuhr narrates this exchange in direct speech relating the memory's vividness: "[I asked] 'Where is this coming from?' 'Well,' she said, 'you are the only one who dared say anything today'—found that interesting." The lecturer was looking for a master's student for a research project on church youth groups and the FDJ in the 1950s, when the Lutheran Youth (Junge Gemeinde) had been persecuted by the state. Although his new supervisor was confident they would gain access to materials on the censored topic, she was clear that the thesis may well be written to be kept "under lock and key" (*für den Panzerschrank*). Fuhr notes again, "That was interesting." This episode signals the beginning of a period during which Fuhr's *Bildungsroman*-like self-development gathered pace as he gained almost unlimited access to information about the East German state.

The life story then describes this period of research focusing on the limited-access collections at the library, which included West German literature, and on incidences that foreshadow the end of the GDR in 1989. The latter appear tellable because of their prophetic character. In one case, after reading West German news pieces, Fuhr commented to a friend that the GDR was no longer viable. Another time a fellow student pointed him in the direction of dissident groups. Fuhr's reflection on this is telling:

> I was very surprised, that there are organizations in the GDR that exist outside of the normal state structures. That individuals are in opposition to the state, that someone wants to leave the country [I knew], I had lots of friends who wanted to leave and some did, and some got into trouble with the state and went into prison. . . . But I didn't think it possible that there would be real organizations, because I always assumed that the state would prevent that.

This moment sets up an unrealized turning point as Fuhr decided not to join these groups, instead adding this information to his growing knowledge. He evaluates the episode with the adjective "surprised" instead of "interesting." A similar change of rhetoric occurs when the narrator reflects on his MA thesis. Marked after 1989, it gained a second, which Fuhr considers "good" for the work of someone who had been socialized and educated in the GDR. This switch in terminology marks a change in the self-portrayal. The narration is no longer about isolated moments of growing knowledge experienced by an observant learner but rather about more fundamental matters of eastern German lives that are now considered by a mature and confident professional.

The story then turns to the *Wende*, which Fuhr begins with his observing the first public protests in 1988. The next narrated turning point, however, concerns the elections of 1989, where the remembered self engaged in more open resistance for the first time: Fuhr insisted on using a confidential booth and striking through all candidates.[6] The narration then becomes faster paced and summarized. After 1989 his wife found work in Tillberg and Fuhr followed her, applying for a post as administrative assistant at the Birthler agency. From there he moved up to the post of head of the local branch, where we meet him today.

Fuhr's episode-rich narration is limited in terms of experiences had with others. However, a few brief comments—one in the excerpt above, another concerning his teenage years—reveal that his social circle, in contrast to his regime-compliant parental home, included a good number of critics. While he does not evaluate this explicitly, he positions himself as different vis-à-vis "ordinary" eastern Germans in a number of places. With regard to his school years, he comments that "in contrast to many others," he noticed noncompliance and repression, like Christian children who were denied opportunities because they did not join socialist organizations. Fuhr's observing demonstrations in Leipzig in 1988, a year earlier than commonly known, also sets him apart as a particularly astute observer. These positionings serve to foreshadow his current position as head of an institution that administers and explores the material traces of state control and dissidence.

Both for the eastern and western German interviewees, life stories fall under a distinct genre, include emblematic experiences, are coherent, and appear carefully crafted. While the life stories of western German officials begin with early political engagement that turn toward East Germany through a growing relationship, they are shaped as narratives of developing regime criticism for their eastern German counterparts. The theme of development is so prevailing that turning points are not turns but rather near-predictable steps toward an understanding of the GDR as dictatorial that foreshadows their present professional work. The main difference between these life stories is political personhood. The genre of *Bildungsroman* within a dictatorship means that political engagement in the GDR through membership of the pioneers or FDJ is not counted as such. Instead, refusing the grasp of the state and dissidence are cast as political activity that is not only individually driven but moreover risked.[7] While a status as citizen and government maker arises for western German narrators from lifelong practice of democratic politics, it arises for their eastern German counterparts from individual struggles for civil rights. Although this seems to challenge the notion of *Prägung*, that the regime shaped passive personhoods that create obstacles for the transition, these life stories rather reinforce the understanding prevalent in this realm that legitimate citizens are those who engage politically in the present based on a firm understanding that the GDR was a dictatorship.

Working with and on the State: Being Journalists

In contrast to the above, the stories told by many journalists seem less purposefully crafted. Rather, they take the form of reflections on lives in journalism interspersed with recollections of events that left impressions. The narrative of Klaus Steinberger, for example, who wrote the editorial on color TV in East and West Germany mentioned in chapter 2, provides an overview of the fifty-year-old senior reporter's professional path from its beginning, a schooltime interest in writing, to the mid-1990s. Episodes that are more detailed appear at four moments, marking turning points or tellable events that resist a more summarized retelling.

Having decided on a career in journalism in his penultimate school year, Klaus applied for an internship at the *Daily Paper*, a requirement alongside university studies. But after losing out in the competitive entrance tests, he followed his parents' advice to study engineering. Yet struggling with math and physics and having to care for his young family, he withdrew. Klaus decided to work as an untrained factory worker. His young family needed the money, but more importantly, the job would change his class background from *intelligentsia*—his parents were administrators—to working class, which could open doors to the sought-after degree in journalism. This period of working on the factory floor prompts the first detailed narration:

> There I really . . . I had learned a lot at school and university, from a highly theoretical perspective about the working class. And the leading role of the working class . . . When I then got to know the working class—I don't know whether I ended up in a less typical brigade, but I suspect not. You can't imagine the kinds of things that went on there. I don't even know where to start. It began with the fact that the young ones or new ones, especially myself as a university dropout, which put me into the lowest cast, we got the jobs that none of the more senior workers wanted.

Klaus talks about chicanes and drunkenness, about hearing of ordinary people's struggles with the shortage economy during lunch breaks. He evaluates this phase as opening his eyes to the "discrepancies" between socialist ideology and reality, particularly with regard to the "heralded working class." This turning point signals Klaus's practical and realistic character and a penchant to observation that suit his later career. He returns to the problem of finding suitable work:

> I really hated that job. I got up with stomach cramps every morning. I needed to do something. By the way, I earned 320 marks monthly . . . The rent was 45 marks, just to see that relation . . . So then you try to manage in that situation. You look at the system for a while, try to see any weak points. And then you try to cut off a bit for yourself.

The trope of the "system," which Klaus employs, describes contexts and structures that stand in a dialectical relationship to individual will and agency, or "spirit" in German dialecticism, according to Dominic Boyer. The trope appears in many journalists' life stories, since, as Boyer's informants note, the notion of "system" was everywhere in the GDR (2005: 8). Interviewees used it most commonly to reflect on the structures they found themselves caught in and attempts to find the best way through those. This includes making compromises with the system and with those who control those contexts. For Klaus, in clear contrast to Fuhr's narrative, difficult situations did not necessarily concern repressive state structures. In a further departure from the life stories in the field of *Aufarbeitung*, Klaus turned to the political realm to solve his problem. He volunteered to develop an FDJ section at his factory department. This secondment gave him considerable freedom while maintaining his income. However, the comments above about making the system work for you remain the only evaluation of this strategic move. Similarly, Klaus passes over his joining the party during military service. When his party membership is queried in the interview, he confirms but his response suggests that questioning it is nonsensical: he wanted to work for the *Daily Paper*, an organ of the SED; joining the party was inevitable.

Of the compulsory eighteen months' military service, Klaus only says that he worked for two army papers. This summary presentation as primarily an opportunity to return to journalism reveals the overriding theme of this life story, which is that of a career in journalism. Upon his return, his renewed application to the *Daily Paper* was successful since, being now both working class and ex-military, he had become a privileged *Kader*.[8] At this point, the life story's second significantly detailed narration follows. It concerns the interview at the Leipzig Polytechnic, where all GDR journalists were trained:

> There was an entrance exam, which I passed with honors. And then the interview, which was attended by the head of the polytechnic, the party secretary, and my *Kader* editor [from the newspaper]. They said, "Yes, that was all very good," and, "We would like to hear why you want to study journalism," et cetera . . . And then the party secretary said, "Eh, something different, what do you do in your spare time?" I said, "Oh well, I watch TV and I read. I read a lot." "What did you read last?" And in that moment I just answered truthfully, and my *Kader* editor, who sat next to me, lost all the color from his face. I said, "I've just finished *The King David Report* (*Der König David Bericht*) by Stefan Heym." And Stefan Heym had just been ousted from the GDR association of authors. But the *König David Bericht* had been published in the GDR. It was under-the-counter [scarce] goods, but it wasn't West German literature—only that Stefan Heym had just become problematic . . . They said, "We can try this again in a year's time, but there are no free places at the moment."

Klaus reports the exchanges that unfolded almost verbatim, indicating that this was an important moment. Yet he introduces it as an aside, a "nice little story" and "something funny," which claims tellability of this stepping-turned-stumbling stone for his career hopes merely for entertainment. As a comedy, the narration illustrates the difficulties of finding a way around ever-changing ideological suppositions, which often created situations of absurdity. The evaluating introduction serves to distantiate the remembered self from such "senselessness." Simultaneously, the remembered self is cast as little concerned with government politics despite a goal to work for the state, suggesting also that Klaus pursued his life course somewhat independently, a point that becomes clearer later on.

Commiserating about his university time (he succeeded at the interview the second time around), Klaus comes to the longest of the four detailed narrations. The event, described by the narrator as a "caesura" (*Zäsur*), is an encounter with the Stasi, when two MfS officers ring the Steinbergs' doorbell one afternoon:

> I remember, in that moment, with them standing there and [saying], "State Security Police," I immediately asked myself, what did you do wrong? Didn't you keep your mouth shut, or did you—I immediately thought there was something. But they remained polite. I let them in. And they said: "Well, we want to get to the point. Have you ever considered changing careers?" And I said: "No, I love being a journalist. I worked very hard for it, I am now studying, and I'll soon finish." "You don't need to tell us," he said. "We know your CV. But let us make you an offer."

This narration includes interjections by the remembering self that offer explications to the interviewer and a high amount of reported direct speech, typical of Klaus's narrative style. He emphasizes this narration moreover with the phrase "I remember," which is often used to claim veracity (Ochs and Capps 1997) and add vividness, drawing the listener into the remembered, if not reexperienced, moment.

Klaus explains that the meeting was a recruitment attempt to a full-time post with the MfS. Perturbed, he spoke with his wife despite the officers' order to keep silent. She was skeptical about the MfS's overt approach and hazarded that this was the West German Security Service in disguise, making its own attempt to recruit him. This prompted Klaus to ask his line manager, then the editor-in-chief at the *Daily Paper*, for advice, who took the matter to a party meeting. The recruitment attempt was confirmed, and the editor-in-chief reprimanded the district chief of the MfS for trying to poach existing party personnel. Klaus received a return visit from the MfS during which he was subjected to a tirade of threats, but no other "negative consequences" followed. He evaluates this episode as a significant junction: "Unknowingly, [this was] one of the singular most important moments in my life." Klaus suggests that without his wife's and line manager's interference, he may have been seduced or pressurized into accepting, which would have put him into a very difficult position in 1989.

In stories of journalists, encounters with the MfS provide those instances when remembered selves negotiate their relationship to the regime, which for interviewees from the governmental realm was the question of SED membership. For example, Renate, a reporter on the business beat, explains how indignant she felt about acquaintances' comments that she could make much more money working for the MfS than for a newspaper. Although clear that they were doing political journalism, interviewees rejected views of themselves as belonging wholesale to the state through such narrations of refusing the secret police. These stories serve a professional self-portrayal by evidencing dedication to the chosen career as much as they signal courage in the face of danger. As such, they highlight the complexity of the seemingly homogenous socialist state system that, even for those on the inside, afforded both risks (in the Stasi) and protection (in Klaus's case, his line manager).

Klaus begins the retelling of 1989 with a moment at the Monday prayers, at which he represented the *Daily Paper* on invitation of the churches' regional superintendent:

> This was the time of the demonstrations and the Monday prayers in Tillberg. [He asked] whether I'd do a question and answer session about the *Daily Paper* during this event in church. Why new groupings, like Neues Forum, get so little space in the newspaper and why concerns of the church are little represented. I said, "OK, I'll do that." I went there in the evening. I remember I stood by the font. The church was full; there must have been a hundred people. And all of them shouting at me. I was the punching ball for the *Daily Paper*, so to speak. If the superintendent hadn't been by my side saying, "Order please, Herr Steinberg volunteered and will answer all questions, but we need to let him speak." I was sweating blood and tears for two and a half hours and then left. And the next day at lunchtime, I get a call from the district chief [of the SED] . . . "Come over immediately" . . . He had heard that I had been at this "Christian revolt."

This episode triggers further recollections of 1989 that together represent the fourth significant event, or "crunch point" in Klaus's words, in this life story. The pace of narration picks up; reported direct speech and reflection begin to run into each other as remembering threatens to overwhelm the storytelling. In these recollections of 1989, important characteristics of Klaus's persona and narrative become even more explicit. Reflections on what he could and could not get away with writing reveal the remembered self's growing awareness of the political realm he worked in and highlight attempts to expand boundaries at work. For example, he published pieces by a pastor (on local history) against arguments of colleagues, "hardliners," that men of the church could never appear in the *Daily Paper*, whatever the topic of their writing. He increasingly sought conversation with the Church during 1989, which led to the difficult moment at the font, because he felt that Christian congregations entailed a large group of readers who should find representation in the *Daily Paper*. This explanation furthers a self-portrayal as someone who not only practiced journalism beyond tight party lines but who also adopted a democratic understanding of his profession before the fall of the regime. The theme of democracy continues in the next detailed recollection of 1989, a lunchtime meeting of reporters to discuss "how the *Daily Paper* could be taken forward":

> I would say that from the main office there was hardly anyone there. There were many experienced journalists there, some of them older, who through their work over decades had their roots in the newspaper and who stood for a particular line of reporting. There were lots of younger colleagues from the districts, so up to thirty years old . . . And we sat down together and had a heated debate . . . And we said that, if possible, we wanted to disconnect from the party and become independent . . . There was an example, they were the first . . . [We] want to do the same.

Klaus continues explaining that the discussion turned to the financial viability of such an undertaking, while staff elected a new editorial leadership.[9] This meeting led to the next decisive moment and another appearance in church, this time the Tillberg cathedral. Hearing of plans that the Monday demonstration intended to take over the editorial headquarters, it was decided that a group of reporters, including Klaus, whose personal connection to the pastor opened the door, should present their proposal for a changed *Daily Paper* at the Monday prayer meeting. Klaus evaluates this moment explicitly as "another one of those crunch points." This phrasing suggests that there were other testing events, but he only refers to one other explicitly as "caesura," making it unclear whether he means other points in his life or more generally of the *Wende*.

After this last recollection, which sets the *Daily Paper* up as a workplace fit for the new times, Klaus moves on to his professional development: "And for me personally, I then thought about how we can make the *Daily Paper* a bit fresher, a bit zestier." This introduction marks a new phase in life that concerns the narrator's further career. Klaus initiated weekly celebrity interviews, which got him promoted to one of three senior reporter posts at the editorial headquarters, then under new ownership and with a western

German editor-in-chief. His first assignment was to report on the Bosnian War from Sarajevo, marking his beginnings as lead reporter on dangerous and contentious topics that would soon include a good number of revelations about the Stasi involvement of public figures.

Klaus Steinberg's narrative shares many concerns with other GDR-trained journalists, including the original interest in journalism, the struggle to access this career, Stasi encounters, the turbulent *Wende* years, and party control versus journalistic freedom. A commonly narrated turning point that Klaus does not discuss but is emblematic of political control concerns the change from the relatively protected position of intern to becoming a reporter. Markus, for example, discusses losing his youthful illusions about the profession when starting to work on the business beat. Visiting plants and cooperative farms, he saw firsthand the dire situation the socialist economy was in yet found himself unable to write about it due to strict party lines. The management of this awareness of significant disjunctures between ideology and reality, which Klaus realized when working on the factory floor, is described by GDR-time journalists as the "scissors in the mind": a continuous reflection on whether what one wanted to write would survive censorship and/or risk one's career (also Boyer 2005). This theme, also reflected when some interviewees speak of attempts to publish more controversial pieces and others about having had more leeway than colleagues had (because they worked for TV or the paper of a bloc party), portrays the narrators as agents who actively struggled with the SED's tight control of their professional practice.

Despite this, the life stories of GDR-time journalists do not provide narratives of regime criticism or developing dissidence. Given the reality of lives lived (Albright 1994; Neisser 1994), a certain closeness to the state has to be reflected. Most do so openly and several by referring to their belief in or sympathy with the main ideals of socialism, which are cast in terms of social justice as equality, fair distribution of wealth, and a social and political system that cared for people. Against the "hidden costs" (Verdery 1996: 10) of the transition to market capitalism, socialist values have proved enduring (Straughn 2009). In reevaluating such ideals and separating them from the faulty and failed "system," these narrators can negotiate habitable self-identities in the look back. The impact of the morally loaded discourse of *Aufarbeitung* is apparent in interviewees' evaluations of occasional attempts for freer practice. In moments of self-revelation, they are, however, clear that such actions were not resistance but rather *Eigensinn*, a stubborn sticking to one's guns (Luedtke 1993). Speaking about their role as party journalists or responding to the additional questions of how GDR-time life stories can be judged from today's perspective, Klaus, Markus, and others note that the worst offense was people presenting themselves as "resistance fighters" when they had sat at every party meeting, just like they had. In the 1990s, such people were often referred to as *Wendehälse* ("turning necks"), whose political convictions turned as easily as leaves when the "wind of change" blew from another direction. What the journalists describe, however, goes beyond a mere dropping of party allegiance. It includes a self-revelation as someone who was oppressed and resisted, a *Betroffener*, and thus an unjustified, to their minds, claim to moral currency. Setting themselves apart from such others, "system-near" (*systemnah*) interviewees use honesty in reflection, rather than nonconformism or dissidence, to portray moral selfhood from past to present.

Becoming Journalists:
From Troubles with the State to Questioning Politicians

Klaus's professional interest is inextricably linked to his love of writing. In GDR times, learning the "craft of writing" was an important part of journalistic training. In the everyday at the press, this craft remains integral to older journalists' self-understanding as they frequently bemoan its loss among their younger colleagues. This new generation seems to hold other values dearer, such as being inquisitive and critical. Having entered the profession after 1989, these journalists have to do less persuasive work to present themselves as socially and morally proper individuals (Linde 1993) in the aftermath of GDR-time complicity. The eastern Germans among them who changed to journalism from a previously different career, however, need to incorporate this personal transition into a coherent narrative.

Thorsten Seifert, a news reporter in his early forties and son of two teachers, had just finished his military service in 1990. His short and summary life story is interspersed with episodic memories of incidences at school, where he got into trouble due to a teenage conviction intent on testing boundaries, as he reflects. He speaks of wearing batik jeans to his finals despite a ban on jeans, for example, and of refusing to sing a specific propaganda song in the music exam. It had recently been discussed in class and rejected by the whole group.[10] Thorsten contrasts these episodes of youthful *Eigensinn* with his later delegation to the inner German border, suggesting a disjuncture between one perception of his self as antiauthoritarian or difficult, by his teachers, and another as reliable and compliant enough to serve at the Berlin Wall. His reflection, which is relayed in a similarly ironic tone to Klaus's recollections of absurdities in state socialism, highlights the contradictions within a system that, in *Aufarbeitung*, is usually considered totally organized—"controlled through"—and, through the Stasi, totally knowledgeable (Wolle 2007).

Given his troubles at school, Thorsten decided not to apply to the EOS but instead sought vocational training with a view to work in a relative's private photography business. But in his apprenticeship he came to work under an insufferable manager. To escape that situation, he volunteered for the longer three years of army service only to find himself sent to the Berlin Wall. This is a difficult period for the narrator, marked by a paucity of narration, heavy pauses, and silences. Thorsten moves on to explain how he requested to be moved elsewhere, threatening to cut his service short. His narration continues with his service at a rural border post, where he joined a unit of border guards who were considered less reliable. He experienced both the autumn of 1989, with its mass demonstrations and the opening of the border, and early 1990 from that station.

Thorsten shares some experiences of this time, for example, how the regiment was told they were to cover local incidents in the autumn of 1989. The soldiers, however, questioned the hidden request to suppress local demonstrations:

> Then the commander . . . came . . . and said: "You are responsible for securing the region . . . You will stay here as the reserve." [He delivered a] talk to the regiment. "In case of any incidents here." And we pricked our ears up and said, "What do you mean, 'incidents'?" "In case of counterrevolution." There was a lot of murmuring, because people said, they don't need to tell me about counterrevolution, that's rubbish, that's what they told people on 17 June too. Nobody believed it.

Thorsten felt particularly wary since he was familiar with the military suppression of the mass protests of 1953 from his grandmother's stories and West German TV programs. Luckily, the soldiers were never commanded to take action, and after eighteen months of service, he returned home. Finding that, with the economic transformation, there was no longer work for him in the photography business and after a short-term job on hourly pay, he followed a friend's suggestion to apply to the *Daily Paper* as a photographer. The narrative's tone of voice changes when he speaks of the interview and unexpected job offer:

> Exactly, so I went [to the *Daily Paper*] to present myself. And they said, "Only taking pictures is not enough; you'd also need to write . . . What marks did you have in German?" Me: "Good usually." "Well, then, let's try." . . . And that was the first time, when I consciously experienced that getting to those contradictions was valued. So not to just tow the line but, in contrast, to look behind the statement. And that was very interesting and a lot of fun. I mean, I didn't care much for the money, you just said that you'd need to get paid for this eventually, but it was so enjoyable. It was an extraordinary

time that you can't compare to today. Because everything was in motion, the GDR was also dissolving. And people were happy and euphoric: [they said,] "Goodness, things are happening."

The narration contains several positive evaluations that distinguish it from other episodes: what he did was "valued," he found it "very interesting," "fun," and "enjoyable." This enthusiastic tone marks this moment as a turning point and reveals the theme that gives Thorsten's story its coherence. It is the personal traits of criticism and inquisitiveness that have now become professional values. This becomes clearer when instead of responding to Sabine's query regarding the *Daily Paper's* seemingly unusual recruitment strategy here, remembering takes over and Thorsten moves on to an episode—"for example, there was this story"—that tells of how he revealed, tipped off by an environmental group, that a high-flying politician had used his position to illegally build a house in a nature reserve. This is followed by a quick-fire series of narrations and reflections on this period, many about the politicians he encountered. From there the narrative moves in a more summarized fashion to his current post at the *Daily Paper*.

The time of 1989 and 1990 is recollected as an impressive event, if not a "crunch point," by all journalists who worked in the profession then. The historically significant *Wende* years provide highly tellable events due to their—believable—extraordinariness. Their beginnings also constituted a time of rupture and potential danger for SED members, yet in the interviews other themes push to the fore. While Klaus describes those months as "anarchy," where people could write whatever they wanted, Markus, Renate, and Steffen portray them as "exciting" and "wonderful." There were a great number of things to write about and an accessibility of leading politicians, especially West Germans, that GDR citizens were not used to. For GDR-trained journalists, this period was most significantly marked by an unprecedented journalistic freedom, which was only curbed once the new West German owner had established their management.

While *Bildungsroman*-like life stories very much conclude for actors in *Aufarbeitung* in the early or mid-1990s, when the object of the learning process ceased to exist, for many journalists and for clerical staff from the political sphere, impressive events and turning points continued. Apart from reflections on working with politicians and the fortunes of the *Daily Paper*, there is also consideration of knowledge gained from their Stasi files that impacted relationships, and recollections of incidents that afforded insights into the new state and society. Martin Gross, another senior editor, for example, discusses his upset about a neighbor, a likeable man, who suddenly brags about showing off his new West German car to his poor Polish relations. Such stories of unhappy experiences with a capitalism that creates social division and seems to bring out the worst in people chime with Martin's expression of attachment to the socialist ideals of equality and social justice later in the narrative. Yet then he juxtaposes these unpleasant moments with recollections of newfound freedom to travel abroad or to write—even if not entirely freely, he expands, with still more freedom than previously. His critical attitude is reflected again when he argues that nowadays people leave principles behind for even lesser reasons, often over job security. The sentiment that "back than you could not criticize Honi [Head of State Erich Honecker], today you cannot criticize your boss" appear in a number of interviews, as do a weighing up of positive and negative aspects of the new order in a reflection not yet fully ordered that wavers between the good and the bad, uncertain about which conclusion to make. Showing reflectiveness is important for journalists, as it portrays selves as critical and observant. Yet it also highlights that for many, making sense of this fundamental regime change—understanding the new realities and their position toward them—is an ongoing process.

* * *

The life stories of managers working in the governmental sphere fall under a specific genre that prompts the exploration of certain themes (Bruner 1987, 1991). Whether stories of professional development in politics that took them to eastern Germany or of growing regime criticism that led to work in *Aufarbeitung*, they focus on events and reflections that support these paths. Instances are recollected not only vividly but also with a drive and a purposiveness predicated upon narrators' present-day positions in governmental realms where "words become actions" (Bourdieu 1991: 26) and persuasion is the task. Through their work, these actors are moreover familiar with stories about the SED dictatorship, and they are likely to have had to account for their own lives in this vein. The discourse of *Aufarbeitung* thus provides the scripts, practice, and morale that lend coherence to life stories. The stories of journalists also share a common theme of professional work in journalism, but this theme does not provide scripts and makes fewer demands on personhoods. And while journalists also encounter life stories in their work, they collect narratives for a much wider range of purposes. This open and flexible context allows for less structured narratives that entail more varied recollections of events that were impressive at the time, for various reasons. It also creates space for the telling of befuddling situations reflected as conundrums (Ochs and Capps 2001), such as Thorsten's secondment to the border despite his seemingly troublesome character. Putting it succinctly, the stories of managers in the political field are more linear and explicit because the narrators "have a point to make" (Oliveira 1999: 40) due to the moral and political demands of the discourse they create and whose key messages they embrace.

Even if GDR-time journalists cannot recollect regime criticism due to their profession, a lack of experiences of serious problems with the state, and a view of the socialist system as complex and ambiguous, the discourse of *Aufarbeitung* still shapes these narratives. Its influence becomes apparent at three specific points: a reflection on moral personhood in comments on what was or was not resistance, expressions of narrators' views of socialist ideals, and the narration of *eigensinnige* struggles against party control. These reflections are due not only to narrators' awareness of the authoritative discourse but also to experiences of challenges to their morality posed by eastern and western Germans during 1989 and 1990, the very historical circumstances that created the *Aufarbeitung* of the East German past. Their lives' context of conformism, *Eigensinn*, and a love of the profession shapes narratives that reveal political citizenship as emerging out of struggles with authoritarian government, not unlike the stories of eastern Germans in *Aufarbeitung*, albeit in different struggles, and as based in professional values of inquisitiveness and criticism. Even if political work must be seen as ideological work for GDR-time journalists, agency is predicated on both compliance and struggles for self-determination that came to be realized without bounds during the almost anarchic *Wende* years that also allowed some journalists to prove themselves as valuable to their new management. These experiences and the professional values arising from and proved through them have come to form the basis of their journalistic work, as well as their understanding of today's political order.

Notes

1. There was a considerable shortage of housing in the GDR. Married couples, couples with children, and single mothers were prioritized; the state also encouraged self-building to help alleviate the pressure on accommodation. Borneman provides a detailed analysis of housing and kinship structures in East and West Berlin (1992).
2. This was further probed in the interview. Wolf means a willingness and aptitude to proactively disagree—to seek and engage in "conflict"—with disliked situations and to search for solutions.
3. The *Tschekist* vow was the vow to silence and secrecy required by the MfS of its unofficial employees (IM).
4. Army service was compulsory in the GDR, but soldiers could refuse to carry a weapon, in which case they joined the corps of *Bausoldaten* (Eisenfeld and Schicketanz 2011). Service at this corps had a poor reputation, as chicanes and abuse were frequent. Complete refusal of service almost certainly meant imprisonment.

5. Early opposition in East Germany often centered on environmental topics; this was also the case for some of Schumacher's oppositional activities.
6. Elections in the GDR took place under much pressure and obvious surveillance. Refusing to participate was often believed to engender potentially dangerous interest of the MfS, as was using a confidential booth or annulling the ballot paper.
7. The life stories of clerical staff in the realm of *Aufarbeitung* differed from their managers'. Most described themselves as "ordinary" East German citizens who did not experience repression. Most, however, also refused to join the SED. Individuals learned about the GDR as dictatorship through their present-day work and agree with aspects of the discourse of *Aufarbeitung*, especially where it concerns the plight of victims. However, these interviewees view the past state and society in differentiated ways, given that their own biographies do not suit an exclusive view of the "GDR as dictatorship."
8. *Kader* (cadre) was the term used for citizens who were primed for careers in the party.
9. To note, in the excerpt there is also the change from singular to plural as the self is subsumed into a collective group. This chimes with a second, less pronounced theme in this life story that concerns a social memory with regard to turning points. I do not have space here to explore this aspect.
10. In consequence, Thorsten's parents were asked to collect his final marks personally to face an uncomfortable conversation with the head of school.

Chapter Six

DEMOCRACY IN TROUBLE
Remembering to Safeguard the Future

As fieldwork moved on, the twentieth anniversary of the fall of the Berlin Wall in 2009 became the main business item for the Working Group *Aufarbeitung*. The anniversary's approach coincided with a large-scale survey on the population's political attitudes, which turned Working Group members' suspicion about widespread nostalgic tendencies and lack of democratic skills into firm concerns. Now, however, these concerns were no longer the Working Group's own. The survey had been commissioned with the State Chancellery, and the Minister President took the helm when responding to its results, in collaboration no less with the Office for Political Education. As the survey findings coincided with the approach of the anniversary, the discourse of *Aufarbeitung* became a tool of political problem-solving, which had a further delimiting effect on the narratives that could now be told.

Following the exploration of the memory discourse the Working Group *Aufarbeitung* creates "to govern souls" through education in chapter 4 and of actors' senses of purpose in relation to the building of democratic governance in Mittelland apparent in the life stories of chapter 5, this chapter explores how narrative production develops when *Aufarbeitung* is appropriated for party-political government. As chapter 1 shows, from its inception in the early 1990s, the notion of the "*Aufarbeitung* of the SED dictatorship" was closely intertwined with the political sphere, which entails specific dynamics in relation to narrative. Particularly, political texts often seek to legitimize goals and actions based in specific understandings of the present and to engender specific imagined futures in ways that tend to simplify complexities, making them amenable to political problem-solving. As a view of the German nation as "overcoming" past "totalitarianism" to "become" free and democratic is increasingly canonized in this discourse, it becomes resistant to change (Schwartz 1991) and has the power to drive not only the production of historical narratives but also perceptions of local people, of regional problems, and of their causes. In Mittelland these dynamics and their impacts become apparent in relation to notions of citizenship, where some forms of citizenship become legitimated while others are delegitimized, when the "reworking of the past" is used for party-political government to safeguard the democracy that actors here are heavily invested in, even if the meaning of this trope remains indeterminate.

Planning an Anniversary

At its spring meeting described in chapter 2, the Working Group decided to form a working party for the preparation of the twentieth anniversary, which met for the first time in the summer of 2007. It was prompted by a request for help by the local TV broadcasting station MDR and followed Frau Wolf's (LpB) and Stasi Commissioner Schumacher's attendance of a conference at the Foundation for *Aufarbeitung* in Berlin, which sought to help "coordinate, network, initiate" anniversary events across the country. The thus formed "Working Party Peaceful Revolution Autumn 1989"—the Berlin foundation had referred to the events of the autumn of 1989 as "the peaceful revolution"[1]—signed responsible for coordinating events across Mittelland and so included institutions that held statewide responsibilities.[2]

At its first meeting, Wolf represented the Office for Political Education (Bohlmann is at an urgent meeting following a right-wing attack on a theater ensemble), Koehler the border checkpoint memorial museum, Herzog the Birthler agency, and the TV station was represented by an Herr Steeg. The meeting was convened by Schumacher. Once the group had settled on the oval table in the Stasi commission's meeting room the meeting opened with a general round of introductions for Steeg's benefit. Schumacher then reported back from the conference in Berlin. Following this, Steeg was invited to outline the plans of the TV station before attendees reported on their institutions' plans for 2009.

The station wanted to produce a series for TV, radio, and CD covering the time from January 1989 to the end of March 1990, when the first free regional elections took place. They aimed to approach topics of "the everyday": "of individuals' quite ordinary but simultaneously fascinating experiences." Steeg's question to the group was whether anyone could assist with film footage or stories. He added that since he was from western Germany, he depended on their support for the eastern German point of view; he had his own differing recollections of the Wende. This comment sparked a discussion during which attendees narrated experiences and knowledge they deemed relevant: the civil rights movement in late 1989, the mass exodus of the summer, "clueless authorities" who approached the opposition for help and solutions amid the Wende, and the plight of victims who continue to encounter former power holders in current-day institutions. While these stories were told by the eastern Germans Schumacher and Herzog, Koehler and Wolf contributed recollections of an exotic yet slightly dangerous GDR gained from school trips into the East (and restrictions to the pupils' movements, the presence of Stasi officers) and of a film of an unusual border crossing conceived first as a dream, which was held in the border memorial's archive.

In the narrative exchanges—which intersected the planning and coordination of events that aim to "celebrate the achievement of democracy," "encourage young people to research the last and falsified elections in the GDR," and train teachers "on life in a democracy and a dictatorship"— prototypical narratives were handed around the table that tell of state control and repression, victims' suffering, and the civil rights movement. Whether based on personal experiences or professional work, the stories came to connect to one another through the shared perception of the past dictatorship, sweeping the group along into an emerging vernacular narrative about the demise of a dissolving state due to civic struggle. This vernacular narrative made demands for topical coherence and suggested certain recollections that are emblematic for this theme, which, combined with the promise of listening others, led individuals to contribute stories that testify to the discourse's overriding canonical message of the "GDR as dictatorship" and, in this moment, its inevitable end. As such, they reconstituted the group, despite individuals' somewhat contrasting experiences and personal reasons for coming to this work (chapter 5), as an *Erinnerungsgemeinschaft*, a memory community (Nünning and Erll 2006), that shares particular understandings of the past through a shared present and is predicated on particular visions of the future.

Eric Hirsch and Charles Stewart capture this intertwining of past, present, and future with the notion of historicity, which is "the manner in which persons[/institutions] operating under the constraints of social ideologies make sense of the past, while anticipating the future" (2005: 262; Hoëm 2005; also Poole 2008). As a story seed, the advancing anniversary returned minds to the upheavals of 1989 that led to unification with the Federal Republic of Germany to establish democratic political practices *also* in East Germany. From this vantage point, socialism's fall seems inevitable, as the narrative tempts interlocutors to interpret post hoc as propter hoc—a feature of narrative Bruner describes as "the imposition of bogus historical-causal entailment" (1991: 19). A view of the GDR as overcome by the civic strife, the "democratic awakening" of 1989, legitimizes the present-day form of government, which many of the people at this meeting helped establish, and enshrines the need to bring this development to its conclusion. The deeper shared concern that underlied the narrative exchanges here was today's democracy, which needed to be safeguarded, for example, through educating the next generation, the issue with which the meeting thus ended. Wolf concluded that she may run additional teacher training events, for example, on "what democracy means and what it means to live in a dictatorship."

At this meeting, Koehler queried which of two timeline mottos that then circulated in national discussions would guide the celebrations. The mottos of 40-40-20 (forty years each of the GDR and FRG, twenty years united Germany) and 60-40-20 (sixty years of the Basic Law, forty years division, twenty years united Germany) were attempts to situate the remembrance of 1989 in a longer-term historical narrative of the nation.[3] Later the conference of Minister Presidents settled on a third variant, 70-60-20, which included the beginning of World War II: a typical western German view, according to Bohlmann, that found little echo in Mittelland's plans. More important locally was instead the notion of the "peaceful revolution," which the working party had included in its self-chosen title. The term set the tone for recollecting the fall of the Berlin Wall as due to an uprising of local people, which, while humane and peaceful, had transformatory will and power. As such, the title encapsulates the theme of civic struggle also apparent in another suggestion at this meeting of mapping the events of 1989 (rather than anniversary celebrations) across the region. The theme moreover highlights local stories and democratic drive at the grassroots, in turn shrouding the significant role played by political elites in the *Wende* (see chapter 1), and thus became the leitmotif in narrations of the GDR past that developed around the anniversary.

The memory of the GDR's ending and unification, which speak to the end of German dictatorships more generally and, propter hoc, democracy's triumph, emerges in these mottos and this meeting as part of a storied view of Germany as *overcoming* "totalitarian" regimes to *become* democratic. As Bill Niven argues with regard to the legacy of the Third Reich, the national socialist past "is everything today's Germany does not want to be" and "forms the essential negative foil to Germany's democratic national identity" (2002: 5). This foundational myth depends on a dichotomic understanding of authoritarian past versus a free and democratic present, which is not limited to Mittelland's government or Germany. As anthropologists have shown, such dichotomic thinking—of East and West, communism/socialism and capitalism, civilization and primitivism, elites and plebs (Buchowski 2006; Dunn 2004)—which arose from Cold War discourses that organized ideas about the world, proliferated in the transition (also Hann et al. 2002; Verdery 1996). In the anthropological literature, these dichotomies are usually related to the transition to capitalism, but in relation to memory politics and political government, what arises is a genre of civic struggle with regard to the past that signifies attempts to "overcome" in order to "become." Through geographical location, "typify[ing] the 'naturalized association of culture with place' (Gupta and Ferguson 1997: 35)" (Buchowski 2006: 465), this sense of development extends into the present, where it enshrines a view of the East as in continuing transition. Genres are not only "conventional ways of representing human plight" but "also ways of telling that predispose us to use our minds and sensibilities in particular ways" (Bruner 1991: 15). Beyond molding intersubjective narrative making in meetings such as above, this genre of civic struggle and founding myth of German democracy as arising from a triumph over the "totalitarianism" of the Third Reich and the GDR have come to guide what is expected of citizens today.

A Population "between Past and Present"

One story we were told repeatedly at the start of fieldwork at the Office for Political Education concerned a school trip to a parliamentary session, routinely organized by department three, gone awry. The students, who had arrived well in time and sat quietly and respectfully in the visitors' gallery, felt put off by parliament members' late arrivals, mobile phone use, and reading of papers during session. A politician they met for a question and answer session also let them wait and answered a question about honesty maybe too honestly with "you can't tell voters everything if you want to be reelected." The students voiced their disgruntlement in a letter to the *Daily Paper*, which led to a full-flung debate on the readers' page about politicians' worth causing much upset in the State Chancellery. When Frau Wolf discussed the incident with me, she highlighted the students' "misperceptions," to her mind, which she felt stemmed from a lack of sufficient knowledge about representative democracy and the time pressures politicians were under. To staff at the LpB, the collective letter was moreover reminiscent of GDR-time practices when school classes' letters about their socialist deeds were published in the party-controlled newspapers, which led them to suspect that this was in fact the teacher's scheme. Although, then again, this particular teacher was someone who had shown the kind of interest and initiative Wolf and Buesing valued.

At the office the story came to stand for wider concerns about the quality of political education in schools, which fit a recent realization that many of Mittelland's social studies teachers, in whose remit political education lay, had not received formal training in the subject and that a good number of them had previously taught the ideological subject of *Staatsbürgerkunde* ("citizenship studies"). These considerations mixed with other concerns, such as a historic low in voter participation in the most recent local elections with just over 40 percent[4] and the continuing threat posed by right-wing extremism, which, as one of the office's remits, confronted LpB staff all too often. In just one such instance that spring, Buesing and her staff found themselves facing a large group of neo-Nazis at the annual Mittelland Day, where she had organized stalls to celebrate multiculturalism. Most disconcerting that year, however, was the violent attack on a theater ensemble that prevented Bohlmann from attending the meeting of the Working Party Peaceful Revolution; several actors were put into hospital. Serving as stark reminders of Third Reich horrors, such racist incidents reinforced concerns about lacking civic skills for LpB staff at an emotive level. These were often linked to the East German past or, as Mittelland's Minister President argued in an interview with the *Daily Paper* in the summer, as resulting from the population's longer-term "lack of experience with democracy."

As concerns about civic skills mounted and democracy education (*Demokratieausbildung*) seemed *en vogue* nationally, Mittelland's State Chancellery took up the issue.[5] A first move was a restructuring of the Office for Political Education away from its five departments to a focus on two main themes: democracy education and initiatives against right-wing extremism. Historical-political topics, such as the Third Reich and the GDR, would be subsumed under these two pillars. Second, the office was tasked with an "education offensive," including further professional training for Mittelland's social studies teachers. Third, following the example of a neighboring state, the Chancellery, in collaboration with the Office for Political Education, commissioned a large-scale survey of the populations' "political attitudes." The LpB was to coordinate the study that would include, as Bohlmann explained at a staff meeting, questions on "young people's knowledge of the GDR, nostalgia," and, importantly, "whether reevaluations of the GDR were linked to right-wing extremist attitudes." Planned during the spring and carried out in the early summer, the eagerly awaited findings began to filter through in late summer, and the official findings were announced in the autumn.

The quantitative study, conducted by a research center in collaboration with one of Mittelland's universities, consisted of approximately fifty questions that explored a range of topics from commuting and senses of belonging to political leanings, understandings of the current political order, attitudes toward the socialist past, and xenophobic, extremist, and anti-Semitic inclinations. The survey report provided a complex picture of the populations' political attitudes. For example, 70 percent of respondents agreed that unification had fulfilled their hopes, 79 percent that democracy was the best form of government. Fifty-four percent agreed that the benefits of unification outweighed its drawbacks in general, and 65 percent held that opinion also with respect to their own lives. However, majority responses also showed that some aspects of life were considered to have worsened in comparison to GDR times, such as social justice, protection from crime, education, childcare, and the health system. This picture of general support for present-day democracy intertwined with reevaluations of certain aspects of the socialist past was taken to indicate unwelcome nostalgic tendencies by both the governmental sphere of Mittelland and, if to a lesser degree, the survey report, which comments:

> In the look back and in regard to the everyday, the GDR, for most citizens—and some of their descendants—takes on traits of a great friend of the populace who maintained a social all-around care and allowed for solidary ways of life in society and in private communities. Although very few people wish the GDR's political system back . . . the dictatorial core of the system and its undemocratic functional logic is mitigated by a selection of "good" and "bad" aspects of the system in retrospect. Through this Cinderella method private life worlds are transfigured retrospectively, and, in tendency, the whole of the GDR is softened.

The survey showed moreover that the prime source of information for the younger generation was the family. Rather than simply taking their elders' views on board, however, young people appeared to draw on older generations' recollections to develop their own opinions. These included, for example, a higher degree of "felt well-being" in present-day Germany and "a more distanced view" of the GDR, so statements such as "not everything was bad in the GDR" and "one was able to live there quite well privately" received notably less strong agreement," so the report. However, while the democratic order and present-day civil rights received majority support and the majority of respondents also indicated they were politically interested, the functioning of the political system received lower ratings. Party political institutions were perceived as relatively unaccountable, especially at the national level. A couple of questions in a rubric on understandings of politics also obtained unexpected responses. For example, 66 percent of respondents agreed that the opposition should support the work of the government, which runs counter to the authoritative understanding of political opposition as ensuring competition to keep governmental powers in check.

The survey results thus revealed rather complex interplays between understandings of the past and opinions and affiliations in the present, as does some of the LpB's day-to-day work. Nevertheless, colleagues there and in the Working Group quickly homed in on a limited number of responses that spoke to existing anxieties. Bohlmann's first conversation with Sabine about the results, for example, focused on how half of the respondents believed the foundation of the GDR state had also had social motives, respondents rated the GDR's health system as better than today's, and people believed to have been safer, all of which evidenced "incorrect understandings" of the East German past to his mind. The statistic cited most often by members of the Working Group, usually in an exasperated tone, was that more than 90 percent of respondents had agreed with the, in members' minds, most nostalgic statement of all that "not everything was bad in the GDR."[6] Frau Wolf in turn was particularly concerned to see that respondents did not seem to understand that the role of political opposition is to query government decisions. The LpB, the wider Working Group, and the State Chancellery thus saw the survey findings as clear indications of a lack of understanding of democracy and widespread rose-tinted views of the GDR. This constellation appeared particularly troublesome due to what seemed to be scientific proof of the predominance of familial memory, which, despite the report's caveats, furthered existing anxieties about looming increases in nostalgic remembering.

The State Chancellery's press release that first announced the survey report's publication nevertheless focused on positive findings: that local people value democracy and, moreover, that young people are even more optimistic and firmer in their attachment to democracy, showing great potential for the state's future. The pessimistic tones returned at the report's public presentation, however, where both the Minister President and the study's author emphasized worries about "trivializations of the GDR" in social memory. This trajectory toward a focus on less welcome findings was reinforced when results from another survey made the rounds in the media two months later (Flohr and Wensierski 2007).[7] Conducted by the Research Center SED State (Forschungsverbund SED-Staat) in Berlin, this study compared pupils' understanding of the GDR past and history of German division in five new and old *Bundesländer* (Deutz-Schroeder and Schroeder 2008). Results of the first, the Berlin study, were widely reported as revealing "shocking" levels of ignorance regarding the dictatorial character of the past state, especially among eastern German youth. This study was taken on board in particular by Mittelland's Minister President, who soon invited the principal investigator, Klaus Schroeder, to an "expert discussion" to help develop policy responses.

Within a few months, following the dichotomic, propter hoc logic of illegitimate past versus legitimate present, rather complex survey findings were read in a more simplistic way as showing the link between reevaluations of the GDR past and lacking understandings of and attachments to the present-day political system that actors in this field had long suspected to exist. Armed with this new authoritative knowledge, previous comments about political *Aufarbeitung* possibly stating its case too strongly or about remembering of the everyday not necessarily leading to reminiscence appeared to be forgotten. The simplifying logics according to which attitudes to past and present are interdependent were increasingly taken on board by members of the Working Group *Aufarbeitung* and used in arguments vis-à-vis the research team. "But the Mittelland survey has now shown . . ." became a refrain Sabine and I heard more often. Similarly, an initial cautiously optimistic review of the survey results by the State Chancellery turned progressively pessimistic as further information was taken on board and political responses developed. Inevitably, these became responses to long-existing concerns and fears rather than to the complex picture the large-scale survey could have offered, although the study continued to be referenced for legitimacy.

Political Problems and Solutions

Around five months after the publication of the survey report and an announcement by the MP that, if citizens distrusted political government, politicians needed to make themselves better understood, the State Chancellery publicized the big political initiative that was to tackle the apparent problems. This was to be a "Campaign for Democracy" (*Demokratieoffensive*) that the Office for Political Education would oversee. The restructuring of the office that was already under way was now recast as part of this initiative, as was the retraining of social studies teachers also already in planning. These two initiatives, along with others such as the twentieth anniversary, now had to be brought together under the banner of the Campaign for Democracy in press releases and governmental texts. Rather than being clear from the outset, the rationale that would make legitimizing connections between these disparate themes was rhetorically fostered over time.

The early 2008 press release that announced the Campaign for Democracy (*Demokratieoffensive*) and its motto, "Get Involved" (*Einmischen*), only partially links the initiative to the survey results, the Minister President's consequent call for action, and the twentieth anniversary. The announcement quotes the MP: "After much preparation we can now start our Campaign for Democracy, which will, so I hope, increase our acceptance of democracy. Convinced democrats are immune against extremism. An open, tolerant society requires people who participate and engage out of democratic conviction." The text goes on:

> [A] part of the campaign will also be the topics of "dealing with the GDR past" and the 20th anniversary of the state of Mittelland in 2010. In this regard the survey has shown that a majority of people view reunification and its effects positively. On the other hand, however, the GDR was selectively evaluated positively in the look back. The Minister President: "The retrospective consideration of the GDR past remains a task. This is also proved by the alarming lack of knowledge of many pupils. Especially young people need to be convinced of the values of democracy early on."

In this text, democracy education, or rather the bringing about of an appreciation of the democratic order, is presented as the sole remedy against extremist attitudes: the threat posed by the continuing attractiveness of neo-Nazi groups to local youngsters. The campaign's motto, *Einmischen*, which can mean either "get involved" or "interfere," speaks to a sense of engendering political pro-activeness, outspokenness, and participation, which, as many fieldwork conversations showed, are considered key attributes of citizenship in a pluralist society by staff at the LpB. A knowledge of history, especially GDR history, is posited as supporting the development of these civic skills without, however, explaining why that should be. Rather, such knowledge is constructed as counterposed to "selectively positive evaluations," suggesting that managing nostalgia would itself lead to engaged citizenship. The text moreover leaves open who it is that is remembering selectively. Although young people are singled out as targets of political action, the only explicit relation made in the text is between young people and their lack of historical knowledge on the one hand and the need for young people to value democracy on the other. According to the Mittelland survey, positive reevaluations of the past were most pronounced among respondents above thirty-four years of age, who had experienced some years of life in socialism; respondents younger than eighteen were not included in the survey's sample. Left open here, future press releases become clearer on the connections between reevaluations in memory, lacking knowledge, and democracy education. The text of invitations to an "expert discussion" of these issues at the State Chancellery in March set the tone:

[S]tudies such as those of the Research Center SED State (Berlin) indicate considerable deficits in knowledge *about* the unjust character of the GDR *especially among* younger people . . . These disconcerting tendencies are keenly noted at a national level. (emphasis added)

In this excerpt, it is clearly those of the younger generation, rather than their parents or grandparents, as the Mittelland survey suggested, who lack an appreciation of the past state's character as a dictatorship. Later texts repeat this argument until an eventual, detailed proposal for political action, of which more below, links the upcoming anniversary to the "disconcerting news" about young people's "lack of knowledge about the unjust character of the SED dictatorship." This "narrative slippage" that conflates the apparent nostalgia of one generation with lacking historical knowledge among another goes hand in hand with a privileging of one kind of empirical evidence, the Berlin study in its popular reception, over another, the Mittelland survey.[8] Such was the case even though the results from Berlin, which had then been presented, were only one part of a wider project that moreover did not include Mittelland. The study enabled the use of a political sleight of hand that reduced two complex matters to one simpler problem to legitimize already envisioned political action.

Government, as Nicolas Rose and Peter Miller put it, is a "problematizing activity: it poses obligations of rulers in terms of the problems they seek to address." Language then becomes a technique that renders reality thinkable in a way that is amenable to political deliberation (Rose and Miller 1992: 181; Inda 2007). In this process, in which agents "seek to transform their visions of the world (and thereby the world itself)," reality necessarily comes to be recast in simpler terms than it may present itself (Bourdieu 1991: 26). Complexities are not so much smoothed over as edited out by representations that allow for solutions that are within the reach of governmental action. As Rose and Miller write:

It is around . . . difficulties and failures that programmes of government have been elaborated. The programmatic is the realm of designs put forward by philosophers, political economists, physiocrats and philanthropists, government reports, committees of inquiry, White Papers, proposals . . . The relation between political rationalities and such programmes of government is not one of derivation or determination but of translation—both a movement from one space to another, and an expression of a particular concern in another modality . . . Such translatability between the moralities, epistemologies and idioms of political power and the government of a specific problem space establishes a mutuality between what is desirable and what can be made possible through the calculated activities of political forces. (1992: 181–82)

Surveys constitute one technique that allows government to garner knowledge, which helps define the problem to be targeted (Miller and Rose 1990; Paley 2001). They inform the authoritative discourses that act as "epistemic enforcers" to define what can be thought and said on certain issues (Said 1988; also Franklin 1990). In the eastern German case, however, a closer look is warranted, as memory discourses must compete with alternate knowledges and understandings, as previous chapters show. This context of increased contentiousness highlights that power in discourse is derived from the social position of interlocutors (Bourdieu 1991). Here, actors in government, and in extension *Aufarbeitung*, are conferred the ability to suggest certain tropes and metaphors as the only correct ones for descriptions of past and present. Those failing to use the right phrases or arguments about democracy, the dictatorial past, and the "controlled-through everyday," or those who apply them inappropriately, become excluded from conversations and narrative making and thus cultural production. In this vein, members of the Working Group saw respondents to the survey as failing to link the right kinds of statements to present-day political practice and the socialist past, which delegitimized these respondents' opinions. Citizens' language use and knowledge were not only considered inadequate but also taken as evidence of inappropriate civic personhoods that were molded (*geprägt*) by life in socialism. The binary terms of *Prägung* and *Bildung* (Boyer 2005) follow the same dichotomic logic as socialist past and democratic present in governmental discourse, whereby *Bildung* ("education") doubles up as the process that creates the bridge between the then and now. The governmental response to the survey thus exemplifies again the view of Mittelland, and in extension eastern Germany, as remaining in transition—in between past and present, as in the survey report's title, "Political Attitudes between Past and Present"—and as only slowly moving toward an all-German normality. The State Chancellery's response also highlights that this perception is not limited to western German actors but rather has become a matter of government and politics. One of the press releases of the time, for example, quotes the (eastern German) Minister President as stating that now that the "transformation of state and judicial structures had been accomplished and the economic transformation had moved out of its slump," politicians needed to turn attention "to the, so far neglected, mental transformation process."

This was then the sphere and the problem that political action was to address. The dichotomic logic underpinning this discursive realm, which presented nostalgia for socialism as one cause of the apparent difficulties, paved the way for a turning to memory-work for solutions, while developments that were already under way, such as the LpB's restructuring but also planning for the anniversary year, lent themselves as efficient tools.

While moving from complex survey results toward a political response, influenced by other knowledges and longer-standing views on the issues, narrative slippage allowed for rhetorical legitimization of a focus on the coming generation that was most at risk to develop extremist attitudes and most receptive to education. Through a double bind of the binary logic at play here, this risk of extremism becomes a threatening echo of the Nazi past and a potential continuity of the *Sonderweg*, although survey questions testing extremist attitudes had received low agreement scores.[9] For the anniversary year, activities and manifestos would therefore be planned that represented and explored the historical events of 1989 and 1990 in ways that would further the civic skills desired by government. To lend structure to the planned activities and clarify the state's approach to the GDR past, the State Chancellery decided to write a "Proposal for Action." With this, *Aufarbeitung* became a tool of "'making up' citizens capable of bearing a kind of regulated freedom" (Rose and Miller 1992: 174). In her work on Poland, Dunn (2004) describes how the remaking of persons was required by the transformation to a market economy; here this remaking is rhetorically linked to the political transition and the need to create citizens who will safeguard the nation's future in freedom. But here as there, this transformation of the self is not open to everyone, as some individuals are remade into vestiges of the past because their "formative period [is considered to have] ended in 1989" (Buchowski 2006: 476; also Dunn 2004; Klumbyte 2010). The *Daily Paper* interpreted the government's Campaign for Democracy in this manner and took issue with it, as chapter 7 shows.

Aufarbeitung to the Rescue: Rewriting Local History to Create Civic Skills

In November, Bohlmann revealed to the Working Group *Aufarbeitung*—over questions of additional financial support for the coordination of anniversary activities—that the government's priority now was to develop a statement on the anniversary. Three key members of the Working Group—Bohlmann, Stasi Commissioner Schumacher, and Schneider from the recently founded Memorial Foundation—came to be closely involved in the writing of a proposal for action to further understandings of democracy (*Demokratieverständniss*). To get the paper under way, the Minister President first invited a number of groups and institutions, including all of the members of the Working Group, for an "expert discussion" to the State Chancellery on 18 March, the anniversary of the first free elections in East Germany in 1990. The paper was to be presented to parliament on the equally symbolic date of 17 June, tying the proposal's development firmly into historical events of the East German past. In the invitations, the expert discussion was presented as a consultation of state and civil society institutions to help shape approaches to the anniversary and inform the Proposal for Action.

On the day of the workshop, the Chancellery's large conference room was prepared with the tables set in a large square, providing space for approximately forty attendees, place cards that pointed guests to their seats, and the usual array of refreshments; agendas were circulated once the meeting began. Herzog, Schumacher, and others from Tillberg's *Aufarbeitung* scene met in the anteroom shortly before proceedings start. Sabine was introduced to a representative from the History/ies-Association, but conversation was dominated by the question of whether listing former IMs by their real names (instead of their MfS codenames) is allowed, thus identifying them in exhibitions. Apart from these *Aufarbeitungs* institutions, the workshop included a range of civil society groups and organizations, such as Tillberg's university, Christian groups and the churches, different ministries, and an association for political education. Two historians—one a local professor and the other Professor Schroeder from Berlin, author of the study mentioned above—who had been invited by the MP, sat left and right of the Minister President and head of the State Chancellery whose table was completed by the speaker of parliament and someone from the Chancellery's press office.

The meeting began with an introduction from the head of the Chancellery, who led the proceedings, followed by a short address by the MP and then talks by the two academics. It was completed by one hour of discussion. While the MP articulated his concerns about lacking historical knowledge, the importance of families in transmitting memories of the GDR that "come to be shaped by these families' discontent," and the need to "relate the sociopolitical ideals of the GDR's foundation to the regime's political arbitrariness," the two historians spoke to their individual preoccupations. Hoffmann commanded the longer slot and came prepared with a handout, which took attendees through his concerns regarding the need for historical sciences to remain independent from politics; for more historical research, especially regional studies of Mittelland; and ideas about possible contributions of the historical sciences to democracy education, for example, by "highlighting the achievements of the public protests in 1989," and a call to use 2009 to "celebrate" these. Schroeder focused on his concerns regarding widespread lack of historical knowledge and "illusions of [the GDR as] a welfare state" in popular remembering. Although the invitation to the event had listed a number of questions to consider in preparation, such as whether attendees saw a need for change in their work given the results of the Mittelland survey and the Berlin study, whether they experienced societal or bureaucratic hindrances to their work, or what particular actions they would suggest, the discussion took the form of largely disconnected comments and observations: a university lecturer in education, for example, criticized that teacher training in history is voluntary; a representative of the Protestant Lutheran Church in Mittelland commented that freedom is both gift and task, that people need to understand that dealing with freedom needs to be learned; the head of the Association of Museums noted that representing events of the very recent past is difficult since people come with their own memories, and similar.

Overall, the concerns raised at this workshop echo discussions on *Aufarbeitung* at other occasions, as previous chapters show. There is the issue of teacher training, for example; the need for historians and others to be able to approach history without getting caught up in moralizing debates; concerns over eastern Germans' civic skills; the, still, hot topic of recognition of victims of the socialist regime and suggestions to commemorate in turn (one attendee had suggested a national commemorative day); and financial issues that were raised almost defiantly and considered "inappropriate" by some of our informants. However, there was no real discussion of any one point, little interaction between the different commentators, and no attempt by the chair to steer commentators into a more focused conversation. Invitees arrived with differing perceptions of what the event was about, and many seemed to capitalize on this rare opportunity of speaking directly with Mittelland's government to drive their concerns home, whether they be institutional or personal, or a mixture of the two, as is often the case. The presence of the two historians lent expertise and professionalism to the event, yet, bar one or two comments, their talks also seemed to go largely unnoticed. The MP left halfway through Hoffmann's presentation, and no minutes appeared to be taken either. At the LpB, however, the event was rated a success. A few days later, for example, the office received letters from groups that did not get the opportunity to speak at the time. A teacher or two wrote in to argue against a suggestion of project weeks about East German history at schools, which were disruptive to teaching and would be very top-down, "just like in GDR times."

Published the following day, a press release appeared to be the workshop's main outcome. The statement articulates again the government's goal of furthering attachments to democracy through disseminating knowledge of East German history, which would be achieved by celebrating the twentieth anniversary of the fall of the Wall, the twentieth anniversary of the first free elections of the People's Chamber (Volkskammer; East German parliament), and of "German unification." These three historic events differ from dates picked previously by the Working Party Peaceful Revolution but suit the emerging narrative and its political realm of production. The fall of the

Wall through its link to the 1989 mass demonstrations stands for struggles for civil rights and created the potential for present-day German unity; the May elections are a first exercise of pluralist democracy in East Germany. Moreover, at elections "the mysterious link between representative and represented (and thus the state and its citizens) is established and renewed in ritual form" (Spencer 2007: 76), which makes these first democratic elections highly symbolic to the realm of party-political government. Third, unification, celebrates the German state as it is now, in turn legitimizing the present. All three therefore serve as story seeds that entail narrations of democratic rights—striven for and exercised—in a narrative that propter hoc foreshadows the present. This theme continues in considerably more detail in the governmental Proposal for Action that followed.

The Proposal for Action, "Twenty Years of the Peaceful Revolution and German Unification—Measures to Further Understandings of Democracy," was originally planned as a fairly short statement of maximally three pages but when completed ran to thirty-six pages over five sections. The proposal was co-authored by Mittelland's ministers and the three members of the Working Group, each signing responsible for the part of the document that applied to their purview. The complete document was agreed upon by all before being presented to Mittelland's parliament. The introduction to the proposal centers on the government's Campaign for Democracy in relation to the twentieth anniversary and the survey results—in particular the "disconcerting news" about young people's "lack of knowledge about the unjust character of the SED dictatorship," which the proposal seeks to address to manage "gaps in knowledge, counter unreflective GDR nostalgia, and provide activating impulses for increased contending with history and the realities of life in the GDR." Section 2 extends the discussion and adds background. Section 3 then provides an overview of lead projects, and section 4, subdivided into ten parts, details these projects by presenting plans for 2009 and 2010 of each relevant institution—the government (state government, parliament, State Chancellery); each ministry (ministry of the interior, ministry of justice, ministry of culture, ministry for health and society, ministry for transport); and the Stasi commissioner, Office for Political Education, and Memorial Foundation (and here each memorial museum)—as well as their efforts to date regarding the reworking of the GDR past. The final section 5 concerns collaboration with other states and the federal republic. Overall, the document echoes the arguments made by the government so far for democracy education and about memories of the socialist past but presents these in considerably more depth, revealing an instrumental historical narrative shaped by its character as a political text that must persuasively legitimize political action in the present.

The second section fulfills the double task of lending background to the proposal and strengthening the argument for action through a telling of Mittelland's history since 1945 over two pages written by Bohlmann, Schumacher, and Schneider. The narrative begins with a sketch of the local situation at the end of World War II, explaining that when the state regained power after centralized control during the Nazi regime, "first democratic forms of government administration developed." However:

> The form of political decision-making developing in the new civic parties CDU and LDPD [Liberal Democratic Party of Germany] went against the SED's will for solitary power. The Soviet administration and quickly establishing SED dictatorship suffocated the beginnings of democratic structures.

These two sentences establish a narrative of struggle between two antagonists, Mittelland and the SED regime, which are rhetorically defined. The state is portrayed as innately democratic yet in the grasp of a regime to which it is diametrically opposed. Thus, the regime's illegitimate and "suffocating" moves are pitted against already existing tendencies to democracy among Mittelland's political parties, which are contrastingly denoted as "civic." The German term *bürgerlich*, meaning "civic" or "bourgeois," relates these parties to the wealthy and educated, urban class of the *Bürgertum* that developed aspirations to political rule during the Bismarck Reich (Hahn 1995). The narrative's theme is again based in the dichotomic logic of socialism versus democracy, signaled most clearly by a description of SED rule as "antidemocratic." The theme is extended in the following sentences by positioning the population in this story:

> The Sovietization forced onto society and economy did not proceed without objection by the population, but attempts to demand *natural* [*selbstverständlich*] civil rights often ended in penitentiary, prison, or Soviet camps. This is evidenced by the memorial museums of former Stasi prisons in today's Mittelland. (emphasis added)

The population is here depicted as both "objecting" to the socialist government, in an agentive manner, and as demanding civil rights, which are evaluated with the term *selbstverständlich*, meaning "natural" or "self-evident." References to material traces of state violence in Mittelland today are positioned as providing evidence and move this narrative of the past closer to readers' present-day worlds. The strongly put illocutionary suggestions about the dictatorial character of the state and its rejection by the population are extended further in the following paragraphs by telling of the "singular escape movement" of citizens from the GDR and the "resignation and apathy" of others due to not only SED rule but also "a growing economic and social gap" vis-à-vis West Germany. Numbers of escapees from Mittelland are added to support an impression of objectivity while furthering a sense of GDR citizens as "voting with their feet," as the MP put it at the commemorative ceremony the previous August (chapter 4). The text then moves to the popular uprising in 1953 that was caused by "poor living and work conditions."[10] Here, evaluative terms suggest that socialist economy was inadequate, pointing forward to socialism's demise and market economy's triumph, which, like the political transition in discussions among the "working party peaceful revolution" at the start of this chapter, are colored with a sense of inevitability.

The narrative is rife with rhetorical phrases, which not only describe a situation and convince others of that description but also put across an "*evaluation* of this situation, so that the rhetoric [becomes] morally compelling" (Carrithers 2012b: 14). While metaphors describe the socialist regime as forceful, if not violent, they cast the population in a positive light. This combined with a positioning of local people as in opposition and resisting, whether through dissent, escape, or resignation, paint the population as heroes in a propter hoc narrative about struggles for civil rights. Local people are cast as active, autonomous, and choice-making agents—in short, as furnished with the civic skills that the political realm would like them to exercise in the present day. Every now and then the rhetoric is reinforced by hyperboles that describe the arising situation as extraordinary, such as the "*singular* escape movement" above, bordering on a glorification of the region and its people in their dictatorship-resisting identity.

The narrative continues with the theme of the oppressive regime by discussing next the fortification of the border, political convictions within Mittelland, and the MfS, which "pervaded all aspects of society." The text then turns to the thorny issue of everyday life and potential contentment, which could so easily challenge the picture of an all-controlling regime and dissenting society painted so far, but that, given the realities of many eastern Germans' lives, needs to be approached:

> Despite all attempts by the state and the state's party to control [society], life in the GDR of course also offered niches and spaces for private everyday life. The majority of people in the GDR had to live under the regime and experienced happiness and contentment at work and in the private realm.
>
> In addition there were brave forms of assertion and resistance. Under the churches' protection new forms of resistance developed, first out of environmental and human right's concerns, which developed into civil initiatives for emigration and for public gatherings.

The text controls the topic's "polluting" potential in three ways (Douglas 1966; also see chapter 4). First, although the text acknowledges the possibility of happiness in the GDR, it locates it in confined areas, "niches" and certain "spaces." This is a reference to Günter Gauss's (1983) notion of "niche society," which describes an apolitical private sphere that citizens used to withdraw from an interfering state (Mueller 2013). Second, the sense that people had to struggle for contentment against the government's dictatorial striving is furthered by phrases suggesting that people lived "under the regime" and that they "had to." The ambiguous topic is thirdly controlled by the brevity of the discussion—two sentences over a two-page text—and its location between two paragraphs that discuss political convictions on the one hand and "brave forms of resistance" on the other.

The last two sentences quoted above begin a discussion of GDR-time opposition, which swiftly leads to the fall of the regime and the transformation, where the text again gives much credit to eastern Germany's, and thus Mittelland's, citizens, now for "making the peaceful changeover." The, so far, empathic view of the population is thus extended into the first years of unification, where virtues now concern political participation:

> The 1990 elections evidenced the population's great willingness to engage in the process of political decision-making—for example, at the parliamentary elections in the reconstituted Mittelland, the first free such elections since 1933.

This sentence brings to mind the high participation rates of the 1990 elections and relates them to East Germany's longer-term dictatorial and, following the dichotomic logic of this discourse, unfree and nondemocratic history. The evocation of the horrors of the Nazi past lends further value to this civil right that people had striven for, then embraced, but which they now seem to have forgotten. Free elections are thus moreover constituted as a distinctive ingredient of democracy vis-à-vis dictatorial regimes.

From this positive narrative of innate democratic drive and civic skills in the region, the text turns to the present-day problems that the proposal seeks to address. These occupy the following two and a half pages. With this move, the text also changes tone of voice quite considerably: earlier praise of the population is replaced by a view of eastern Germans as unable to appreciate democratic rights due to their past:

> The twenty years of rebuilding in the East of Germany required from a population shaped by forty years of a dictatorship a great deal of ability to learn, flexibility, and change in thinking. The required self-precaution and self-initiative needed to replace the all-determining state and welfare dictatorship.
>
> Democracy depends on participation and engagement; it needs to be learned, practiced, and developed. However, as quickly as democracy was taken for granted—and economic needs pushed to the fore—memories of the dictatorship, and the civil courage that toppled it, faded. Alleged

benefits of GDR society—taken out of context—are suddenly brought up as desirable and as worthy of imitation.

While paying homage to the flexibility required of local people in the transformation in the first sentence, the second sentence casts local personhood as *geprägt* by the dictatorship, which rationalizes a need for change to a personhood that is in contrast characterized by initiative and self-dependency. Following this, the second paragraph, like previous texts and also discussions in the Working Group, relates problems with an appreciation of democracy to apparent nostalgia for socialism, stating explicitly that a devaluation of democracy goes hand in hand with an unrealistic reevaluation of the socialist past—"*alleged* benefits", "taken out of context" (emphasis added). The following section provides a bulleted list of the action proposal's principles with regard to the anniversary activities, which follow this historical narrative: to explore this most recent history more using multiple perspectives to allow societal dialogue, to organize actions that focus on students and young people and that fit an all-German and European framework,[11] to "highlight happiness about the great bliss of unity in freedom and peace," and for all activities to be clear about "the great value of democracy."[12]

Although seemingly related to academic research and civil society consultation, the Proposal for Action rather clearly bears the signs of a text of the political realm. It employs strong rhetoric to try to make its meaning self-evident. However, the plethora of evaluative phrases takes away from an objective and factual tone, rather giving the impression of an attempted self-fulfilling prophecy that wills local civic drive and political engagement into existence by telling of them. It seeks to endow its addressees "with a will, a plan, a hope, or quite simply, a future," as Bourdieu notes political texts do (1991: 191). The purposefully worded document outlines the state's vision of its own past, present, and future and their attendant problems, legitimizing political action for problem-solving. These are solutions that suit the political leaders' worldview, particularly the Minister President's, whose conservative outlook, according to some of our informants, for example, preferred education and economic development over the redistribution of resources to address inequality. And they are solutions that are economical (Rose and Miller 1992). The proposal therefore details activities that ministries and relevant institutions were already organizing—concerts, talks, school project days, teacher training, the Night of Democracy organized annually by LpBs across the country. Only some of the listed activities are outcomes of this exercise, such as the installation of three "memorial teachers," which the Memorial Foundation had fought for, as its director Schneider told us later. Although different kinds of activities made it into the proposal, the most interventionist actions, as previous texts foreshadowed, focus on young people. This emphasis follows here well-established patterns and moreover targets generations that, in contrast to their parents, were not *geprägt* (molded) by life "under the regime" and that the state has access to through the schools under its purview.[13] Finally, despite its strong rhetoric and emotive phrasings, the Proposal for Action was a compromise document, as Schneider highlighted on more than one occasion. He strongly criticized some ministers' requests to tone down the narrative's rhetoric regarding nostalgia and the SED dictatorship, which caused him to suspect that even within the government, there were individuals intent on "whitewashing" the previous regime. According to the narrative told here, this tendency threatened democratic freedom, yet among all the rhetoric, what democracy actually *is* remained unclear.

"Our Democracy Is Proving Difficult"

Another day, another commemoration for members of the Working Group *Aufarbeitung*, this time in November. It was the day before the annual, national Volkstrauertag (people's day of mourning) at which victims of wars and dictatorial regimes are remembered.[14] Benches had been arranged in the courtyard of the former Stasi prison memorial museum, towered over by the prison walls, for a brief ceremony. About forty people had gathered, wrapped up in winter coats and jackets in subdued colors on this crisp morning. Many were from the Victim Association, but there were also members of the Working Group *Aufarbeitung*, political representatives, and associations such as the War Graves Commission (Volksbund Kriegsgräberfürsorge). On this day, Chairman Stiehl of the Victim Association led the ceremony. After a minute of silence and laying of wreaths, he gave a short address that included a plea against unnecessary and inappropriate victim competition—an issue that occasionally raises its ugly head as victim associations to the Nazi and the socialist regimes vie for political and financial support (Boll 2001: 419)—and a warning that history may repeat itself due to extremist threats from not only the right, very much the focus of political action, but also the left. There were continuities in personnel from GDR times, he explained, and these "enemies of democracy" were becoming ever more brazen. When Stiehl finished, the Stasi commissioner, who seemed to feel he needed to comment, stepped to the microphone. Schumacher began by reminding the audience that this month was the time of the "revolution" (of 1989) when people had fought for democracy. "This democracy is now, however, proving difficult," he continued, especially when one had to work with people from the Left

Party. However, he concluded, such difficulties meant one was required to approach *Aufarbeitung* more consciously, which in turn was a good thing.

In their somewhat opaque manner, the two speeches referred to a current political issue that would take Mittelland's parliament several months to resolve. It concerned membership of the advisory committee to the recently established Memorial Foundation. The committee consisted of members of parliament and relevant civil society groups, such as the Victim Association. Political delegates had been voted onto the committee in one block, among them a politician from the Left Party who had acted as a Stasi IM at a young age and went on to work for the GDR state's prosecution services on political cases.[15] These aspects of the representative's biography were well known but seemed to have been forgotten, some suspected, when parliament seconded the group to the advisory committee. The Victim Association, which is almost exclusively made up of former political prisoners, lost no time to voice their protest. They held their committee membership in abeyance requesting that the politician in question be replaced.

The case caused considerable debate among political parties, the Working Group, and the local media, where the concern was not the past but rather understandings of the present. A number of politicians and a member of the Working Group *Aufarbeitung* noted that the Victim Association needed to learn what democracy was; after all, the representative had been properly elected. Others, including editors at the *Daily Paper*, criticized the parliament's blindsidedness and in turn the politician's lacking sensitivity. Franke, whose memorial museum frequently collaborates with the Victim Association that has its office in the same building complex, wrote to the *Daily Paper*, strongly rejecting any criticism of the group. "The association does not need tuition in democracy," he said. They had always been "willing to engage with a broad spectrum of political parties in the interest of democratic freedom." He concluded that indeed their work transmitted values of pluralism and democracy to younger generations.

The debate reveals that democracy is not a clearly defined term even among members of the Working Group, which is surprising given how frequently the term is invoked and how fiercely fought for. Rather, it is a trope that individuals put to a variety of usages. In many conversations at the Office for Political Education and in its training events, values such as tolerance, responsibility, and initiative come to the fore, in particular when the focus is on countering right-wing extremism. A similar sense of democracy as civic virtues is apparent in Franke's reader letter, where he suggests that the Victim Association's work in testifying about a dictatorial regime fostered democratic values. Concerns at the LpB about the incident with the pupils in parliament, shock at survey respondents' apparent lack of knowledge about the role of opposition, and criticism of the Victim Association for not understanding the workings of representative democracy all reveal in contrast an emphasis on a processual understanding of the representative and parliamentary form of government that has been practiced in the FRG for the past sixty years, in which a number of actors in this realm have lifelong investments (see chapter 5). That the trope democracy is nevertheless able to rally individuals with different understandings into joined action is due to its resistance to "univocal interpretation" (Strecker and Tyler 2012b: 5). Its multivocality combines with heartfelt concerns about the nation's future in freedom and this memory community's attendant view of the East German past as dictatorship to create a sense of common endeavor when these policymakers come together. What brought the disagreement about the Victim Association's action to the fore is in turn the association's relatively powerful position within this semantic realm. This arises from their experiences of suffering at the hands of the SED dictatorship. The moral currency this creates is reinforced by their present-day work for *Aufarbeitung* that moreover makes for ethical ties into the Working Group. This position conferred political and linguistic power, which allowed this small group to question a situation created by the proper and due political processes that actors in this realm seek to safeguard, when other people's criticism may have been read as ill informed or inappropriate due to their "lacking experience" with democracy.

* * *

The nearing of the twentieth anniversary of the fall of the Berlin Wall and German unification returned minds to the extraordinary happenings of the autumn of 1989. The anniversary provided an opportunity for governmental institutions to legitimize and thus foster the present-day political and economic order. From the vantage point of the governmental realm, where some actors participated in the East German opposition and others supported first steps toward democratic politics and all are in a position of power in a system they helped create, these historical events take on a character of inevitability. This gives rise to a genre of propter hoc stories of the failing of an illegitimate regime underpinned by a simplistic dichotomy of illegitimate, dictatorial past versus legitimate, democratic present, which simultaneously enshrines a view of the region as formerly East German and in development toward an all-German normality modeled on the FRG's experiences. This genre, which guides not only narrative production but also perceptions, created a situation where complex information about local people's political attitudes was read in ways that supported existing concerns now regarded as evidenced by scientific research. As responding to the survey results was taken up by the head of state, political solutions followed this path, which immediately suggested particular problems that moreover seemed amenable to political solutions (Rose and Miller 1992; also Inda 2007), partly, because they were already under way. When the memory-work of *Aufarbeitung* was, in turn, appropriated by party-political government, its linear and morally certain stories produced a rhetorically loaded political text that sought to realize its aims and goals by taking on the features of an overdetermined self-fulfilling prophecy. The propter hoc story of Mittelland as always already predisposed to the present political order in the Proposal for Action thus emerges as a tool to remake person-hoods, as in other postsocialist contexts (Buchowski 2006; Dunn 2004; Junghans 2001; also Berdahl 2009b; Zigon 2010), and to govern citizens. Both T. Richardson for the Ukraine (2008) and Buchowski for Poland (2006) show how this transformation of the person is predicated upon edu-cation and thus people's own will to remake themselves. This process then excludes those who reject the understandings, knowledges, and specific tropes this discourse entails, in turn denying them status as citizens and thus voice in narrative production. Underpinning this narrative making is the politically constitutive, all-German founding myth of *becoming* a free and democratic society through *overcoming* "totalitarianism"—a feature that makes this narrative increasingly resistant to change (Schwartz 1991), which points to an imagined future within which democracy has been protected by those engaged and interested citizens whose souls could be successfully governed in the present (Foucault 2010). This means that the struggle over hegemony of the socialist past, which many of our informants from the Working Group insisted was at the heart of their work, is rather a struggle over the meaning of the multivocal yet cherished trope and practice of democracy, which plays out on the battleground of citizenship.

Notes

1. Given its terminological ambiguity, this is not an uncontentious phrase, especially for historians, but it is much less emotionally fought over than other phrases applied to the GDR (e.g., Sabrow 2009).
2. A second working party concerned with events in the city itself was formed in the summer and consisted of locally relevant institutions, such as the former Stasi prison memorial museum and the Citizen Initiative.
3. The latter two mottos, which reach further back, were at least partly an attempt to generate interest in the western German states that felt less invested in a celebration of 1989. Given the plethora of mottos at the time, it seems unsurprising that they are confused as 40-20-20 in the minutes of one meeting and as 60-40-60 in another.

4. In *Landtagswahlen* (elections of state parliaments) voter turnouts of approximately 50 to 65 percent are more common in other new and old *Bundesländer*.

5. As chapter 2 shows, one initiative in democracy education had already taken place in Mittelland led by the Institute for Teacher Training and Educational Research. The issue was taken up at the LpB while other states, including western German ones, simultaneously developed similar initiatives.

6. The survey questionnaire itself is indicative of the governmental discourse's preoccupations and deserves further exploration.

7. Soon others, such as the yellow press paper the *Bild*, followed with their own "quick and dirty" surveys, while other media commented on these, increasing the topic's circulation in public discourse (Franke 2007).

8. I use this term here in a different sense than that of Holstein and Gubrium (2000), who employ it to describe elastic ways personal narrative draws on cultural categories to make their argument. Rather, I employ narrative slippage to describe a slippage in phrasing over time that here allows legitimisation of predetermined political action.

9. Questions regarding anti-semitic attitudes received lower agreement scores than the western German average.

10. Similarly, Mary Fulbrook observes in relation to a work by historians Stefan Wolle and Armin Mitter (1993) that the GDR is depicted as in a "state of incipient civil war," where the "dictatorship of the party . . . was continuously opposed by the heroic people below . . . Thus 1989 was a direct continuation of 1953" (1997: 185).

11. In 2009 the European Parliament adopted a resolution on "European conscience and totalitarianism" (2009). However, the inclusion of Europe here does not seem to relate to this development, which was not mentioned during fieldwork, but rather Germany's commitment to the European Union more generally.

12. The sense of needing to celebrate the success of 1989 and thus democracy was also noteworthy at working party meetings. It is reminiscent of David A. Kideckel's observation that workers' voices about their troubles with the transition are drowned out by an "abundance of rhetoric proclaiming the joys of market democracy" (2008: 11).

13. In Germany, individual states rather than the federal government preside over educational and cultural matters.

14. Introduced in the 1920s, the Volkstrauertag became a "Heroes Day of Commemoration" in the Third Reich and was reintroduced under its original name in the FRG in 1950 (Moeller 2006: 33).

15. The politician had been vetted, and her short-term IM activity was deemed to pose no barrier to fulfilling a public office. Her work for the GDR prosecution will have played no role, as it was a legally valid position at the time. The debates rather concerned a lack of understanding that someone with such a background should not work directly with *Betroffene* of the GDR. The politician in contrast wanted to contribute to *Aufarbeitung*, specifically with regard to the Nazi regime under which her family had suffered.

Chapter Seven

MEMORY FOR CITIZENSHIP
The Trouble with Democracy

Speaking in a democracy workshop at the University of
Chicago many years ago, Wayne Booth . . . observed that
freedom of speech is guaranteed in America only to the
extent that no one is listening; that while everyone has a
right to talk, nobody has an obligation to pay attention;
that democracy disempowers by encouraging the kind of
cacophony in which voices cancel each other out.
— John L. Comaroff and Jean Comaroff (1997: 123)

While the Working Group *Aufarbeitung* was preoccupied with preparations
for the twentieth anniversary of the fall of the Berlin Wall and unification,
and becoming increasingly concerned that communities and city councils
were not engaging, the *Daily Paper* was concerned with rather different
matters. These consisted of a varied mix of local incidences, economic
news, and some debacles, including the Mittelland survey and the government's political response, the Campaign for Democracy. The *Daily Paper*
had a very different perspective on these latter issues, considering the
results of the survey, for example, as saying more about people's present-day
situations than their relationship to the East German past.

Chapter 3 shows how the *Daily Paper* reported a news event that concerned the East German past directly. Given its interpretively more open
discourse and explicit aim to serve local people's concerns, the same people

who ensure the newspaper's financial viability, this chapter asks how the *Daily Paper* portrays Mittelland in its eastern, and formerly East, German character. In this respect, as chapter 6 shows, the Working Group *Aufarbeitung* increasingly considered local people's East German upbringing as creating obstacles for the conclusion of the region's transition. This understanding arises from an othering of the local population that is an outcome of the aim to govern. The *Daily Paper* on the other hand depends on its ability to draw readers in and is itself part of the region it portrays on its pages. Moreover, news work does not usually have the past at its center but rather focuses on the present, which shines a light on the devaluation entailed in arguments about the GDR-time *Prägung* of personhoods. This chapter therefore considers how memory emerges in everyday work at the newspaper and the generative powers it harbors in those moments in terms of facilitating senses of belonging, community, and enabling present and future-focused "linguistic politics" (Crocker 1977) that are based in different concerns about democracy, its political practice, and understandings of local people as citizens other than the realm of government.

"Mittellanders are unsatisfied with the performance of politicians" and "Large survey: Majority of population neither hostile to democracy nor right-wing extremist" are page 1 headlines in late September. Following the report's public presentation the previous afternoon, the Mittelland survey was *the* news item that day, covered by a page 1 news piece, a page 3 in-depth report, and an editorial. The page 1 headlines suggest a very different reading of the survey results compared to the State Chancellery and the Working Group. There appears to be a greater focus on positive findings with regard to people's attitudes and on statistics that point to respondents' unhappiness with party politics. However, in contrast to the headlines, the front-page piece largely mirrors the public presentation that had been organized by the State Chancellery. The article thus refers to the government's resolution to continue countering right-wing extremism, although survey results suggested that such attitudes were on the wane. The piece mentions the findings that a minority of respondents rejected democracy entirely and that social studies teachers were to receive further training through the Office for Political Education. The final paragraph, however, returns to the issue that "a considerable majority of people in Mittelland are unsatisfied with the performance of politicians and the [limited] intelligibility of politics." The issue is pursued in more depth in the page 3 report, which conversely headlines "Many are satisfied, but also 15 percent of losers," and the editorial, where it becomes one of "Three problems."

Bourdieu describes journalists as looking at politics like "Thersites, the ugly, cowardly, 'thrower of words' in the *Iliad* who abuses everyone and 'argues nothing but scandal'" (1996: 4). This perspective is due to journalists' ambiguous position in the political field: although influential actors, they are not fully fledged members. This leads to a focus on the tactical game rather than the issues at stake and thus a cynical view of politics reflected in journalists' political arguments (Bourdieu 1996). The second main factor that shapes journalistic writing, according to the theorist, are the market forces of audiences and advertisers. As chapter 3 shows the *Daily Paper*, in an attempt to bind its readers, accords local and regional matters considerable importance. One way this is done is through playing to "going concerns," which Everett C. Hughes (1984) sees as publicly shared or institutionalized issues—troubles, independence, success—produced in the discursive environments of talk shows, self-help books, and the media (Holstein and Gubrium 2001). Whichever form they take, going concerns are usually of the present, which is also customarily the media's purview. Barbie Zelizer (2008) goes so far as to speak of a "division of labor" between journalists, who take care of the present, and historians, who take care of the past. She also, however, shows that the past often pushes into newswriting focused on the present day, for example, in reports on commemorations, as background to stories or as news such as the order to shoot (chapter 3), where it allows news outlets to fulfill one of their main prerogatives: to enable readers to better "understand the [present] world and their positions within it" (Richardson 2007: 223). In this manner newswriting attends to the "historicity" (Hirsch and Stewart 2005) of present-day issues, revealing the "immanent" character of the past (Birth 2006). Using this notion, Kevin Birth suggests that although the past exists in the present, it retains powers of its own. It is in their interaction that past and present enable meaning making:

> Although the phenomenological existence of the past is in the present . . . the present does not determine the immanent past. In some cases, the conspicuous nature of vestiges from the past demand attention; in other cases, such vestiges haunt and subtly structure intersubjective relations; and in still other cases, present experience evokes unwanted, anxiety-provoking flashbacks . . . In significant ways the past in the present structures the reproduction of knowledge and subjectivity, as much as present concerns can shape the past. (2006: 186)

The survey's representation in the realms of government and journalism produces stories of Mittelland and the population that have their own historicities but differ with regard to their "going concerns." For the governmental realm, these are the idea and processes of representative democracy and their projection into the future, which are threatened by people's attachments to the past. For the *Daily Paper*, they are local people's concerns, or what the newspaper assumes these to be, which are of the present but imply the past. These differing foci position these institutions differently to their audiences. The mechanics of government necessarily entail an othering of local people, while the *Daily Paper* creates narratives that seek to foster the bond to its readers and bring them closer, which is predicated upon the *Daily Paper*'s goals expressed in its journalistic guidelines of serving the local population (chapters 2 and 3), the economic need to sell issues (Bourdieu 1996), and staff's local belonging.

Writing News of the Present: The *Daily Paper* as Readers' Advocate

The *Daily Paper*'s coverage of the Mittelland survey highlights how its position as a local medium leads to the construction of narratives that are not just news pieces but very consciously also representations of the region and its population, within which the *Daily Paper* positions itself as a narrator/advocate for its readers. This is most evident in the in-depth report, which takes the entire third page and is introduced by the boldface preface as follows:

> The politics department at Wellau University concludes after the survey: Most people in Mittelland consider democracy to be the best form of government, but are unsatisfied with the performance of politicians. Seventy-two percent of respondents are also happy with their own situation, but 15 percent feel like losers. And: The state is less on the political right than the East as a whole.

The article identifies three newsworthy findings: attitudes to democracy and politics, a group of people who seem to have "lost out," and the question of racist/right-wing extremist attitudes. Discussion begins with the final point that is taken in the broader meaning of *Ausländerfeindlichkeit*, "hostility toward foreigners" (xenophobia), coupled with anti-Semitism. The main statements of this section are that right-wing attitudes are on average less pronounced in Mittelland than in eastern Germany and that, as an in-text headline announces, "anti-Semitism [is] more pronounced in the West" than here. These points are made succinctly in the piece's first sentences through citation of the survey report:

> The researchers state: "In national comparison, right-wing extremist attitudes of Mittelland's population are considerably lower than the average for the new *Bundesländer* and differ only somewhat from the old *Bundesländer*. In particular areas, such as anti-Semitism, they fall below the East and the West German average."

After a summary of statistics concerning individual survey questions on xenophobia, the article turns to some of the report's detail, which had found little discussion in Mittelland's government. The article notes that attitudes differed depending on educational attainment, between age groups and regions. A table and a chart, two of eight visual representations of survey statistics that accompany the written text, support the discussion. These visuals bear succinct captions that make clear the report's illocutionary intent. The graph on "attitudes toward foreigners," which presents statistical averages for the old and new states compared to Mittelland, is thus captioned: "Comparison shows that Mittelland is no right-wing stronghold." This is the fourth reiteration of the finding that Mittelland is generally not right-wing extremist, which was also raised in the article's preface, first paragraph, and subheading, marking it as the most newsworthy and therefore, from the *Daily Paper*'s perspective, most significant outcome of the study.

Like the governmental realm, as previous chapters show, public discourse since unification has usually described eastern Germany as in continuous transformation and thus troubled—with regard to a lagging economy, high unemployment, right-wing violence, population flight, deprivation, and identity issues—while the old *Bundesländer* have provided the standard that the new states should catch up to. This is already indicated by the simple fact that the terms Ostdeutschland and Osten (East Germany and East) appear in the news, including the *Daily Paper*'s reporting, very frequently, while the respective terms West Germany and West are rarely used. The most significant marker of Mittelland's eastern German character, echoed at the LpB (chapter 6), is right-wing extremist violence. In this context, the survey results take on important symbolic meaning. Based in independent, scientific research, thus allowing claims to truth, they paint Mittelland as less troubled than its neighbors in this respect and with that as less "transitional," potentially less "eastern German," and *even* more progressive than western Germany. Behind the article's defiant insistence on this finding's significance thus stands an attempt to rhetorically re-identify (Burke [1950] 1969, 1973) the region and to signal this both internally to local people and externally to observers, such as other media outlets.

The second half of the article, with the subheading "No return to the socialism of the GDR," concerns results on politics and democracy, which are presented here again in a different light than they were perceived by Working Group members and the State Chancellery:

> A considerable majority, specifically 79 percent, of Mittellanders consider democracy to be the best form of government. But 57 percent are unsatisfied with its functioning. What is the problem? Not the system, since three

quarters of Mittellanders agree with the Basic Law and the political system it enshrines. Just as many reject a return to the socialism of the GDR. Non-voters also agree mostly with the political system. "The dissatisfaction is rather contextually determined," the researchers state. What did they find?

In the *Daily Paper*'s typical unembellished style, the article argues that the democratic order is widely supported. This suggests in turn that the cause of people's reported dissatisfaction with the political system must be sought elsewhere. In three boldface bullet points the article notes the main issues. These include the finding that many people are unhappy with politicians' performance, described dryly as "poor marks for politicians." Their unhappiness concerns specifically, so the article, "areas that are of importance to people: such as unemployment, fair wages, population flight, or declining birth rates." The second bullet point regards "perceived injustice," which concerns the finding that a majority of respondents sees much of what goes on in Germany today as unfair. Third, there is the 15 percent of "losers," also highlighted in the article's headline: "if the group of those unsatisfied, hopeless, and those that feel treated unjustly are put together, a group emerges that has been left behind, a losing class." A graph presents demographics of this group. The final bullet point highlights "gaps in political education." The text notes that many respondents, particularly younger generations, reported struggling to understand political processes. Two more charts, one of which explores whether hopes in the political *Wende* have been fulfilled, illustrate this part of the article. The other visual concerns "satisfaction with democracy," the caption to which repeats that:

> Many are unsatisfied with how democracy is functioning. This, however, does not carry over to the constitution, since 80 percent agree with democracy and 72 percent are happy with the Basic Law.

The page-long spread is interspersed with three graphs on themes that are not discussed in the text. These concern respondents' sense of belonging to the state and attitudes toward potential boundary changes; perceptions of Mittelland's economic situation, captioned succinctly, "an upward trend is notable"; and the number of self-declared voters compared to voter turnout in recent elections.

Despite the recounting of numerical data, quotations from the report, and a listing of survey findings, which signal the objectivity, expertise, and trustworthiness that journalism aims for (de Burgh 2005; Fairclough 1995), the report is suggestive of particular views. Evaluative terms, metaphors, conversationalized language, and an emphasis on certain findings present the survey report as indicative of local people's discontent. This is most obvious in the evaluatively explicit phrase "poor marks for politicians" to describe one set of statistics and in the listing of issues that respondents did not trust party politics to address unemployment, deprivation, and population flight. Although the survey report also mentions these same issues, this is not a quotation. The list in the article employs phrases commonly used in the newspaper's reporting, signaling that their mentioning is rather based in the *Daily Paper's* knowledge of local problems. Discussion of respondents' dissatisfaction with their political representatives' day-to-day work in turn is forefronted by news that respondents overwhelmingly supported the Basic Law (Grundgesetz) that is at the heart of the free democratic order. In thus acknowledging the value of constitutional patriotism (*Verfassungspatriotismus*) for German culture, this rhetorical move portrays survey participants first of all as civic, as *Bürger*, and thus legitimate protagonists, to then suggest they are critical of particular practices, a view that differs markedly from that taken, for example, by the Office for Political Education (chapter 6). This reading of survey results as respondents' rightful critique of the party-political realm necessarily means locating responsibility for solving the apparent issues also with the political realm. This illocutionary intent is made explicit in the editorial, which declares that the survey results highlight "Three problems." It is worth citing at length:

> First: most avow democracy, but are deeply disappointed with politics. Politicians, who often promise more than they can fulfill, have considerable stake in this. After all, in a market economy the state cannot force businesses to create jobs.
>
> Second: the better educated, the greater is acceptance of democracy. Especially *Hauptschüler* [students in basic schooling at secondary level] tend to the extremes. But to simply get rid of *Hauptschulen* will not make anybody cleverer.[1] It might make more sense to support all children, including the less able, from early on and depending on their capabilities. Investment into kindergartens and schools appears to be investment into democracy.
>
> Third: Mittelland is no haven of right-wing attitudes. But the minority should not be underestimated. If only half of the 8 percent of democracy rejecters among the young people is willing to resort to violence, the region has a problem.

The editorial explores three areas: trust in politics, education and political leanings, and right-wing extremism. With regard to the first, the text not only places the blame for lacking trust squarely with the political field but also employs emotive terms that signal an empathic understanding of such sentiments: people are "deeply disappointed," politicians have "considerable stake" in this. This theme of sympathy for issues raised in the survey continues in the second paragraph, which addresses providing support for local people, referring the problem to unnamed higher authorities that can, however, only be Mittelland's government in whose purview education falls. But the final paragraph drops the sympathetic voice. Marked by a semantic change from active to passive voice, it reminds of the continuing threat posed by right-wing violence.

In these three pieces, the *Daily Paper* takes a position that stands for the region and signals empathy toward survey respondents, who, since the survey was a representative study, are taken by the newspaper, just as they were by Working Group members and the State Chancellery, to stand for the population and thus the *Daily Paper*'s readership as a whole. Since "problematic" findings are narrated as a criticism of politics, the emerging vernacular story paints local people as protagonists and the political realm as antagonists in a dispute of which the press becomes the sympathetic narrator/advocate. This sense is conveyed in sections that focus on lacking trust in politics and a concern with the "group of losers" who come to stand for the most deprived and most powerless in the region, crystallizing wider-spread socioeconomic problems and felt injustice. The discussion of known going (reader) concerns (the issues respondents did not trust politics to address, concerns about potential boundary changes, perceptions of the state's economic performance, and senses of belonging represented in the graphs) add rhetorical power to the reporting by intimating a familiar closeness and, paraphrasing Margalit (2002), thickish relations between the *Daily Paper* and its readers. This ethical empathizing is predicated on the fact that the *Daily Paper* itself is an integral part of the region it represents on its pages. Consequently, here the "'looking good' principle" that interlocutors employ in self-narratives to position themselves as morally superior to others (Ochs et al. 1989; Ochs and Capps 2001) comes to be applied to the *Daily Paper*'s area of distribution. Another issue shines through this representation, which did not find much expression in the government's texts and was only mentioned indirectly in the Proposal for Political Action: free market capitalism. Relayed implicitly in the discussion of the group of losers and a graph about confidence in economic growth, it is addressed explicitly in the editorial. Here the author not only raises the issue but also puts his finger decisively on the difficult relationship between electoral politics and the government of a free market economy. The East German past in turn, such an important topic for the Working Group, seems sidelined in the *Daily Paper*'s reporting. The finding that most respondents "do not wish to return to the GDR" appears as a subheading, where it is, however, used as a further piece of evidence that Mittelland has managed the *Wende* and thus completed the transition to become a "normal" *Bundesland*—in other words, that this *Land* no longer is a project in need of development—rather than as a topic of its own.[2]

The issue of memory is instead pursued in an opinion piece two weeks later, which seems at first to run counter to the positive picture of Mittelland painted in the original articles. But even this piece soon mediates a sharply raised concern with nostalgic tendencies. The article by Otto, headed "Ugly dictatorship with nice aspects," begins thus:

> More than every fifth Mittellander wishes the GDR back. This showed a recent survey . . . Seventeen years after unification this is a shocking and, at firsthand sight, hardly explainable wish . . . Of course it is good to hear and the more important result that the vast majority, 77 percent to be precise, do not wish for the Workers and Peasant State [Arbeiter und Bauern Staat] to return. Yet the 21 percent show that it has not been possible to create the basis for a satisfying, fulfilled, and happy life for all people. Beyond that it becomes clear that not enough is done in society and in schools to transmit an adequate picture of the GDR.

In plain-speaking, emotive language, the author conveys his concern with the considerable minority that seems to wish for a return to socialism. Rather than focusing solely on this as problematic, however, as our informants in the realm of *Aufarbeitung* did, the piece relates the phenomenon to problems in the present, media's purview (Zelizer 2008), which are relayed again in an empathic vein as a collective failure to enable everyone to be happy. The article continues in the manner of the reporting of the order to shoot (chapter 3), which, while condemning the past state, avoided judging wider society:

> For sure, in the look back it is necessary to highlight first of all that the GDR was an oppressive state, which countered any enemies, most of which were its own citizens, without mercy . . . This dirty aspect of the GDR must never be forgotten. We all owe this to the victims of the GDR dictatorship. On the other hand, it is possible that this reduction of the GDR to Stasi, oppression, and total SED rule is a cause of the frustration of some people who rather associate a "nice community feel" with the GDR. This aspect also needs to be taken into consideration in the *Aufarbeitung* of the GDR past. They did exist, the famous niches into which GDR citizens could retreat at the end of the working day. This is where they lived, loved, drank, and were happy until the next morning. That both phenomena—the oppression and the withdrawal [from it]—belong together, is rarely considered today.

Although the text is clear about the GDR's character as an oppressive state, signaled by the terms "oppressive," "dirty," "total" rule, and the story seed "victims" giving the GDR's metaphorical identification a moral edge, Otto goes on not only to moderate this black-and-white description but even to warn against it. And while the piece shares the government's concern with nostalgic attitudes—the MP and the study's principal investigator are quoted as saying that the GDR is trivialized in memory—it does not share the governmental realm's perception of the root of the problem: upset about the economic hardship that arose after socialism's fall according to the Proposal for Action (chapter 6). Instead, Otto suggests that the cause of some people's frustration may be the uncompromising discursive powers of *Aufarbeitung* and its overtly linear and morally certain narrative of the "GDR as dictatorship." The piece thus appeals in an empathic manner, signaled by a rhetoric that describes life in the GDR almost lyrically, for a view of the socialist past as encompassing both dictatorial rule and a niche-like private sphere removed from the grasp of the state. These themes are repeated in the piece's final paragraphs, which go on to suggest that support of local people "who . . . have not managed to get settled after the *Wende* . . . has to become more of a task for politicians." It is suggested that this support, combined with improved history teaching in schools and training for social studies teachers, may help solve the problem of nostalgic reminiscing. As previous reporting, the piece concludes by moving the pointed finger of responsibility for approaching the issue away from the population to government.

The rhetorical embellishment of the piece suggests that the author's view of the problem goes beyond empathy, and a look at Otto's biography explains how so. As indicated in chapter 3, Otto's father's escape from the GDR provided the young man with a critical view of the East German state. Otto nevertheless joined the journalistic profession to work for the paper of a bloc party. He married young. In the interview Otto speaks particularly fondly of his GDR-time social circle, which was sizeable and very close. "Kingdom Tillberg-Lamme" is what they called their patch in Tillberg where the group, as he puts it in the opinion piece, "lived, loved, drank, and was happy until the next morning." So Otto can write about the "famous niches," because he led an example niche life. In the life story he emphasizes further that he was the first local journalist to write about the 1989 Monday demonstrations in Tillberg despite being ordered not to and that he later made sure to view his not insubstantial Stasi file. This narrative focus suggests a self-understanding of at first silent and then outspoken regime critic, which lends to his writing about life in the GDR not only the authority of experience but also a moral currency derived from a status as *Betroffener*.[3]

Citizenship has often been described as based in both membership of a community and participation in its public life (Marshall 1992; Steenbergen 1994). According to James Holston and Arjun Appadurai, however, participation should extend to government, the "business of rule" (1996: 191, 193), so that citizens become subjects who are not only governed but who also govern in turn. Such confident, participatory citizenship is inextricably intertwined with "the meanings and practices of belonging" (200). The *Daily Paper*'s rhetoric of advocacy for local people reveals a view of and simultaneously constructs Mittelland's population as significant players in the region and vis-à-vis the political realm. In and through these texts, readers become citizens who belong locally, a sentiment that implies past and hints to future belonging.[4] On this basis, the *Daily Paper* positions local people as rightfully raising criticisms and making demands. These are not always demands that individual editors can support, as the below will show, but at least in the newspaper's published pieces ones that are taken seriously since they are based in the *Daily Paper*'s implication in its own news, which gives rise to an ongoing "talking-relationship" (Collins 2010; Rapport 1987, 1993), if by proxy, between the medium's authors and their audience. According to Nigel Rapport, such relationships develop out of social interaction over time so that interlocutors come to share notions of conversational propriety, of turn-taking, as well as topics of concern, even though they may not share the same understandings as the indeterminacy of language allows for multivocality (1993: 154). At the *Daily Paper* such talking relations arise out of an ongoing process of trying both to grasp readers' worlds and to develop a sense of what kind of a place Mittelland is, to then facilitate readers' understanding of the world and their place in it.

Many of the stories that the *Daily Paper* followed that summer and autumn—for example, on neo-Nazi violence, changes to benefits, a train driver strike lasting several weeks, the éclat about the advisory committee of the Memorial Foundation mentioned in the previous chapter, mismanagement at a sewage utility company, and baby homicides—entailed suggestions about Mittelland, ranging from, minimally, a state where "something like this can happen" to being right-wing extremist and lacking moral standards. These are impressions that the *Daily Paper* needed to manage carefully. This is apparent in high degrees of reflexivity about readers and their worlds that was always ongoing in the working everyday. Michael, an editor on the politics beat, for example, after commenting over lunch in response to my explanation of the project's research questions that, in his experience, people mostly spoke positively about life in the GDR, pointed out that sometimes, however, too much is made of the past. The MP had recently argued that problems with right-wing extremism stemmed from the fact that local people had not experienced democracy since 1933. That made no sense to him: "Who is he talking about, the ninety-year-olds? They don't take to the streets."

Changes to benefits conversely entertained several 1 PM conferences due to the great number of local people on minimum benefit. Economic hardship is an important aspect of the semantic context of news production here. For example, a meeting of a team of editors responsible for the weekly feature the "readers' advocate," a rubric in which reader problems are addressed, whether they concern job centers, bills, or housing, soon turned into a conversation about which relative or family friend recently found work or is still without. On another occasion at the 1 PM conference, staff discussed at length how the topic of child poverty could be approached by the *Daily Paper*, which for the editors raised questions of how to live off just 6 euros a day, people's consumption choices that may not always be advisable, financial support and some people's lack of knowledge or unwillingness to enquire about this, among others. Editor-in-chief Arnold mentioned a neighbor who had been in political imprisonment in the GDR but did not want to request compensation because he was "finished with the system," so he made do with his meager pension. However, even if editors share in the experiences of unemployment and financial struggles through family and friends, they do not view readers uncritically, as the above indicates. Erica, who leads the "readers' advocate" team, but also Markus, whose desk is close enough to overhear many of Erica's phone conversations, for example, found that many people ask for too much. For her this contrasts with GDR-time attitudes when "people worked and bought what they could afford [rather than wanting more]." And "there was less skiving and 'I-can't-be-asked-ness,'" as she explained to Sabine one afternoon. At the same time, however, she has much empathy for some local people's desperate situations and takes pride in her team's work to help those in need.

In these reflections, news production at the *Daily Paper* also emerges, like narrative making more generally, as a social process beyond that which goes on in the newsroom, staff conferences, and meetings with the editor-in-chief. Here readers are interlocutors as paper buyers and thus addressees but also potential respondents—receiving angry reader reactions is something most editors seek to avoid. The mantra at the 1 PM conference is thus regularly, "But the readers" or—directed at the editor of readers' letters—"What do our readers think?" In turn, invoking readers and their concerns gives editors rhetorical purchase when suggesting stories or lines of argument. Like when the weekend supplement lead editor's explanation at a 1 PM conference, that their "guide-to" next week would concern how to choose bedding, was criticized by two senior editors with the words "as if local people have got that much money." Energy prices had been at the rise, so a guide to tariffs seemed more appropriate to them. As Dietzsch (2014) shows is the case for work involved in creating "publics" more generally, considerations of what readers may be interested to know and what kinds of stories may be appropriate when are key to this news production. They are based in editors' expertise, their views of themselves as both writers and readers in addition to encounters with local people in and outside of work, reader feedback through letters, phone calls, and a good part educated guesswork. An important aspect of this style is the creation of a balanced edition with a good mixture of "nice, little" stories, as they are often described, and the often more negative news. Here the influence of management becomes more apparent, which at times deliberately steers staff in the direction of more positive stories to lighten up a page. Particularly, the economics section can look dire with news of closures, bankruptcies, or unemployment figures. Over a period in the autumn, the vice editor-in-chief's daily mantra, usually eliciting a pained grin from the economics editors, was thus, "And, can we give our readers something positive too? A positive story from economics?" Even if not all editors always agree that readers should be served in every aspect, editors-in-chief try to ensure that the printed paper maintains largely a sympathetic view of the local population and its concerns in order to safeguard the economically all-important ethical conversation by proxy in which, as the above also show, the East German past is immanent and keeps pushing into the present.

About the Past: East or Eastern German Stories?

The question of the relationship between the region's and wider eastern Germany's present and past came to the forefront that autumn with regard to a heated debate about baby homicides. It evolved around a comment the Minister President gave during an interview after findings appeared in national media that the number of baby homicides, some of which had recently made sad news in Mittelland, were considerably higher in the new *Bundesländer* than in the old.[5] In an interview with a political magazine, the MP, a former gynecologist, mused that this was related to a differing evaluation of early life in eastern Germany, since the GDR's liberal abortion policy had made abortion available as a "means of family planning." One comment in particular, that in GDR times women would choose abortion if the prospective delivery date threatened to interrupt their holiday plans, did not go down well with the public. Feelings ran high as interest groups, politicians, and individual citizens spoke out against the MP's evaluation. Having published the news on this faux pas and angry reader reactions—the *Daily Paper* had received approximately twenty-five letters concerning this issue in just one week—the newspaper explored opportunities for a story. And Oliver, editor in the Mittelland section, began researching East and West German abortion policies.

Having returning to his computer after printing off an article, Oliver discussed the story with a colleague on a nearby desk. His arguments travelled through the open-plan office: "The picture of East Germany that emerges here is completely wrong . . . All thanks to the MP." And "it wasn't that different . . ."he added in reference to the abortion legislation in East and West Germany in the 1970s. Oliver planned his article in this vein as a piece on the history of abortion legislation. At the 1 PM conference, however, Arnold was looking for a wider discussion. He asked the staff group what the topics at the heart of this issue were and what "positive news" the Daily Paper could transport. With this interjection the discussion soon moved away from Oliver's plans and on to questions about loss of values, moral decline, and familial breakdown in German society more generally, which could feed into a story about present-day baby homicides, rather than GDR and FRG abortion practices "back then." And one editor insisted this was, decidedly, not an East–West German topic.

Meanwhile, the Minister President apologized for his remarks, blamed inadequate proofreading of the interview by his press office, and tried to explain what he had meant at the time, which changed the more the harsher he was criticized. The Daily Paper in turn changed tack to following the éclat's political aftermath, which manifested next in a debate in parliament where the Left Party requested the resignation of the Landesvater ("state father"), as the MP is often benevolently referred to.[6] A page-long spread reported the discussion by presenting summaries of the speeches of the main four parliamentary parties. Much space is given to the speaker of the Left Party, who is quoted as opening the debate by noting that:

> "In our opinion you were very clear in the interview." The former clinician spoke, who knows how things worked in the GDR. "And anyone who disagrees presumably does not know what they are talking about, is too young, or has too positive a picture of the GDR."

The politician is reported as adding that the MP's comments led to national news, which cast the former GDR as devoid of values with regard to unborn life. Like other observers of the debate, and staff at the Daily Paper, the politician is also quoted as arguing that further factors ought to be considered in these tragic cases, such as the role of partners, the character of relationships, and economic hardship. It is the theme of the implicit picture of the GDR, and thus present-day eastern Germany, however, that is carried forward in the article with a quote of the SPD speaker, who makes her point poignantly:

> One may well think that we eastern Germans are a particular species of German citizens whose behavior needs to be studied. As if growing up in the GDR caused a genetic disease that will carry on for generations.

Of all the material presented in the page-long piece, this quote of the SPD politician is used as the headline: "As if we eastern Germans are a particular species."

There is much that people can take issue with in the MP's comments, including the very fact that comparing baby homicides to abortion means condemning people who choose the latter as murderers. But in the political debate and the *Daily Paper's* reporting of it, it is the wholesale judgment of eastern German people that ruffled feathers. Stories that make references to GDR times to explain present-day problems, such as the MP's comments about the East German roots of right-wing extremism criticized by Michael at the start of this chapter, are keenly noted because they are understood as narratives that concern not the past but present and future. They belong to a genre of narratives that employ the simplistic dichotomy of illegitimate past versus legitimate present, stretching it to aspects of personhood that touch people intimately by not only asking but, drawing on the powers of wider discourses, also suggesting "what is good . . . and how one ought to live (and have lived) in the world" (Ochs and Capps 2001: 45).

The most infamous of these narratives appeared in the early 2000s: an assertion by a western German–based criminologist, Christian Pfeiffer, that right-wing extremism in the new *Bundesländer* was linked to authoritarian education in the GDR beginning at kindergartens. Part of the to-be-blamed educational techniques was, according to the academic, collective potty training, a statement that provided the media with snappy headlines and easy visuals so was thus overemphasized, but the image stuck. Although now over a decade ago, the name and story remain on people's minds as story seeds that describe situations where powerful narratives—because they are "scientific" and come from hegemonic western Germany—appear to judge eastern German lives and present them both as problematic, or broken, and as impossible to change due to the lasting impact of *Prägung* (the "molding" of personhood by external factors; Boyer 2005) on mentalities and behaviors—like "a genetic disease that will carry on for generations," as the SPD politician put it. The MP's comments were read as belonging to this genre, since he made them in response to research findings, spoke from the powerful governmental realm, and implied a judgment, here of eastern German women, along with the unfortunate fact that this research project had once again been one of Pfeiffer's. In this context a story about abortion practices, as Oliver had envisioned, would have contributed to the implicit construction of a forever-transitional eastern Germany. At the very least the narrative would have had to engage with it. This concern would have motivated Arnold's question of what "positive messages" could be included in such a story, beyond the fact that discussing the topic in any detail would have made for a very bleak read. Focusing instead on the parliamentary debate allowed the *Daily Paper* to engage with the issue indirectly, adding scope for an exploration of party-political frictions. This was certainly a less sad topic that also helped protect the *Daily Paper*'s role as the region's sympathetic storyteller/advocate.

The MP's comments, which at their heart concerned the East German past, gained rhetorical force moreover because of their association with the powerful discourse of *Aufarbeitung*. This threatened to make them impossible to argue with since any criticism of statements based in the categorizing truth discourse can be rejected with the repost that interlocutors lack an appropriate understanding of the GDR (as dictatorship), as chapter 6 shows. That rhetorical force increases, however, does not mean that persuasive power also grows, as the incident at a talk in chapter 4 shows. Rather, these implications may further irk listeners who already disagree with the comments' basic premise if they thus feel silenced. This is precisely what the speaker of the Left picks up on. Using irony, he turns the narrative's logic on its head and points its "charge of energy" (Carrithers 2012b: 7) back at the MP in an equally moralizing argument that questions the legitimacy of narratives that judge people without allowing them to answer. Although this may seem a dubious move if we consider who is speaking—the Left Party has a history of rejecting the dictatorial character of the GDR state at times appearing to relegitimize the oppressive regime (Beattie 2008: 43; Jones 2014: 19–20)—the speaker put his finger on a central issue in this debate.[7] Devaluing personhoods in the past in a manner that prevents voice and thus participation in the present means denying citizenship, which in turn rattles on democracy's own foundations. Before exploring this question further, however, we will consider how memories of the East German past can support notions of belonging in everyday working practices at the *Daily Paper*.

The Immanent Past and Belonging

Despite the heatedness of the discussion, it soon blew over. A week later news at the *Daily Paper* concerned a demonstration against right-wing extremism, the environmental badge for cars,[8] a wine festival, among others. In national politics there was news about a United States–Germany agreement on the transfer of electronic data. The politics editor, Markus, presented this accord at the morning planning meeting with the words, "Of course it's meant to concern things like fingerprints, DNA. Like the Stasi . . .," to which a colleague added that if the Stasi had had the technology, such databases would long be in existence.

Rhetorical invocations of the East German past such as this are frequent at the *Daily Paper*, as are comments that concern the East German past as the ethnographic snippets of office talk above already show. They often appear in conversations between editors, mostly of those generations that experienced the GDR from whichever side of the border. One winter day, for example, Markus explained that he was "collectively" shoveling snow with his neighbor the day before, invoking the GDR-time practice of collective labor to improve communal facilities. Similarly, news of patients queuing at a recently opened optician's office was greeted by reporter Susanne with the words, "like with the welcome money"—the one hundred West German deutsche marks that had been handed out to East German visitors and caused long queues in the winter of 1989. In these moments, rather than constituting a going concern in its own right, the East German past appears because it "'gnaws' into the present and future," as Birth puts it (2006: 180) in Henri Bergson's phrase ([1908] 1991: 150). References to aspects of the GDR, from the form of government to everyday experiences and culture, support senses of belonging by affirming a shared sense of continuity. In the short moment of their invocation, they make memory communities visible (Nünning and Erll 2006). What allows this despite the contentiousness of this past is the "wide margin of indeterminacy and interpretive leeway in communication" (Strecker and Tyler 2012b: 5). In the case above, for example, there is no need to engage in a conversation about what collectivity in East Germany meant; a smile at the recognition of the terminology is all that Markus may expect. Such rhetorical invocation thus enables people with different experiences of and opinions on life in socialism to *belong with* each other, while they also leave room for frowns or pulled faces if a colleague recognizes the phrase but considers such lighthearted comments to be too trivializing.

The use of references to the GDR past at the *Daily Paper* is not confined to the newsroom either. Most commonly it appears in local news making that tells of events and people whose biographies extend into the past, whether they concern local luminaries, golden weddings, the future of GDR-time buildings, and so on. With some regularity they also appear on the main Mittelland pages, such as when a book reading on FKKs, the East German nude beaches, is announced as a "nude reading" on April Fool's Day (it was a joke); when an editorial on Moscow's government having ordered thousands of mice bears a headline in Cyrillic; and when the story of the overly popular optician's is more predictably entitled "Queuing for bananas? No! For an optician's appointment!" In these cases, references to GDR-time rhetoric or practices are made as part of the conversation by proxy between the *Daily Paper* and its readership, as editors assume that their audience shares this cultural background and its semantics with them. Just as in conversations in the newsroom, semantic collocations in newswriting can support senses of belonging through facilitating the imagination of a larger community, as Benedict Anderson describes it (1983), which on the regional paper's pages is Mittellandish and has an East German biography. Like the *Ostalgie* practices of the 1990s, such news stories provide a way of "remembering the GDR and of connecting personal biographies to the passing of time and a state" (Berdahl 1999a: 202), thus also facilitating senses of coherence important to individual selves but without the assertion of a defensive East German identity.[9] These seemingly lighthearted references to the East German past do not, however, constitute "unreflective nostalgia." Rather, they are a kind of "working through," a reckoning, required for meaning-making after fundamental regime change. As Birth writes, "The past in the present structures the reproduction of knowledge and subjectivity," and as such it "allows . . . the creation of new possibilities" (2006: 186), views, or insights that can concern present, past, and future (Gallinat 2012)—such as when two colleagues consider, however briefly, how far the Stasi would have gone if they had had today's computing technologies or what it says about the provision of services in some rural areas if people queue for optician appointments as they did for the desirable deutsche marks (or bananas) in 1989.

We Need to Talk about Democracy

The US–German agreement on data storage was not the first time political decisions about electronic data had been related to GDR-time experiences or upset the jovial fifty-something-year-old Markus. Just a few months earlier, as we were lunching in the downstairs eatery, the senior editor had lamented the recent EU decision on electronic data storage. We were with Michael and Renate, discussing the latest on this agreement. Michael thought the media were exaggerating the issue, but I also found it problematic if data storage was coupled with special legislation, like around terrorism in the United Kingdom. Markus was even more worried: "Here democracy is slowly demolishing itself, but the people don't notice!" he cried out. "In 1989 they went on the streets for more freedom. Now the freedom is being taken away and they don't notice, just because they can still buy their bananas and oranges." He was angry. We wondered how such a wealth of data, which will be greater than anything the MfS amassed, was ever going to be explored and by whom, for what purpose. Markus thought there might be commercial usage, just so companies could push ever more products on consumers.

In these exclamations an eastern German background served as starting point for a cause that went beyond belonging. Our lunchtime conversation had started with another topic that had already aggravated the outspoken editor. When I joked about the press's outsourcing of its catering, as we were digging into our lentil soup and pasta in tomato sauce, Markus responded in a grave tone of voice, "Negative news about the publishing house won't be printed." He pointed to the lack of reporting in the *Daily Paper* on a proposal by the SPD for minimum wage: "Why is that? Think about who delivers the newspaper," suggesting that this is a taboo topic because the publishing house would be implicated in any critique of low-wage labor. Getting aggravated, he exclaimed that he would like to write an opinion piece on this, but colleague Renate was quick to caution against it. Markus retaliated: "But then today is no better than back then when you could only write what suited politics. You've still got the scissors in the mind today." And the issue of data storage was not much better, he went on, making the comments cited above. Halfway through the conversation, the younger but equally headstrong Michael, who often struggled with some of his senior colleagues' positions, especially where they seem to bear toward the political left, got up and left. Markus commented that Michael always left when the topic of conversation was the GDR. He "can't be asked with that," Markus added, and why should he: "He didn't experience it—that the supplement you'd written went into the bin because of your political opinion, that editorials were not printed because of the political opinion."

Linguistic figurations, whether metaphors, story seeds, or irony, are "at once *thought* and *felt*" (Crocker 1977: 46) because the persuasion that rhetoric affects engages both intellectual attention and emotive responses. This seemed clear when Markus used strongly put rhetoric that likens situations of the present to aspects of the socialist past in a rather sweeping manner to lend moral force to heartfelt arguments. Following Fernandez's model (1986: 8–9), by relating GDR-time censorship to journalism today, he moved his daily work into the domain of cultural production, placing it at the undesirable end of the continuum where the arbitrary political censorship of the SED dictatorship resides to suggest that today's control of news work is overly restrictive. Markus reinforced this illocutionary intent by invoking the "scissors in the mind" trope that refers to GDR-time journalists' sense of a disjuncture between "reality out there" and what could be written about it. Similarly, he created an association between political agreements about electronic data today and surveillance practices of the past MfS, the epitome of the SED state's control. Markus thus used GDR-time terminology as metaphors and story seeds in a deliberately controversial layering of past over present to make a case for the protection of freedom, civil rights, and democracy. That this was indeed a moment of linguistic politics for present and future (Crocker 1977), instead of a reevaluation of the past, becomes clearer when considering his more moderate comments in the one-on-one interview:

> [1990] was a time of terrible insecurity. On the one hand, finally this pressure gone. I worked sixteen-hour days and longer, and it was so much fun . . . You could write what you wanted. *Finally.* That lasted about a year, right? Then it got more difficult. But it was still manageable. It was still better than GDR. It still *is* better than GDR, GDR journalism. Absolutely. But it's also got its problems.

Markus makes his evaluation of present-day journalism here when speaking about his experiences of 1990, when the *Daily Paper* was free of the socialist party's influence but not yet under new management, allowing for unprecedented and never-to-be-repeated journalistic freedom. This, combined with the moment of political linguistics above, highlights that Markus's concern is with a democracy of values (rather than process; see chapter 6) that at its heart includes open discussion, freedom of opinion, and thus free press. This sense also speaks to journalists' professional identity, of inquisitiveness and criticism as we see in chapter 5, and as such was shared more widely.

The question of what constitutes democracy moved to the center of attention when details of the state government's Campaign for Democracy became public. In the articles and opinion pieces on the Mittelland survey, there had been support for the initiative due to a concern, which the *Daily Paper* shared with the State Chancellery, about lacking understandings of political processes, especially among young people. Yet later in the autumn, when the MP published full details of the initiative in a government declaration, the view at the *Daily Paper* changed significantly.

"We've had a good response to the call for the democracy debate," vice editor-in-chief Schäfer announced at a 1 PM conference in mid-October. "The MP probably did not mean this by his Campaign for Democracy, but if he thinks he needs to teach his *Landeskindern* ["state children"] democracy, then he'll have to put up with it," he added. The government declaration had been discussed controversially at the *Daily Paper*. Editors had felt that the initiative, which aimed to improve local understandings of democracy, was patronizing. Schäfer's ironic reference to local people as the MP's "children" points to this sense of the initiative being born out of a ruler's overbearing father complex.[10] The *Daily Paper* had thus called for letters from readers to discuss the question of how, whether, and in what ways democracy could or should possibly be taught. The debate ran over five issues and included around twenty published letters. It was started by an editorial by Schäfer entitled "Democracy understandable" (*Demokratie verständlich*). In this editorial the vice editor-in-chief undertakes, even more explicitly than in the articles on the Mittelland survey, a critique of government that simultaneously claims an advocacy role for the newspaper:

> A large survey recently revealed what few would have doubted anyway: a large proportion of Mittellanders have lost interest in politics; frustration with parties and politicians is rising. Instead of active democratic participation, shaking heads and resignation in the face of bureaucracy monstrosities, never-ending debates (such as the law about dangerous dogs), inconsistencies (such as in childcare), unlawfulness (such as the management of sports funding), or dissatisfaction (with personal circumstances). And: twenty-five to twenty-six thousand people do not leave the country every year [just for fun].
>
> The unpleasant truths, which—among the many positive news—could be derived from the survey alarmed the state government. Too right, I think. Despite all troubles that dampen the mood, the state does not need to hide, given what has been maintained and newly created in the last few years. But then one also needs to cherish these achievements. The MP says that representative democracy is in need of explanation. Openness and transparency of political decision-making, sensitivity for the significance of processes and agreements, truthfulness vis-à-vis voters—this is where the . . . explanation of democracy has to start. Only this coupled with economic success, which makes itself known also in people's purses, can stop extremists in their tracks.
>
> By the way, the media have not only made "modest attempts" (so the MP) to accompany the "clarifying process of discussion" since the *Wende*; they often started it, gave it direction, and led it—and they will continue to do so.

The editorial is program. Irked by the MP's suggestion that the media have not played their role in making politics transparent, it sets out to explain rather how politics has failed citizens. This is again done through a demonstration of the thick relationship between paper and readers by listing going concerns, issues that have entertained the *Daily Paper* both through news reporting and in readers' letters that are thus constructed as local people's gripes: the law for dangerous dogs, embezzlement of sports funding, deprivation, out-migration. This, coupled with some strategic inconsistencies—claiming that people are dissatisfied but then pointing to the report's "positive news," which included the finding that satisfaction levels had risen considerably—and the *Daily Paper*'s powerful position that allows it to talk back at government, reinforces the newspaper's role as local people's advocate. In response to the MP's request, the *Daily Paper* calls for a debate that hands its power of voice over to readers, but not without the *Daily Paper*'s intervening mediation, to showcase civic participation. A detailed call for the debate appeared repeatedly on the readers' page alongside the self-fulfilling prophecy that "the debate continues."

A number of themes emerged on the readers' page over those five days: most readers, including two who self-identify as members of political parties, criticized a lack of closeness between politicians and voters, and political representatives' lack of accountability. Many argued for more direct democracy that allows citizens to have greater influence on political decisions. Several blamed broken election promises for disenchantment with politics, while others linked political disengagement to socioeconomic problems in reference to a neoliberal style of government that allows politics to rescind responsibility for the free market. Two main concerns crystallize in the letters. One is with deprivation and financial hardship. The other is lacking accountability of politicians and the distance of political processes, which take place behind closed doors and are shaped by internal party politics, from voting citizens.

After a flurry of publications, the debate seemed to have ended by the following Monday. Recent letters had only been laments and lists of complaints, Erica from the readers' page explained when I asked whether two more submissions she had mentioned at the staff conference would appear in the *Daily Paper*. No, she and Schäfer had decided that the democracy debate was now concluded, she added. Yet discussion of what democracy entailed continued at the editorial office that day. A bigger story had just been announced: a refuse water utility company had lost millions due to mismanagement. Given the potential weight of this news, Schäfer suggested at the 1 PM conference that it receive an editorial. Martin Gross, a senior editor, added that the commentary should make reference to the democracy debate: "The MP wants to teach us what democracy is and then millions are wasted like this." Michael disagreed; it goes too far in his opinion, why democracy here? "Taxpayers' money," Martin explained, but he found little support for his view, and on the way out another editor drily asked "what a utility company has to do with politics please?" Martin was upset about the unwelcome reception his suggestion had received. These are the kinds of stories, he explained over a smoke later, "where the people say: 'but the MP wants to teach *us* politics. That's our money that was wasted there.'" Indeed, this issue seemed to be no more or less about democracy than the embezzlement at the publicly funded sports association mentioned in Schäfer's editorial. But more than a failure to convince his colleagues, Martin was upset about the manner in which his suggestion had been brushed aside. Conversely, when a good half hour of the 1 PM conference several weeks earlier had been spent discussing how to approach the issue of child poverty, he had announced in a rather good mood afterward that it had been a very good discussion. The importance of open discussion not just for its own sake but also as an integral aspect of democratic practice was also raised at one of the project workshops at the end of fieldwork. On this occasion Markus tried to calm a rather heated argument about readers—how indicative letters to the editor are of the readership in general and whether there is even such a thing as "the readers" (Dietzsch 2014: 122–134)—by reminding his colleagues that readers' letters contribute to the discourse, the debate, that democracy is built on. A similar comment was made about the project workshops themselves.

Rather than as particular political procedure, democracy emerges in these moments as a matter of values. These values are based in the modern notions of liberty, equality, and fraternity applied to the issue of communication that is expected of the political field in a governmental order that is "representative." The term itself implies the existence of relations, of ethical ties between these politicians and their voters, the citizenry. From this perspective it seems logical that democratic practice should entail talking-relationships through visible discussion. Participatory citizenship (Marshall 1992; Steenbergen 1994) is thus seen as being able to speak, having voice, and, crucially, of that voice being heard. It is not the freedom of speech that no one has to listen to, as in the quotation at the start of this chapter. This view that acknowledges the procedural workings of representative democracy but jars with political practices that turn discussions opaque if not invisible or insubstantial, leaving both the press and local citizens confounded, is not limited to journalists or eastern Germans of a certain age either (Markus and Martin belong to the older age groups in the editorial office). For example, the western German director of the former Stasi prison memorial museum, Franke, explained in his interview how interested he was to see, when working with the East German opposition in 1989, how political discussion was carried out: that people "really talked to each other, they really listened," instead of falling into inherited party-political positions. This sense of civic engagement through "dialogical" relationships (Collins 2002, 2003, 2010) also goes some way in explaining the "shocked commentary—from Poles and East Germans for instance, at the emphasis of sound bites and candidate packaging to the detriment of debate over principles and ideas" that Verdery observed in the early 1990s (1996: 11).

A view of a dialogical citizenship is, however, predicated upon an acknowledgment of local people as political subjects *from* past *to* present. Not only is such recognition required for senses of continuity and local belonging as the above has shown but moreover as an acknowledgment of political personhoods being predicated upon managing life in a controlling state (Dunn 2004; Jarausch et al. 1997) and on experiences of direct political action in the *Wende* years—when journalists could finally write, when the *Daily Paper* had to be accountable at the pulpit, when a group of editors "elected" its manager, when politicians were accessible to queries, when citizens sat at Round Tables with local power holders (chapters 1 and 5)—in short, when citizens participated "in the business of rule" (Holston and Appadurai 1996: 191, 193).[11] The self-understanding of being citizens with legitimate claims to participate that arise from those experiences were reinforced by national narratives of 1989, such as in the Proposal for Action (chapter 6), as a time of civic triumph and an acknowledgment of the *Wende* years as difficult that circulated at regional and national levels in the run-up to the twentieth anniversary. However, if local people are already democratic citizens and can rightfully expect to be listened to, a suggestion that they need educating about politics, such as in the Campaign for Democracy, was always going to fall on deaf ears.

* * *

Just like the governmental realm, the *Daily Paper* has a certain power to dominate discourses and suggest appropriate language (Bourdieu 1996). This power lends the *Daily Paper* the voice that allows it, Thersites-like (Bourdieu 1991), to talk back at government, which it does to cast itself as local people's advocate. This narrative positioning safeguards the economically important bond to readers but is moreover bound up with editors' personal implications in the stories they write through their biographies and ethical relationships to local people. In the arising narrative production, representations of Mittelland are carefully negotiated, especially where they concern the region's devalued identity as eastern, and previously East, German. Through the *Daily Paper*'s talking relationship by proxy to its readers in which the past is immanent (Birth 2006), local people are cast as agents who legitimately belong from past to present and as such should be enabled to "participate in the business of rule" (Holston and Appadurai 1996: 191, 193). The *Daily Paper* facilitates such belonging through its presentation of the region and reader participation in its debates that hand linguistic power to "the people," albeit after careful mediation. This is seen as supporting the free expression of opinion that many editors regard as the basis of present-day democracy, if debates include listening, while simultaneously exemplifying the *Daily Paper*'s position as a significant player in democratic government. In such debates, but also in conversations in the newsroom just as in newswriting, the East German past becomes a resource that is exploited semantically to make arguments about the present. Rhetorical invocations of the past defy the straightjacket of the dichotomic logic of illegitimate past versus legitimate present that would reject such comparisons as nostalgic and inappropriate. Instead, they insist on a recognition of political agency that not only crosses the *Wende* of 1989 and 1990 but was also practiced during those anarchic and exciting times, turning it into an important aspect of individuals' self-understandings and into a resource for the production of new knowledge and understandings that inform alternate discourses. While notions of democracy as based in dialogical recognition arise at the *Daily Paper* at least partly from a professional journalistic practice that creates confident narrators who expect to be heard, the *Daily Paper*'s strategy and linguistic power, derived from its social position (Bourdieu 1991), creates a semantic environment where these understandings suggest themselves. The *Daily Paper* thus expresses and facilitates a sense of a "normal," a non-transitional, citizenship *from* past *to* present through narratives that entail East German semantics to discuss present-day issues in the construction of an imagined community that has a certain history.

Notes

1. The German system is divided into three types of schools at secondary level. *Hauptschulen* provide the lowest level of secondary education, which students leave aged fifteen to sixteen. *Realschule* or *Sekundarschule* are selective schools that see students through to year 10. The selective *Gymnasium* instead takes students to the A level equivalent of the *Abitur* after twelve or thirteen years of education (varies regionally).
2. The anthropological literature uses the notion of "normal" in differing ways. Sigrid Rausing (2004) discusses Estonians' attempts to become "normal" through aspirations for Western, and Swedish, culture. Buchowski (2006) finds arguments that eastern states need to "become normal" by completing the transition in discourses on the economic transformation.
3. Readers may ask whether someone who was able to live largely unperturbed and build a career in the political sphere of journalism should be described as a *Betroffener*, or moral witness. I am suggesting the term here based on arguments made in the self-narrative, rather than on the basis of my judgment of lives lived.
4. Dietzsch makes the connection between readership and citizens by suggesting starting with the opposite premise that "citizens are for example readers" (2014: 131). Rather than asking more generally how the status of citizenship relates to being a reader, my concern here is with how local people, whom the *Daily Paper* always immediately sees as its readers—in similar moves from the particular to the general as explored by Dietzsch—come to be portrayed as citizens in news texts.
5. In many cases these were newborns or very young infants, of usually young mothers, whose bodies were found abandoned in litter bins or rivers.
6. This reference is reminiscent of Verdery's depiction of the socialist state as paternalistic (1996). However, it has a longer-term history and relates to the notion both of the *Landesherr* ("lord") of the middle ages and of the *Vaterland* ("father country";

homeland) of the nineteenth century. It conveys a Prussian sense of the state as taking care of country and people in a fatherly, benevolent or strict, educational manner.

7. During the period of fieldwork, the Left Party, for example, explained that there was no need for a freedom monument in relation to the twentieth anniversary of the fall of the Berlin Wall: "We were free in the GDR. If colleagues in West German felt unfree, they can have a monument in Bonn." On the topic of the Berlin Wall itself, a western German politician from the Left explained that the wall had been necessary to keep West Germans from buying up all the cheap East German produce.

8. The environmental badge, at the time in planning and introduced later in 2008, categorizes cars into groups by the pollution levels their exhaust fumes cause. Those in categories deemed highly polluting are charged for access to certain inner-city areas.

9. This link between East German rhetoric and senses of belonging is nevertheless a tenuous one, since with growing distance to 1989 increasingly fewer readers will share this experiential background, while others read these references as nostalgically trivializing a dictatorial regime. Just like life stories (Linde 1993: 3), practices of local newswriting therefore also need to be constantly revised.

10. See note 6 above.

11. See T. Richardson (2008) on the impact of the Orange Revolution on Ukrainians' sense of agency.

CONCLUSION

≥•≤

"There is no such thing as a clean slate," write James R. Millar and Sharon L. Wolchik in *The Social Legacy of Communism* (1994: 28). And anthropologists have long highlighted the impossibility of a linear and legacy-free transition from socialism to free market capitalism and democracy. I suspect that our informants from both the Working Group *Aufarbeitung* and the *Daily Paper* would also agree. Yet, where they would take that argument next would differ in important ways. Members of the Working Group are likely to suggest that what is required is for people to face up to their personal pasts, especially if they collaborated with the MfS. Others need to realize that all their experiences, whether with the health system, schooling, or their careers, depended on the state's dictatorial character. These and similar arguments, which we heard frequently during fieldwork, are caught up with forward-looking governmentality that seeks to create particular kinds of democratic actors for present and future.

The discourse of *Aufarbeitung* is a young one that developed in the aftermath of fundamental change, a context that caused intense reflection on such public memory representations in their meaning to individuals and groups. This book has shown that these reflections continue. As chapter 1 explored, the discourse arose in the context of West Germany's experiences of dealing with the Nazi past, anxieties over potential accusations of a third guilt—now of silencing the East German past—and West German constitutional patriotism. As Fulbrook observes in relation to the inquiry commissions into "the history and consequences of the SED dictatorship" in the early 1990s, for some West Germans "the task of energetically 'overcoming' the East German dictatorship was in some sense the measure of their own political maturity as seasoned democrats" (1997: 179). The memory-work of *Aufarbeitung*, which is to commemorate, explore, and educate about East Germany "as a dictatorship," has therefore become inextricably intertwined with understandings of Germany's development as a free and democratic nation. A national foundation myth has developed according to which Germany is *overcoming* totalitarianism, twice over, and the German *Sonderweg* that allowed these regimes to rise, to *become* free and democratic. In this understanding, as literature on memory suggests is the case more generally (Hirsch and Stewart 2005; Poole 2008), specific versions of the past and the future are forever entangled with each other: the past is defined as dictatorial, enabling the development of democracy, attachments to human rights, and constitutional patriotism also in the former East of Germany, as this is the region that, following this logic, has yet to shed the shackles of its dictatorial past.

The antitotalitarian consensus that is an outcome of this sense of the need to reckon with the "double burden in history" to move forward received a further sharpening when *Aufarbeitung* was shaped by party politics at the inquiry commissions in the 1990s, when the conservative party pushed for a delegitimization of the previous regime that would also serve to discredit political rivals on the left (Beattie 2008). Underpinning this founding myth is then a simpler dichotomy of illegitimate, dictatorial (East German) past versus democratic, free united German present, which echoes the binary thinking of the Cold War. This dichotomy has important effects in that it shapes the creation of representations of the past, as well as perceptions and thinking in the realm of governmental *Aufarbeitung*. Problems in the present, such as neo-Nazi violence, thus come to be seen as reverberations of previous regimes and worrying indications of continuities of the frightful *Sonderweg*. These dynamics are catalyzed in institutions of government because of government's character as a problematizing activity, as Rose and Miller remind us: "It is around . . . difficulties and failures that programs of government have been elaborated" (1992: 181). Government is therefore a continuously forward-looking action that drives development by defining problems amenable to political solutions that it then seeks to solve.

This book has shown that these dynamics of government are embodied by the actors who work in this realm. Their experiences of shaping Mittelland's new institutions of government and reckoning confirm a perception of the region as a transitional project in which, due to the founding myth of *overcoming* to *become*, memory-work regarding the East German past looms large. Their work in government and education brings these actors face to face with regional problems—of local people's political disenchantment, of right-wing groups, of teachers' reluctance to broach GDR history—that become pressing concerns as individuals have internalized the moralizing positions entailed in the discourse through personal experiences with the past state from either side of the border, in relationships with the authoritarian state's victims, and with the embodiment of remembrance at commemorative events. In institutional collaboration these actors thus create narratives about the East German past that suit the wider discourse, as well as their own experiences that have further been shaped through reflections within this memory community. These narratives in turn must have transformatory power "to convince citizens of the need to obey . . . at least in that aspect . . . which is precisely the citizens' individual life and the life of their soul" (Foucault 2010: 204–5). More specifically, the aim is to affect changes in people's memories of the shared East German and of their individual past to allow the production of citizens "capable of bearing a kind of regulated freedom" to complete Mittelland's transition (Rose and Miller 1992: 174).

There is then a great sense of purpose here, which means that narratives have to be highly persuasive and as such are created to bear the characteristics of "good stories": they are causally linear, based in a certain moral stance, and categorically clear regarding past and present. This is not to say that only narratives created for government must convey clear messages. The life stories of moral witnesses, *Zeitzeugen*, such as those of members of Tillberg's Victim Association, also aim to clearly portray their central message of the dictatorial character of the GDR state (Gallinat 2006a), but the narratives of governmental *Aufarbeitung* have to espouse even greater effects as they target an entire population. They moreover require the development of particular genres that tell of the now desirable civic skills. These genres in turn suggest the use of certain emblems and the development of particular plots (Bruner 1991). And although content is not fully predetermined, this dynamic of narrative production accounts for considerable consistency across the wide field of *Aufarbeitung*, as certain topics, texts, and films suggest themselves while others come to be seen as unsuitable, if not as potentially polluting, to the discourse's central messages. In Mittelland, the resources that support the telling of these stories at events and in memorial museums were developed in the 1990s, when publicly funded *Aufarbeitung* had a particularly strong focus on the atrocities committed by the MfS, and, when budgets are tight, institutions make judicious use of existing materials, which at the time of fieldwork meant a reification of locally produced narratives about the "GDR as dictatorship."

Messages about civic skills are apparent in stories about GDR-time oppression and resistance that recognize unjust suffering, celebrate acts of refusal, and note the particular agency shown by escapees whether they attempted to flee across the inner German border or left, "voting with their feet," via Hungary in 1989, while it remains understood that such actions were conducted by a minority of the population and/or only for a limited period of time. The story of East Germany's democratic awakening in the peaceful revolution of 1989 is a further powerful narrative championing and evidencing civic will, yet the democratic awakening itself is similarly considered unconcluded, as local people are seen to lack the specific skills and attitudes actors in this realm associate with life in a pluralistic society. Most importantly for the LpB, not enough people attend elections. Speaking generally, East Germans (Ostdeutsche) are rather seen as having been molded into passive personhoods in order to avoid the attention of repressive authorities, which, following the discourse's dichotomic logic, leads to a lack of proactive political engagement in the present. These views are an outcome of the genre of these stories, since, as Bruner points out, genres are not only "conventional ways of representing human plight" but "also ways of telling that predispose us to use our minds and sensibilities in particular ways" (1991: 15). They are internalized in actors' self-understandings, that is, their regime criticism in the GDR for eastern German actors and their longtime party-political involvement and interest in East Germany for western Germans. Stories of GDR-time resistance are thus both understood and told to suggest that a rejection of the previous regime entails an embracing of the current form of government and with that a political agency that should now fuel civil society engagements that support the present-day political order.

Inevitably, this governmental work legitimizes certain visions of citizenship while delegitimizing others on the basis that they bear too many traces of past dispositions—that they are still *of* the past having yet to arrive *in* the present. Similar dynamics regarding the remaking of personhoods in postsocialism, and the resistance this tends to cause, have been observed by Dunn (2004) in relation to the shop floor as a site of the production of capitalism, by Junghans (2001) in relation to civil society initiatives, and by Neringa Klumbyte (2010) in relation to memory. As individuals are asked to align themselves with the new conditions, to recognize the truth of the "GDR as dictatorship," and to reject socialist legacies, those who fail to employ the language and knowledge that have become defined as appropriate by the discourse become rhetorically identified as vestiges of the illegitimate past (Buchowski 2006) and are inadvertently excluded from civic participation. In this regard we have seen how complex survey results about people's political attitudes were quickly understood as indicating too much nostalgia, which was seen as precluding attachments to democracy, and how a school class's disgruntlement at, what they perceived as, politicians' disrespectful behavior was regarded as lacking understandings of politicians' work demands—problems that were seen as having to be addressed through increased efforts in historical education to create the attachments to present-day political practice that would allow the learning of "correct" understandings. In short, this education is to affect the necessary remaking of citizenship. At times this dynamic extends further and hegemonic narratives arise that cast local personhood as generally deficient due to the region's East German biography, as in the case of the MP's comments about baby homicides, which, since such understandings locate the population's formative period in the past, cannot be made good. In those moments, eastern Germans appear to be collectively denied morality in a way that only long-term generational change can address.

I imagine that senior editor Markus would add to the comment, "There is no such thing as a clean slate" a tongue-in-cheek "and that's a good thing" (*und das ist gut so*). As previous chapters showed, the East German past is also a concern for the *Daily Paper* but is moreover regarded as an inevitable part of Mittelland's biography and as bearing potential. While the work of government entails an othering of the local population, the newspaper depends on drawing readers in. To serve the "local and regional concerns of the people in its area of distribution" is the explicit central aim of this regional daily. At the same time, the *Daily Paper* is just as concerned about democracy as the governmental realm, largely because the newspaper itself, through the practice of free press, forms an integral part of Mittelland's democratic governance structures. This position is underpinned by some eastern German staff's experiences of helping shape the transition of 1989 and 1990 at different media outlets after many years of *eigensinnige* struggles against tight party control of their work. Following the national antitotalitarian consensus, the *Daily Paper* also rejects "all forms of totalitarianism," which includes both the Nazi past and the SED dictatorship, and it reports critically and regularly on issues such as right-wing extremism. However, this is where important distinctions lie. As a regional paper that conducts itself as local people's advocate and embraces a critical position toward government, as most media do (Bourdieu 1996), the *Daily Paper* becomes implicated in the representations of Mittelland that it creates on its pages. The paper itself is a part of the region, a fact that is personified not just in many editors' local origins but moreover in their awareness that their family connections link them to Mittelland's social fabric.[1]

Moreover, both the paper and much of its staff share an East German biography with Mittelland, which has two important implications. One is that, since self-narration tends to be driven by the "'looking good' principle" that allows narrators to claim moral soundness (Ochs et al. 1989; Ochs and Capps 2001), the *Daily Paper* seeks positive stories where Mittelland as a whole and its population more generally are concerned. The other implication is that this approach extends to news stories about the East German past where editors tread carefully to avoid creating images that extend the notion of the dictatorship to the whole of the GDR. Their focus rather remains on the culpability of authorities and the MfS, shielding wider society from collective judgment. This is necessary to avoid putting large parts of the readership off, but this position also echoes many actors' life stories—the fact that they worked for the state and "the system" and were party members—and relates to other editors' ethical relationships with these colleagues, which suggest to them that black-and-white views of the "GDR as dictatorship" cannot account for the diversity of possible lives and situations. This context of news production, which also includes the need to appeal to a diverse readership, from the critically minded university lecturer to the pensioners often painted as uneducated out in the state's large rural hinterland (Dietzsch 2014: 122–34), creates a discourse on the East German past that is marked by an interpretive openness achieved by the use of diverse texts, carefully chosen readers' letters that espouse varying viewpoints, and opinion pieces. Instead of suggesting very particular definitions of the past state, as the discourse of *Aufarbeitung* does, the *Daily Paper* uses an approach of ongoing debate akin to the living narratives of everyday life that support meaning-making (Ochs and Capps 2001). The use of personal memory narratives in news pieces and readers' letters further facilitates this social production of meaning as these provide snippets of the kinds of lives that individuals could lead in the past and the ways these may sit within wider, retrospectively created stories about the past GDR. This approach supports the development of readers' understandings of the world and their place in it, which J. Richardson suggests is one of journalism's central aims (2007). Furthermore, a suggestion that the past needs to be publically deliberated also means the *Daily Paper* ought to be bought and read, as the debate continues on its pages.

This discursive openness on understandings of the East German state and society and many editors' local background allows this past to seep into the present of news production in many different ways. The past becomes immanent in Birth's sense (2006) so that references to various aspects of life in the GDR are made in conversations during the working everyday—as jokes or in comments on present circumstances—and on the *Daily Paper*'s pages for a similar variety of purposes. Such invocations of shared memories, however superficial, and the use of references to the past for linguistic politics that criticize present-day issues support the creation of imagined communities that, given the association of history with place here (Buchowski 2006: 465), belong locally. This imagination moreover builds on the senses of identity that developed at the grassroots of East German society, where they were based in social solidarity and senses of accomplishment (Jarausch et al. 1997; Palmowski 2009). These notions were furthered by the shared experiences of a difficult transition and cultural devaluations by a hegemonic western Germany during unification

(Berdahl 1999a; Gallinat 2008). The playful inclusion of the East German past in everyday working practices and the *Daily Paper*'s aim to serve its readers therefore facilitate the construction of local people as legitimate citizens *from* past *to* present. This citizenship is enabled more specifically by the *Daily Paper*'s position as narrator/advocate, within which it plays to many of local people's "going concerns" (Hughes 1984; also Holstein and Gubrium 2001)—though not all, as editors insisted—and by the publication of carefully selected and thoroughly edited readers' letters. In this discourse, democracy and citizenship then arise as issues of voice. Regarding civic agency Holston and Appadurai observe the following:

> In effect, procedural liberalism leaves citizens more entangled in obligations they do not choose and less attached to common identifications that would render these obligations not just bearable but even virtuous. Thus, it produces citizens who are predominately passive in their citizenship. They are, for the most part, spectators who vote. Yet, without active participation in the business of rule, they are citizens whose citizenship is managed, for better or worse, by an unelected bureaucracy. (1996: 193)

In their argument two conditions need to be fulfilled to enable more meaningful citizenship. One of these is belonging based in local communities and modes of identification; the other is participation in the business of rule, at least through voting as in the quotation above. Both of these conditions appear to be met in the *Daily Paper*'s practices, as suggested above: its journalistic style provides means of identification, supports the imagination of local community, and allows participation in mediated debates. However, beyond facilitating mediated voice, the narratives thus created also demand to be listened to—they request dialogue and thus an extension of participation that goes from voicing concerns to influencing politics. A dialogical view of political practice suits journalism's more general goal to support the free development of opinion, fits the *Daily Paper*'s economic needs by keeping the conversation going, and sits well with working practices here, as well as some actors' historical experiences. The daily 1 PM staff conference, for example, intends to facilitate such open dialogue and is seen by many staff as achieving this at least some of the time. Eastern German employees moreover bring to this their experiences of the *Wende*, when questions of accountability were raised with them and they were able to raise them in turn with former and new power holders.

These experiences of dialogical relations to colleagues, of direct democracy and almost anarchic freedom during 1990, continue to drive many senior editors' perceptions of and concerns about political practice today, and they stand in stark contrast to the procedurally focused view of politics among many LpB staff. The differences apparent here are akin to those noted by former civil rights activists in the early 1990s, who, having fought for the "peaceful revolution," found themselves caught in the administrative system of representative democracy and the *Rechtsstaat*, a bureaucracy that struggles to accommodate the passion that both calls for justice and accountability entail (Herzfeld 1992) and, beyond the ability to vote, renders citizens passive (Appadurai and Holston 1996). A dialogical citizenship would moreover be based in ethical relationships that, however, depend on the recognition of local people as legitimate political actors. This position is integral to the *Daily Paper*'s discursive practices, but it appears to be prevented by the discursive practices of the governmental realm that entail a problematization of the local population.

The introduction to this book raised questions of morality and ethics in narrative more generally, and after fundamental regime change more specifically. These themes also emerged in most chapters in one form or another. For *Aufarbeitung*, questions of morality appear to be key. These concerns with more general questions that seek to provide guidance for "thin relations" to "the stranger and the remote" are part and parcel of a truth discourse about history that seeks categorical clarity and wide applicability (Margalit 2002: 7). Within this, the dignity of victims appears time and again as a central concern. As we have seen, in moments where disagreements arise over the content of events (the teacher training event) or texts (the memorial concept), this is a powerful argument that helps safeguard the central message of the "GDR as dictatorship" and through that the discourse's internal coherence. The book, however, has shown further that this concern with the victims, which crystallizes the canonic understanding of the "GDR as dictatorship," is closely intertwined with social relationships. Individual testimony, which is used heavily in memorial museums, for example (Jones 2014), and their present-day renderings entail relationships. The managers of institutions of *Aufarbeitung* also know many victims personally; they have worked with them over many years. It is therefore ethical memory, which concerns human "relations to the near and dear" (Margalit 2002: 7), that drives the discourse's moral messages at the coalface of discursive production. In championing personal memory narratives, the *Daily Paper*'s discourse also enables ethical memory. Moreover, the newspaper's drive for dialogue and dialogical relations continuously invokes ethics in terms of responsibility and accountability, while the newspaper seems to avoid espousing larger moral principles that would risk judging too many readers too overtly.

Overall, then, morality arises in this book primarily as a quest for narrative unity (MacIntyre 1981; Ochs and Caps 2001). Chapter 5 showed how narrators work to create coherence in the telling of their lives to bridge the considerable challenge brought by the end of the GDR and unification, which entailed a change of the value framework by which people should lead their lives. These life stories were driven, as Ochs and Capps argue, by reflectively considered moral stances, "predisposition[s] about what is good or valuable and how one ought to live in the world" (2001: 45), which we have seen moreover in the self-reveal employed in interviews and readers' letters of someone as having been someone specific in socialism (chapter 3). Moral stances are, however, changeable and can be "indeterminate and unstable" (Ochs and Capps 2001: 50). For Alasdair MacIntyre, morality thus arises in the continuous searching for goodness through reflection, in decision-making and action. It is this quest that "provide[s] moral life with its unity" (1981: 219). Insisting on the narrative character of this quest, MacIntyre echoes the points raised by Ochs and Capps (2001) and Bruner (1987, 1990, 1991; also Carrithers 2012a; Collins 2002, 2003, 2010) and those explicated in this book that narrative is at the center of meaning-making, personhood, the creation of habitable identities, and community, not only but most crucially in the aftermath of unsettling, intense change. As "culture in the making," narrative allows actors to approach the ambiguities, uncertainties, and challenges that continue to be created by the afterlife of socialism (T. Richardson 2008: 103). In this regard, references to the anthropology of postsocialism throughout this book have highlighted that there are considerable parallels across the region in terms of the dynamics that the fall of socialist governments created. What is distinctive about eastern Germany is the speed of change, which intensified public reflection, and the unification by accession, which brought questions of ownership of the transformation into sharp relief. These two issues interplay in the production of memory, which plays a central role in eastern Germany's transition since history has been closely intertwined with national identity in both German states. Anthropologists agree that forty years of socialism "created a distinctive historical context" that cannot simply be done away with (Creed 1998: 278), but moreover, beyond socialism, both the afterlife of fundamental regime change itself (see Verdery 1996) and longer-term historical trajectories continue to socially and culturally impact hopes and fears for the future, thus shaping action and agency in the present.

Notes

1. Ulf Hannerz (2004) also observes this relation between journalists' local relationships and their reporting in his work on foreign correspondents.

GLOSSARY

Alltag   everyday life

Arbeiter und Bauern Staat   Workers and Peasant State

Ausländerfeindlichkeit   xenophobia

authentische Orte   authentic sites

Befehl   order; *befehlen* to order

Betroffene   individuals "affected by" certain circumstances (here by the SED regime)

Bildungsauftrag   duty to educate

Bildungsbürgertum   educated bourgeoisie

BStU (Bundesbeauftragter für die Stasi-Unterlagen)   Federal Commissioner for the Documents of the State Security Police, BStU; also Birthler agency at the time of fieldwork, Jahn agency at the time of writing; short, commissioner for Stasi files at the time of writing; short, commissioner for Stasi files

Bundesland   federal state

Bundestag   German parliament

CDU (Christlich Demokratische Union Deutschlands)   Christian Democratic Party

Demokratieausbildung   democracy education

Demokratieverständniss   understanding of democracy

Die Linke   the Left; formed through a merger between the western German left-wing group WASG (Wahlalternative Arbeit und soziale Gerechtigkeit e.V.) and the eastern German PDS (Partei des Demokratischen Sozialismus) which was the successor to the previously ruling socialist party SED (Sozialistische Einheitspartei)

die Mauer im Kopf   the Wall in people's minds

Diktaturvergleich   system comparison of dictatorships

doppelte Vergangenheit   double burden in history

durchherrschte Gesellschaft   controlled-through society

Eigensinn   a sense of one's own interests

FDJ (Freie Deutsche Jugend)   Free German Youth; socialist mass organization for young people from age fourteen

freie Meinungsbildung   free development of opinion

FRG   Federal Republic of Germany (West Germany)

FDP   Liberal Democratic Party

Gedenken   remembrance

Gedenkstätte   memorial

GDR   German Democratic Republic (East Germany)

Grundgesetz   Basic Law

Heimat   notion of home and home country

IM (*Inoffizieller Mitarbeiter*)   unofficial employee of the State Security Police

LpB (Landeszentrale für politische Bildung)   Office for Political Education

LStU (Landesbeauftragter für Stasi-Unterlagen)   State Commissioner for the Stasi Files; short, Stasi-Beauftragter (Stasi commissioner)

Meinungsfreiheit   freedom to express opinion

MfS (Ministerium für Staatssicherheit)   Ministry for State Security; short, Stasi

Neues Forum   New Forum; political opposition in East Germany

NDPD (National-Demokratische Partei Deutschlands)   National Democratic Party of Germany; an East German bloc party

Opfer   victim

Ossi   "Eastie" (East German)

PDS (Partei des demokratischen Sozialismus)   Party of Democratic Socialism; successor to the SED

Prägung   molding or shaping of individuals

Schiessbefehl   an order to shoot

SED (Sozialistische Einheitspartei Deutschlands)   Socialist Unity Party; East Germany's ruling party

Sonderweg   exceptionalism ("special path")

SPD (Sozialdemokratische Partei Deutschlands)   Social Democratic Party of Germany

Staatsbürgerkunde   citizenship studies in GDR school teaching

Vergangenheitsaufarbeitung   the reworking of the past; short, *Aufarbeitung*

Vergangenheitsbewältigung   the management of the past; short, *Bewältigung*

Unrechtsstaat   state of injustice/unjust state

Vereinigung   unification; also *Wiedervereinigung* (reunification)

Verfassungspatriotismus   constitutional patriotism

Wende   political turn around of 1989

Wendehälse   "turning necks"

Wessi   "Westie" (West German)

Zeitzeuge   historic witness

Zentralkomitee   central committee (of the SED)

Zersetzung   MfS method of "dissolution"

Bibliography

≥•≤

"9. November: Bundestag will Einheitsdenkmal in Berlin." 2007. *Spiegel Online*, 9 November. Retrieved November 2015 from www.spiegel.de/politik/deutschland/9-november-bundestag-will-einheitsdenkmal-in-berlin-a-516368.html.

Adler, Nanci. 2012. "Reconciliation with—or Rehabilitation of—the Soviet Past?" *Memory Studies* 5(3): 327–38.

Adorno, Theodor. (1959) 1963. "Was bedeutet: Aufarbeitung der Vergangenheit," in *Eingriffe: Neun kritische Modelle*. Frankfurt am Main: Suhrkamp.

Ahonen, Paul. 2006. "Victims of the Berlin Wall," in B. Niven (ed.), *Germans as Victims*. Basingstoke: Palgrave Macmillan.

Albright, Daniel. 1994. "Literary and Psychological Models of the Self," in U. Neisser and R. Fivush (eds.), *The Remembering Self*. Cambridge: Cambridge University Press.

Amit, Vered. 2010. "Serendipities, Uncertainties and Improvisations in Movement and Migration," in P. Collins and A. Gallinat (eds.), *The Ethnographic Self as Resource*. New York and Oxford: Berghahn.

Anderson, Benedict. 1983. *Imagined Communities: Reflections on the Origin and Spread of Nationalism*. London: Verso.

Antze, Paul, and Michael Lambek. 1996. *Tense Past: Cultural Essays in Trauma and Memory*. London: Routledge.

Applegate, Celia. 1990. *A Nation of Provincials: The German Idea of Heimat*. Berkeley: University of California Press.

Apthorpe, Raymond. 1997. "Writing Development Policy and Policy Analysis Plain or Clear: On Language, Genre and Power," in C. Shore and S. Wright (eds.), *Anthropology of Policy*. London: Routledge.

Arendt, Hannah. 1958. *The Origins of Totalitarianism*. Cleveland, OH: World Publishing.

Arnold-de Simine, Silke. 2011. "'The Spirit of an Epoch Is Not Just Reflected in Pictures and Books but Also in Pots and Frying Pans': GDR Museums and Memories of Everyday Life," in N. Hodgin and C. Pearce (eds.), *The GDR Remembered*. Rochester, NY: Camden House.

———. 2013. *Mediating Memory in the Museum: Trauma, Empathy, Nostalgia*. Basingstoke: Palgrave.

Arnold-de Simine, Silke, and Susanna Radstone. 2013. "The GDR and the Memory Debate," in A. Saunders and D. Pinfold (eds.), *Remembering and Rethinking the GDR*. Basingstoke: Palgrave.

Assmann, Aleida. 2006. *Der lange Schatten der Vergangenheit. Erinnerungskultur und Geschichtspolitik*. Munich: C.H. Beck.

Assmann, Aleida, and Ute Frevert. 1999. *Geschichtsvergessenheit—Geschichtsversessenheit: Vom Umgang mit deutschen Vergangenheiten nach 1945*. Stuttgart: Deutsche Verlagsanstalt.

Auerbach, Thomas, and Wolf-Diether Sailer (eds.). 2000. *Vorbereitung auf den Tag X: Die geplanten Isolierungslager des MfS*. Berlin: BStU.

Bach, Jonathan. 2002. "'The taste remains': Consumption, (N)ostalgia, and the Production of East Germany," *Public Culture* 14(3): 545–56.

Bartmanski, Dominik. 2011. "Successful Icons of Failed Time: Re-Thinking Post-Communist Nostalgia," *Acta Sociologica* 54(3): 213–31.

Beattie, Andrew H. 2006. "The Victims of Totalitarianism and the Centrality of Nazi Genocide: Continuity and Change in German Commemorative Practices," in B. Niven (ed.), *Germans as Victims*. Basingstoke: Palgrave Macmillan.

———. 2008. *Playing Politics with History: The Bundestag Inquiries into East Germany*. New York and Oxford: Berghahn Books.

Behnke, Klaus and Jürgen Fuchs. 1995. *Zersetzung der Seele: Psychologie und Psychatrie im Dienste der Stasi*. Hamburg: Rotbuch Verlag.

Berdahl, Daphne. 1999a. "'(N)ostalgie' for the Present: Memory, Longing and East German Things," *Ethnos* 64(2): 192–211.

———. 1999b. *Where the World Ended: Re-Unification and Identity in the German Borderland*. Berkeley: University of California Press.

———. 2000. "Introduction: An Anthropology of Postsocialism," in D. Berdahl, M. Bunzl, and M. Lampland (ed.), *Altering States*. Ann Arbor: University of Michigan Press.

———. 2008. "Expressions of Experience and Experiences of Expression," *Anthropology and Humanism* 30(2): 156–70.

———. 2010a. *On the Social Life of Postsocialism: Memory, Consumption, Germany*, M. Bunzl (ed.), Bloomington: Indiana University Press.

———. 2010b. "The Spirit of Capitalism and the Boundaries of Citizenship in Post-Wall Germany," in M. Bunzl (ed.), *On the Social Life of Postsocialism*. Bloomington: Indiana University Press.

Berdahl, Daphne, Matti Bunzl, and Martha Lampland (eds.). 2000. *Altering States: Ethnographies of Transition in Eastern Europe and the Former Soviet Union*. Ann Arbor: University of Michigan Press.

Bergson, Henri. (1908) 1991. *Matter and Memory*. Trans. N.M. Paul and W.S. Palmer. New York: Zone Books.

Betts, Paul. 2000. "The Twilight of Idols: East German Memory and Material Culture," *Journal of Modern History* 72(3): 731–65.

Birth, Kevin. 2006. "The Immanent Past: Culture and Psyche at the Juncture of Memory and History," *Ethos* 34(2): 169–91.

Boll, Friedhelm. 2001. *Sprechen als Last und Befreiung: Holocaust Überlebende und politisch Verfolgte zweier Diktaturen*. Bonn: Verlag J.H.W. Dietz.

Borneman, John. 1991. *After the Wall: East Meets West in the New Berlin*. New York: Basic Books.

———. 1992. *Belonging in the Two Berlins: Kin, State and Nation*. Cambridge: Cambridge University Press.

——. 1997. *Settling Accounts: Violence, Justice, and Accountability in Postsocialist Europe.* Princeton, NJ: Princeton University Press.

Bourdieu, Pierre. 1991. *Language and Symbolic Power.* Cambridge: Cambridge University Press.

——. 1996. *On Television and Journalism.* London: Pluto Press .

Boyer, Dominic. 2005. *Spirit and System: Media, Intellectuals, and the Dialectic in Modern German Culture.* Chicago: University of Chicago Press.

——. 2006. "Ostalgie and the Politics of the Future in Eastern Germany," *Public Culture* 18: 361–81.

Boym, Svetlana. 2001. *The Future of Nostalgia.* New York: Basic Books.

BpB. n.d. "Chronik der Mauer." Retrieved September 2014 from www.bpb.de/geschichte/deutsche-einheit/deutsche-teilung-deutsche-einheit/43886/zeitleiste.

BpB. 2014. "Die soziale Situation in Deutschland: Zahlen und Fakten." Retrieved December 2014 from www.bpb.de/nachschlagen/zahlen-und-fakten/soziale-situation-in-deutschland/61718/arbeitslose-und-arbeitslosenquote.

Bruner, Jerome. 1987. "Life as Narrative," *Social Research* 54(1): 11–32.

——. 1990. *Acts of Meaning.* Cambridge, MA: Harvard University Press.

——. 1991. "The Narrative Construction of Reality," *Critical Inquiry* 18: 1–21.

——. 1994. "The 'Remembered' Self," in U. Neisser and R. Fivush (eds.), *The Remembering Self.* Cambridge: Cambridge University Press.

——. 2002. *Making Stories: Law, Literature, Life.* Cambridge, MA: Harvard University Press.

Brussig, Thomas. 1991. *Wasserfarben.* Berlin: Aufbau Verlag.

BStU. 2014. "Debate um IM-Zahlen." Retrieved September 2014 from www.bstu.bund.de/DE/BundesbeauftragterUndBehoerde/Aktuelles/20140623_im-zahlen_inoffizielle-mitarbeiter_forschung.html.

Buchowski, Michal. 1997. *Reluctant Capitalists: An Anthropological Study of a Rural Community in Western Poland.* Berlin: Centre Marc Bloch.

——. 2004. "Hierarchies of Knowledge in Central-Eastern European Anthropology," *The Anthropology of East Europe Review* 22(2): 5–14.

——. 2006. "The Specter of Orientalism in Europe: From Exotic Other to Stigmatized Brother," *Anthropological Quarterly* 79(3): 463–82.

Burawoy, Michael, and János Lukács. 1992. *The Radiant Past: Ideology and Reality in Hungary's Road to Capitalism.* Chicago: University of Chicago Press.

Burke, Kenneth. (1950) 1969. *A Rhetoric of Motives.* Berkeley: University of California Press.

——. 1973. *The Philosophy of Literary Form.* Berkeley: University of California Press.

Carrithers, Michael. 2005a. "Anthropology as a Moral Science of Possibilities," *Current Anthropology* 46(3): 433–46.

——. 2005b. "Why Anthropologists Should Study Rhetoric," *Journal of the Royal Anthropological Institute* 11(3): 577–83.

——. 2006. "'Witnessing a shipwreck' German figurations in facing the past to face the future," *Revista de antropología social* 15: 193–230.

——— (ed.). 2012a. *Culture, Rhetoric and the Vicissitudes of Life.* New York and Oxford: Berghahn Books.

——. 2012b. "Introduction," in M. Carrithers (ed.), *Culture, Rhetoric and the Vicissitudes of Life.* New York and Oxford: Berghahn Books.

——. 2012c. "Story-Seeds and the Inchoate," in M. Carrithers (ed.), *Culture, Rhetoric and the Vicissitudes of Life.* New York and Oxford: Berghahn Books.

Childs, David. 2001. *The Fall of the GDR: Germany's Road to Unity*. London: Longman.

Christoph, Klaus. 2013. "'Aufarbeitung der SED-Diktatur'—heute so wie gestern?—Essay," *Aus Politik und Zeitgeschichte* 42–43/2013.

Climo, Jacob J., and Maria G. Cattell (eds.). 2002. *Social Memory and History: Anthropological Perspectives*. Walnut Creek, CA: AltaMira Press.

Cohen, Anthony. 2001. *States of Denial: Knowing About Atrocities and Suffering*. Cambridge: Blackwell.

Collins, Peter. 1998. "Negotiating Lives: Reflections on 'Unstructured Interviewing,'" *Sociological Research Online* 3(3). Retrieved April 2014 from www.socresonline.org.uk/3/3/2.html.

———. 2002. "Both Independent and Interconnected Voices: Bakhtin Among the Quakers," in N. Rapport (ed.), *British Subjects*. Oxford: Berg.

———. 2003. "Storying Self and Others: The Construction of Narrative Identity," *Journal of Politics and Language* 2(2): 243–65.

———. 2010. "The Ethnographic Self as Resource?" in P. Collins and A. Gallinat (eds.), *The Ethnographic Self as Resource*. New York and Oxford: Berghahn Books.

Collins, Peter, and Anselma Gallinat. 2010. *The Ethnographic Self as Resource: Writing Experience and Memory into Ethnography*. New York and Oxford: Berghahn Books.

Comaroff, John L., and Jean Comaroff. 1997. "Postcolonial Politics and Discourses of Democracy in Southern Africa: Anthropological Reflections on African Modernities," *Journal of Anthropological Research* 53(2): 123–46.

Connerton, Paul. 1989. *How Societies Remember*. Cambridge: Cambridge University Press.

Cooke, Paul. 2005. *Representing East Germany since Unification*. Oxford: Berg.

Creed, Gerald W. 1998. *Domesticating Revolution: From Socialist Reform to Ambivalent Transition in a Bulgarian Village*. University Park: Pennsylvania State University Press.

Crocker, J. Christopher. 1977. "The Social Functions of Rhetorical Forms," in J.C. Crocker and J.D. Sapir (eds.), *The Social Use of Metaphor: Essays on the Anthropology of Rhetoric*. Philadelphia: University of Pennsylvania Press

D'Andrade, Roy G. 1992a. "Schemas and Motivation," in R.G. D'Andrade and C. Strauss (eds.), *Human Motives and Cultural Models*. Cambridge: Cambridge University Press.

———. 1992b. "Cognitive Anthropology," in T. Schwartz, G.M. White, and C.A. Lutz (eds.), *New Directions in Psychological Anthropology*. Cambridge: University of Cambridge Press.

———. 1995. *The Development of Cognitive Anthropology*. Cambridge: Cambridge University Press.

de Burgh, Hugo. 2005. *Making Journalists: Diverse Models, Global Issues*. London: Routledge.

Deutscher Bundestag. 1999. "Unterrichtung der Bundesregierung: Konzeption der künftigen Gedenkstättenförderung des Bundes und Bericht der Bundesregierung über die Beteiligung des Bundes an Gedenkstätten in der Bundesrepublik Deutschland," Drucksache 14/1569.

———. 2008. "Fortschreibung der Gedenkstättenkonzeption des Bundes: Verantwortung wahrnehmen, Aufarbeitung verstärken, Gedenken vertiefen," Ducksache 16/9875.

———. 2013a. "Bericht der Bundesregierung zum Stand der Aufarbeitung der SED-Diktatur," Drucksache 17/13698.

———. 2013b. "Deutscher Bundestag, Stenografischer Bericht 232. Sitzung," Plenarprotokoll 17/232.

Deutz-Schroeder, Monica, and Klaus Schroeder. 2008. *Soziales Paradies oder Stasi-Staat? Das DDR-Bild von Schülern—ein Ost-West-Vergleich*. Stamsried: Verlag Ernst Vögel.

Dietzsch, Ina. 2005. "Die Erfindung der Ostdeutschen," in E. Schäfer et al. (eds.), *Irritation Ostdeutschland*. Münster: Westfälisches Dampfboot.

———. 2014. "The Everyday Life of Publics: An Ethnographic Study," Habil. thesis. Basel: University of Basel.

Douglas, Mary. 1966. *Purity and Danger: An Analysis of Concepts of Pollution and Taboo*. New York: Routledge.

Dunn, Elizabeth C. 2004. *Privatising Poland: Baby Food, Big Business, and the Remaking of Labor*. Ithaca, NY: Cornell University Press.

Dunn, Elizabeth C., and Katherine Verdery. 2011. "Dead Ends in the Critique of (Post) Socialist Anthropology: Reply to Thelen," *Critique of Anthropology* 31(3): 251–55.

Einigungsvertrag. 1990. "Vertrag zwischen der Deutschen Demokratischen Republik und der Bundesrepublik Deutschland über die Herstellung der Einheit Deutschlands (Einigungsvertrag)," 31 August, BGBl. 1990 II. Retrieved December 2014 from www.gesetze-im-internet.de/einigvtr/BJNR208890990.html.

Eisenfeld, Bernd, and Peter Schicketanz. 2011. *Bausoldaten in der DDR: Die "Zusammenführung feindlich-negativer Kräfte" in der NVA*. Berlin: Christoph Links Verlag.

Erpenbeck, John, and Johannes Weinberg. 1993. *Menschenbild und Menschenbildung: Bildungstheoretische Konsequenzen der unterschiedlichen Menschenbilder in der ehemaligen DDR und in der Bundesrepublik*. Münster: Waxmann Verlag.

"European Conscience and Totalitarianism." 2009. European Parliament resolution of 2 April 2009, P6_TA(2009)0213. Retrieved November 2015 from www.europarl.europa.eu/sides/getDoc.do?pubRef=-//EP//TEXT+TA+P6-TA-2009-0213+0+DOC+XML+V0//EN&language=EN.

Evans, Richard J. 2005. "Zwei deutsche Diktaturen im 20. Jahrhundert? Essay," *Aus Politik und Zeitgeschichte* 01–02/2005.

Fairclough, Norman. 1995. *Media Discourse*. London: Arnold.

Falser, Michael. 2008. "1945–1949: Die 'Stunde Null,' die Schuldfrage, der 'Deutsche Geist'; und der Wiederaufbau in Frankfurt am Main," in M. Falser (ed.) *Zwischen Identität und Authentizität: Zur politischen Geschichte der Denkmalpflege in Deutschland*. Dresden: Thelem Verlag.

Faulenbach, Bernd. 1993. "Probleme des Umgangs mit der Vergangenheit im vereinten Deutschland: Zur Gegenwartsbedeutung der jüngsten Geschichte," in W. Weidenfeld (ed.), *Deutschland: Eine Nation—doppelte Geschichte*. Köln: Verlag Wissenschaft und Politik .

———. 1999. "Geteilte Vergangenheit—eine Geschichte? Eine Bestandsaufnahme," in C. Kleßmann, H. Misselwitz, and G. Wichert (eds.), *Deutsche Vergangenheiten—eine gemeinsame Herausforderung*. Berlin: Christoph Links Verlag.

Fernandez, James W. 1986. *Persuasions and Performances: The Play of Tropes in Culture*. Bloomington: Indiana University Press.

——— (ed.). 1991. *Beyond Metaphor: The Theory of Tropes in Anthropology*. Stanford, CA: Stanford University Press.

———. 2012. "Rhetoric in the Moral Order: A Critique of Tropological Approaches to Culture," in M. Carrithers (ed.), *Culture, Rhetoric and the Vicissitudes of Life*. New York and Oxford: Berghahn Books.

Fessen, Bertold. 1995. "Ressentiment und Fehlwahrnehmung: Deutsche Mühen mit der Vereinigung," *Berliner Debatte INITIAL* 4/5: 132–44.

Flohr, Markus, and Peter Wensierski. 2007. "Honecker's paradiesische Diktatur," *Spiegel Online*, 9 November, Retrieved January 2015 from www.spiegel.de/schulspiegel/wissen/grosse-schueler-studie-honeckers-paradiesische-diktatur-a-516534.html.

Foucault, Michel. 1977. *Discipline and Punish: The Birth of the Prison*. London: Allen Lane.
———. 1981. *The History of Sexuality*. London: Penguin Books.
———. 1991. "Governmentality (Security, Territory and Population)," in G. Burchell, C. Gordon, and P. Miller (eds.), *The Foucault Effect*. Chicago: University of Chicago Press.
———. 2010. *The Government of Self and Others: Lectures at the Collège de France*, F. Gros (ed.), Basingstoke: Palgrave Macmillan.
Francois, Etienne, and Hagen Schulze. 2001. *Deutsche Erinnerungsorte*. Munich: C.H. Beck.
Franke, Caroline. 2007. "Was wissen junge Leute heute über die DDR? 'Bonn war die Hauptstadt und Hitler war der Boss,'" *Die Bild*, 20 August. Retrieved December 2014 from www.bild.de/news/2007/wissen-vergangenheit-2319976.bild.html.
Franklin, Sarah. 1990. "Deconstructing 'Desperateness': The Social Construction of Infertility in Popular Representations of New Reproductive Technologies," in M. McNeil, I. Varcoe, and S. Yearley (eds.), *Popular Representations of New Reproductive Technologies*. London: Macmillan.
Frei, Norbert. 2003. *Vergangenheitspolitik: Die Anfänge der Bundesrepublik and die NS-Vergangenheit*. Munich: Deutscher Taschenbuchverlag.
Friedland, Lewis. 2003. *Public Journalism: Past and Future*. Dayton, OH: Kettering Foundation Press.
Friedrich, Carl, and Zbigniew Brzezinski. 1966. *Totalitarian Dictatorship and Autocracy*. New York: Praeger.
Fulbrook, Mary. 1997. "Reckoning with the Past: Heroes, Victims and Villains in the History of the German Democratic Republic," in R. Alter and P. Monteath (eds.), *Rewriting the German Past*. Atlantic Highlands, NJ: Humanities Press.
———. 1999. *German National Identity after the Holocaust*. Cambridge: Polity Press.
———. 2005. *The People's State: East German Society from Hitler to Honecker*. New Haven, CT: Yale University Press.
———. 2007. "Historiografische Kontroversen seit 1990," in P. Barker, M-D Ohse, and D. Tate (eds.), *Views from Abroad*. Bielefeld: W. Berthelsmann.
Gallinat, Anselma. 2002. "Negotiating Culture and Belonging in Eastern Germany: The Case of the *Jugendweihe*: A Secular Coming-of-Age Ritual," PhD thesis. Durham: Durham University.
———. 2005. "The Ritual Middle Ground? Personhood, Ideology and Resistance in East Germany," *Social Anthropology* 13(3): 291–305.
———. 2006a. "Difficult Stories: Public Discourse and Narrative Identity in Eastern Germany," *Ethnos* 71(3): 343–66.
———. 2006b. "Menacing buildings . . .": Former Political Prisons and Prisoners in Eastern Germany, *Anthropology Today* 22(2): 19–20.
———. 2008. "Being 'East German' or Being 'at Home in Eastern Germany'? Identity as Experience and as Rhetoric," *Identities: Global Studies in Culture and Power* 15(6): 665–86.
———. 2009a. "Intense Paradoxes of Memory: Researching Moral Questions about Remembering the Socialist Past," *History and Anthropology* 20(2): 183–99.
———. 2009b. "'Victims' of the GDR Talk and Argue about the Past," in J. Obertreis (ed.), *Oral History in Postsocialism*. Essen: Klartext Verlag .
———. 2010a. "Playing the Native Card: The Anthropologist as Informant in Eastern Germany," in P. Collins and A. Gallinat (eds.), *The Ethnographic Self as Resource*. New York and Oxford: Berghahn Books.
———. 2010b. "Controlling Creativity and Creating Professionals? Mind 'the Line' at a Newspaper Editorial Office," *Intergraph: Journal of Dialogic Anthropology* 3(1). Retrieved December 2014 from www.intergraph-journal.net/enhanced/home.htm.

————. 2011. "The Rush to (East) German History: Recognising Memory and Belonging," in J. McLaughlin, D. Richardson, and P. Phillimore (eds.), *Contesting Recognition*. Basingstoke: Palgrave.

————. 2012. "Memory Matters and Contexts: Remembering for Past, Present and Future," in A. Saunders and D. Pinfold (eds.), *Remembering and Rethinking the GDR*. Basingstoke: Palgrave.

Gallinat, Anselma, and Sabine Kittel. 2009. "Zum Umgang mit der DDR-Vergangenheit: Einige anthropologische Überlegungen," in T. Großbölting (ed.), *Friedensstaat, Leseland, Sportnation?* Berlin: Christoph Links Verlag.

Galtung, Johan, and Mari Holmboe Ruge. 1965. "The Structure of Foreign News: The Presentation of the Congo, Cuba and Cyprus Crises in Four Norwegian Newspapers," *Journal of Peace Research* 2: 64–91.

Garforth, Lisa. 2012. "In/Visibilities of Research: Seeing and Knowing in STS," *Science, Technology and Human Values* 37(2): 264–85.

Gauck, Joachim. 1994. "Dealing with a Stasi Past," *Daedalus* 123(1): 277–84.

Gauss, Günter. 1983. *Wo Deutschland liegt. Eine Ortsbestimmung*. Hamburg: Hoffmann und Campe.

Geertz, Clifford. 2001. *Available Light: Anthropological Reflections on Philosophical Topics*. Princeton, NJ: Princeton University Press.

Giordano, Ralph. 1987. *Die zweite Schuld, oder Von der Last Deutscher zu sein*. Hamburg: Rasch und Röhring.

Glaeser, Andreas. 2000. *Divided in Unity: Identity, Germany and the Berlin Police*. Chicago: University of Chicago Press.

Gordon, Colin. 1991. "Governmental Rationality: An Introduction," in G. Burchell et al. (eds.), *The Foucault Effect*. Chicago: University of Chicago Press.

Großbölting, Thomas (ed.). 2009. *Friedensstaat, Leseland, Sportnation? DDR-Legenden auf dem Prüfstand*. Berlin: Christoph Links Verlag.

————. 2013. "Geschichtskonstruktion zwischen Wissenschaft und Populärkultur—Essay," *Aus Politik und Zeitgeschichte* 42–43/2013.

Gupta, Akhil, and James Ferguson. 1997. "Culture, Power, Place: Ethnography at the End of an Era," in. A. Gupta and J. Ferguson (eds.), *Culture, Power, Place*. Durham, NC: Duke University Press.

Habermas, Jürgen. 2010. "Keine Demokratie kann sich das leisten," *Süddeutsche*, 19 May. Retrieved November 2014 from www.sueddeutsche.de/kultur/juergen-habermas-keine-demokratie-kann-sich-das-leisten-1.892340.

Halverson, Erica. 2008. "From One Woman to Everyman: Reportability and Credibility in Publicly Performed Narratives," *Narrative Inquiry* 18(1): 29–52.

Hahn, H.J. 1995. *German Thought and Culture: From the Holy Empire to the Present Day*. Manchester: Manchester University Press.

Hann, Chris. 2012. "Transition, Tradition, and Nostalgia: Postsocialist Transformations in a Comparative Framework," *Collegium Antropologicum* 36(4): 1119–28.

Hann, Chris, Caroline Humphrey, and Katherine Verdery. 2002. "Introduction: Postsocialism as a Topic of Anthropological Investigation," in C. Hann (ed.), *Postsocialism*. London: Routledge.

Hannerz, Ulf. 2004. *Foreign News: Exploring the World of Foreign Correspondents*. Chicago: University of Chicago Press.

Hastings, Donnan, and Graham McFarlane. 1997. "Anthropology and Policy Research: The View from Northern Ireland," in C. Shore and S. Wright (eds.), *Anthropology of Policy*. London: Routledge.

Haukanes, Haldis, and Susanna Trnka (eds.) 2013. "Recasting Pasts and Futures in Post-socialist Europe," *Focaal* 66.

Havel, Vaclav. 1985. "The Power of the Powerless," in J. Kean (ed.), *The Power of the Power-less*. Armonk, NY: M.E. Sharp.

Herzfeld, Michael. 1992. *The Social Production of Indifference: Exploring the Symbolic Routes of Western Bureaucracy*. Oxford: Berg.

———. 2005. *Cultural Intimacy: Social Poetics in the Nation-State*. London: Routledge.

Hirsch, Eric, and Charles Stewart. 2005. "Introduction: Ethnographies of Historicity," *History and Anthropology* 16(3): 261–74.

Hoëm, Ingjerd. 2005. "Stealing the Water of Life: The Historicity of Contemporary Social Relationships," *History and Anthropology* 16(3): 293–305.

Holstein, Jaber F., and James Gubrium. 2000. *The Self We Live by: Narrative Identity in a Postmodern World*. Oxford: Oxford University Press.

——— (eds.). 2001. *Institutional Selves: Troubled Identities in a Postmodern World*. Oxford: Oxford University Press.

Holston, James, and Arjun Appadurai. 1996. "Cities and Citizenship," *Public Culture* 8(2): 187–204.

Holtmann, Everhardt. 2010. "Die DDR—ein Unrechtsstaat? Bundeszentrale für Politische Bildung." Retrieved September 2014 from www.bpb.de/geschichte/deutsche-einheit/lange-wege-der-deutschen-einheit/47560/unrechtsstaat?p=all.

Howard, Marc Allan. 1995. "Die Deutschen als Ethnische Gruppe? Zum Verständnis der neuen Teilung des geeinten Deutschlands," *Berliner Debatte INITIAL* 4/5, 119–131.

Hüppauf, Bernd. 1981. "Einleitung," in B. Hüppauf (ed.) *"Die Mühen der Ebenen": Kontinuität und Wandel in der deutschen Literatur und Gesellschaft 1945–1949*. Heidelberg: Winter.

Hughes, Everett C. 1984. *The Sociological Eye*. New Brunswick, NJ: Transaction Books.

Humphrey, Caroline. 2002. "Creating a Culture of Disillusionment: Consumption in Moscow 1993, a Chronicle of Changing Times," in *The Unmaking of Soviet Life*. Ithaca, NY: Cornell University Press.

Huyssen, Andreas. 1995. *Twilight Memories: Marking Time in a Culture of Amnesia*. New York: Routledge.

———. 2003. *Present Pasts: Urban Palimpsests and the Politics of Memory*. Stanford, CA: Stanford University Press.

Hyland, Claire. 2013. "'Ostalgie Doesn't Fit!': Individual Interpretations of and Interactions with Ostalgie," in A. Saunders and D. Pinfold (eds.), *Remembering and Rethinking the GDR*. Basingstoke: Palgrave Macmillan.

Inda, Jonathan X. (ed.). 2007. *Anthropologies of Modernity: Foucault, Governmentality and Life Politics*. Oxford: Blackwell.

Jackson, Michael. 2002. *The Politics of Storytelling: Violence, Transgression, and Intersubjectivity*. Copenhagen: Museum Tusculanum Press.

Jarausch, Konrad H. 1988. "Removing the Nazi Stain? The Quarrel of the German Historians," *German Studies Review* 11(2): 285–301.

———. 1994. *The Rush to German Unity*. Oxford: Oxford University Press.

——— (ed.). 1997. *After Unity: Reconfiguring German Identities*. New York and Oxford: Berghahn Books.

———. 1999. *Dictatorship as Experience: Towards a Socio-Cultural History of the GDR*. New York and Oxford: Berghahn Books .

Jarausch, Konrad H., Hinrich C. Seeba, and David P. Conradt. 1997. "The Presence of the Past: Culture, Opinion and Identity in Germany," in K.H. Jarausch (ed.), *After Unity*. New York and Oxford: Berghahn Books.

Jones, Sara. 2014. *The Media of Testimony: Remembering the East German Stasi in the Berlin Republic.* Basingstoke: Palgrave Macmillan.

———. 2015. "(Extra)Ordinary Life: The Rhetoric of Representing the Socialist Everyday After Unification," *German Politics and Society* 33(1–2): 119–34.

Judt, Matthias. 1997. *DDR: Geschichte in Dokumenten. Beschlüsse, Berichte, interne Materialien und Alltagszeugnisse.* Berlin: Christoph Links Verlag.

Junghans, Trenholme. 2001. "Marketing Selves: Constructing Civil Society and Selfhood in Post-Socialist Hungary," *Critique of Anthropology* 21(4): 383–400.

Kalb, Don. 2002. "Afterword: Globalism and Post-Socialist Prospects," in C.M. Hann (ed.), *Postsocialism.* London: Routledge.

Kaneff, Deema. 2004. *Who Owns the Past? The Politics of Time in a "Model" Bulgarian Village.* New York and Oxford: Berghahn Books.

Keightley, Emily, and Michael Pickering. 2006. "The Modalities of Nostalgia," *Current Sociology* 54(6): 919–41.

Kideckel, David A. 2008. *Getting by in Postsocialist Romania: Labor, the Body, and Working-Class Culture.* Bloomington: Indiana University Press.

Kitch, Carolyne. 2008. "Placing Journalism Inside Memory—and Memory Studies," *Memory Studies* 1(3): 311–20.

Kittel, Sabine. 2006. *"Places for the Displaced": Biographische Bewältigungsmuster von weiblichen jüdischen Konzentrationslager-Überlebenden in den USA.* Hildesheim: Georg Holmes Verlag.

Klein, Olaf G. 2001. *Ihr könnt uns einfach nicht verstehen: Warum Ost- und Westdeutsche aneinander vorbeireden.* Frankfurt: Eichborn Verlag.

Kleine, Lisa. 2013. "Kanzlerin Merkel und ihr Leben in der DDR," *Focus Online* 13 May. Retrieved November 2014 from www.focus.de/wissen/mensch/geschichte/tid-31168/kanzlerin-merkel-und-ihr-leben-in-der-ddr-fdj-fdgb-und-dsf-wie-die-ddr-die-massen-organisierte_aid_988138.html.

Kleßmann, Christoph. 1988. *Zwei Staaten, eine Nation: Deutsche Geschichte 1955–1970.* Bonn: Bundeszentrale für Politische Bildung.

Klumbyte, Neringa. 2009. "Post-Socialist Sensations: Nostalgia, the Self, and Alterity in Lithuania," *Lietuvos Etnologija* 9(18): 93–116.

———. 2010. "Memory, Identity and Citizenship in Lithuania," *Journal of Baltic Studies* 41(3): 295–313.

Koch, Thomas. 1996. "The Renaissance of East German Group Awareness since Unification," in M. Gerber and R. Woods (eds.), *Changing Identities in Eastern Germany.* Lanham, MD: University Press of America.

Kocka, Jürgen. 1982. "Der 'deutsche Sonderweg' in der Diskussion," *German Studies Review* 5(3): 365–79.

———. 1994. "Ein deutscher Sonderweg: Überlegungen zur Sozialgeschichte der DDR," *Aus Politik und Zeitgeschichte* 40/1994.

Kornai, János. 1980. *Economics of Shortage.* Amsterdam: North-Holland.

Kühnl, Reinhard. 1997. "The German Sonderweg Reconsidered: Continuities and Discontinuities in German History," in R. Alter and P. Monteath (eds.), *Rewriting the German Past.* Atlantic Highlands, NJ: Humanities Press.

Kürti, Laszlo. 1996. "Homecoming: Affairs of Anthropology in and of Eastern Europe," *Anthropology Today* 12(3): 11–15.

———. 2000. "Uncertain Anthropology: Ethnography of Postsocialist Eastern Europe," *Ethnos* 65(3): 405–20.

Labov, William, and Joshua Waletzki. 1967. "Narrative Analysis: Oral Versions of Personal Experience," in J. Helms (ed.), *Essays on the Verbal and Visual Arts*. Seattle: University of Washington Press.

Lampland, Martha. 2000. "Afterword," in D. Berdahl, M. Bunzl, and M. Lampland (eds.), *Altering States*. Ann Arbor: University of Michigan Press.

Lawler, Stephanie. 2008. *Identity: Sociological Perspectives*. Cambridge: Polity Press.

Linde, Charlotte. 1993. *Life Stories: The Creation of Coherence*. Oxford: Oxford University Press.

———. 2000. "The Acquisition of a Speaker by a Story: How History Becomes Memory and Identity," *Ethos* 28(4): 608–32.

Longerich, Peter. 2001. *Hitler und der Weg zur "Endlösung."* Munich: Piper.

Luedtke, Alf. 1993. *Eigen-Sinn: Fabrikalltag, Arbeitererfahrungen und Politik vom Kaiserreich bis in den Faschismus*. Hamburg: Ergebnisse Verlag.

———. 1994. "'Helden der Arbeit'—Mühe beim Arbeiten: Zur mißmutigen Loyalitat von Industriearbeitern in der DDR," in H. Kaelble, J. Kocka, and H. Zwahr (eds.), *Sozialgeschichte der DDR*. Stuttgart: Klett-Cotta.

MacIntyre, Alasdair. 1981. *After Virtue*. Notre Dame, IN: University of Notre Dame Press.

Margalit, Avishai. 2002. *The Ethics of Memory*. Cambridge, MA: Harvard University Press.

Martin, Marko. 2013. "Wieviel DDR steckt noch in diesen Politikerinnen?" *Die Welt*, 28 May. Retrieved November 2014 from www.welt.de/debatte/article116591422/Wieviel-DDR-steckt-noch-in-diesen-Politikerinnen.html.

Marshall, T.H. 1992. "Citizenship and Social Class," in T.H. Marshall and T. Bottomore (eds.), *Citizenship and Social Class*. London: Pluto Press.

McAdams, James A. 2001. *Judging the Past in Unified Germany*. Cambridge: Cambridge University Press.

McNair, Brian. 2005. "What Is Journalism?" in H. de Burgh (ed.), *Making Journalists*. London: Routledge.

Meyn, Hermann. 1996. *Massenmedien in der Bundesrepublik Deutschland*. Berlin: Landeszentrale für politische Bildungsarbeit Berlin.

Millar, James R., and Sharon L. Wolchik. 1994. "Introduction: The Social Legacies and the Aftermath of Communism," in J.R. Millar and S.L. Wolchik (eds.), *The Social Legacy of Communism*. New York: Woodrow Wilson Centre Press.

Miller, Barbara. 1998. *Narratives of Guilt and Compliance in Unified Germany: Stasi Informers and their Impact on Society*. London: Routledge.

Miller, Peter, and Nicolas Rose. 1990. "Governing Economic Life," *Economy and Society* 19(1): 1–31.

Mironenko, Sergej, Lutz Niethammer, and Alexander von Plato (eds.). 1998. *Sowjetische Straflager in Deutschland 1945–1950*. Berlin: Akademie Verlag.

Mishler, Elliot. 2006. "Narrative and Identity: The Double-Arrow of Time," in A. de Fina, D. Schiffrin, and M. Bamberg (eds.), *Discourse and Identity*. Cambridge: Cambridge University Press.

Mitscherlich, Alexander, and Margarete Mitscherlich. 1967. *Die Unfähigkeit zu trauern: Grundlagen kollektiven Verhaltens*. Munich: Piper.

Moeller, Robert G. 2006. "The Politics of the Past in the 1950s: Rhetorics of Victimisation in East and West Germany," in B. Niven (ed.), *Germans as Victims*. Basingstoke: Palgrave Macmillan.

Monteath, Peter. 2004. "The German Democratic Republic and the Jews," *German History* 22(3): 448–68.

Mueller, Gabriele. 2013. "Re-Imaging the Niche: Visual Reconstructions of Private Spaces in the GDR," in A. Saunders and D. Pinfold (eds.), *Remembering and Rethinking the GDR*. Basingstoke: Palgrave Macmillan.

Müller, Jan-Werner. 2001. "East Germany: Incorporation, Tainted Truth, and the Double-Division," in A. B. De Brito, C. González-Enríquez and P. Aguilar (eds.), *The Politics of Memory*. Oxford: Oxford University Press.

Narayan, Kirin. 1993. "How Native Is a Native Anthropologist?" *American Anthropologist* 95(3): 671–86.

Neisser, Ulric. 1994. "Self-Narratives: True and False," in U. Neisser and R. Fivush (eds.), *The Remembering Self*. Cambridge: Cambridge University Press.

Neisser, Ulric, and Robyn Fivush (eds.). 1994. *The Remembering Self: Construction and Accuracy in Self-Narrative*. Cambridge: Cambridge University Press.

Niven, Bill. 2002. *Facing the Nazi-Past: United Germany and the Legacy of the Third Reich*. London: Routledge.

——— (ed.) 2006a. *Germans as Victims*. Basingstoke: Palgrave Macmillan.

———. 2006b. "Introduction; German Victimhood at the Turn of the Millennium," in B. Niven (ed.), *Germans as Victims*. Basingstoke: Palgrave Macmillan.

Nothnagle, Allan. 1999. *Building the East German Myth: Historical Mythology and Youth Propaganda in the German Democratic Republic, 1945–1989*. Ann Arbor: University of Michigan Press.

Nünning, Ansgar, and Astrid Erll. 2006. "Concepts and Methods for the Study of Literature and/as Cultural Memory," in A. Nünning, M. Gymnich, and R. Sommer (eds.), *Literature and Memory*. Tübingen: Francke.

Ochs, Elinor, and Lisa Capps. 1997. "Narrative Authenticity," *Journal of Narrative and Life-History* 7(1–4): 83–89.

———. 2001. *Living Narrative: Creating Lives in Everyday Storytelling*. Cambridge, MA: Harvard University Press.

Ochs, Elinor, Ruth Smith, and Carolyn Taylor. 1989. "Detective Stories at Dinnertime: Problem-Solving through Co-narration," *Cultural Dynamics* 2: 238–57.

Olick, Jeffrey K., and Joyce Robbins. 1998. "Social Memory Studies: From 'Collective Memory' to the Historical Sociology of Mnemonic Practices," *Annual Review of Sociology* 24: 105–40.

Oliveira, Miguel. 1999. "The Function of Self-Aggrandizement in Storytelling," *Narrative Inquiry* 9(1): 25–47.

Paley, Julia. 2001. *Marketing Democracy: Power and Social Movements in Post-dictatorship Chile*. Berkeley: University of California Press.

Palmowski, Jan. 2009. *Inventing a Socialist Nation: Heimat and the Politics of Everyday Life in the GDR, 1945–90*. Cambridge: Cambridge University Press.

Pearce, Caroline. 2011. "An Unequal Balance? Memorializing Germany's 'Double Past' since 1990," in N. Hodgin and C. Pearce (eds.), *The GDR Remembered*. Rochester, NY: Camden House.

Pine, Frances, Deema Kaneff, and Haldis Haukanes. 2004. *Memory, Politics and Religion: The Past Meets the Present in Europe*. Münster: Lit Verlag.

Poole, Ross. 2008. "Memory, History and the Claims of the Past," *Memory Studies* 1(2): 149–66.

Quint, Peter E. 2000. "The Border Guard Trials and the East German Past—Seven Arguments," *The American Journal of Comparative Law* 48(4): 541–72.

Rapport, Nigel. 1987. *Talking Violence: An Anthropological Interpretation of Conversation in the City*. St. John's, NL: ISER Books.

Rapport, Nigel. 1993. *Diverse World Views in an English Village*. Edinburgh: Edinburgh University Press.

Rausing, Sigrid. 2004. *History, Memory and Identity in Post-Soviet Estonia: The End of a Collective Farm*. Oxford: Oxford University Press.

Reed, Edward S. 1994. "Perception Is to Self as Memory Is to Selves," in U. Neisser and R. Fivush (eds.), *The Remembering Self*. Cambridge: Cambridge University Press.

Reichel, Peter. 2007. *Vergangenheitsbewältigung in Deutschland: Die Auseinandersetzung mit der NS-Diktatur von 1945 bis heute*. Munich: C.H. Beck.

Rethmann, Petra. 2009. "Post-Communist Ironies in an East German Hotel," *Anthropology Today* 25(1): 21–23.

Richardson, John E. 2007. *Analysing Newspapers: An Approach from Critical Discourse Analysis*. Basingstoke: Palgrave Macmillan.

Richardson, Tanya. 2008. *Kaleidoscopic Odessa: History and Place in Contemporary Ukraine*. Toronto: University of Toronto Press.

Roellecke, Gerd. 2009. "War die DDR ein Unrechtsstaat?" *Frankfurther Allgemeine Zeitung*, 15 June. Retrieved September 2014 from www.faz.net/aktuell/feuilleton/debatten/zeitgeschichte-war-die-ddr-ein-unrechtsstaat-1813196.html.

Rose, Nicolas, and Peter Miller. 1992. "Political Power Beyond the State: Problematics of Government," *The British Journal of Sociology* 43(2): 173–205.

Rosenthal, G. 2004. "Biographical Research," in C. Seale, G. Gobo, and D. Silvermann (eds.), *Qualitative Research Practice*. London: Sage.

Ross, Corey. 2002. *The East German Dictatorship: Problems and Perspectives in the Interpretation of the GDR*. London: Arnold.

Rumsey, Alan. 2012. "Rhetoric, Truth and the Work of Trope," in I. Strecker and S. Tyler (eds.), *Culture and Rhetoric*. New York and Oxford: Berghahn Books.

Sabrow, Martin. 2007. "Historisierung der Zweistaatlichkeit," *Aus Politik und Zeitgeschichte* 3/2007.

———. 2009. "Wende oder Revolution? Keinesfalls nur eine scholastische Frage: Der Herbstumbruch vor 20 Jahren im deutschen Geschichtsbewusstsein," *Neues Deutschland* 21/22.

———. 2010. "Der vergessene dritte Weg," *Aus Politik und Zeitgeschichte* 11/2010.

Sabrow, Martin et al. 2007. *Wohin treibt die DDR Erinnerung? Dokumentation einer Debatte*. Bonn: Bundeszentrale für Politische Bildung.

Said, Edward. 1988. "Michel Foucault 1926–1984," in J. Arac (ed.), *After Foucault*. New Brunswick, NJ: Rutgers University Press.

Saunders, Anna, and Debbie Pinfold. 2013. *Remembering and Rethinking the GDR: Multiple Perspectives and Plural Authenticities*. Basingstoke: Palgrave Macmillan.

Schiffrin, Deborah. 1984. "How a Story Says What It Means and Does," *Text* 4(4): 313–46.

Schmidtchen, Gerhard. 1997. *Wie weit ist der Weg nach Deutschland? Sozialpsychologie der Jugend in der postsozialistischen Welt*. Opladen: Leske + Budrich.

Schönball, Ralf. 2016. "Einheitswippe wird nicht errichtet," *Der Tagesspiegel* 12 April, retrieved June 2016 from http://www.tagesspiegel.de/berlin/denkmal-in-berlin-einheitswippe-wird-nicht-errichtet/13438360.html.

Schröter, Eckhard. 1994. "When Cultures Collide: The Case of Administrators from East and West Berlin," in M. Gerber and R. Woods (eds.), *Understanding the Past, Managing the Future*. Lanham, MD: University Press of America.

Schubert, Klaus, and Martina Klein. 2011. *Das Politiklexikon*, 5th edn. Bonn: Dietz Verlag.

Schütz, Alfred. 1962. *Collected Papers 1: The Problem of Social Reality*. The Hague: Martinus Nijhoff.

Schwartz, Barry. 1991. "Social Change and Collective Memory: The Democratization of George Washington," *American Sociological Review* 56(2): 221–36.

Shoshan, Nitzan. 2012. "Time at a Standstill: Loss, Accumulation, and the Past Conditional in an East Berlin Neighborhood," *Ethnos* 77(1): 24–49.

Simon, Annette. 2014. "1989: Wende? Revolution!" *Zeit Online*, 23 October. Retrieved December 2015 from www.zeit.de/2014/44/1989-wende-revolution.

Skultans, Vieda. 1998. *The Testimony of Lives: Narrative and Memory in Post-Soviet Latvia.* London: Routledge.

———. 2001. "Arguing with the KGB Archives: Archival and Narrative Memory in Post-Soviet Latvia," *Ethnos* 66(3): 320–43.

Smith, Jennifer. 2006. "Narrative in Sociolinguistic Research," in E.K. Brown, R.E. Asher, and J. Simpson (eds.), *The Encyclopedia of Language and Linguistics.* Amsterdam: Elsevier.

Spencer, Jonathan. 2007. *Anthropology, Politics and the State: Democracy and Violence in South East Asia.* Cambridge: Cambridge University Press.

Steenbergen, Bart van (ed.). 1994. *The Condition of Citizenship.* London: Sage.

Steinbach, Peter. 1999. "Im Schatten des dritten Reiches: Die beiden deutschen Staaten als postnationalsozialistische Systeme im Zugriff historisch-politik-wissenschaftlicher Forschung und Deutung," in C. Kleßmann, H. Misselwitz, and G. Wichert (eds.), *Deutsche Vergangenheiten—eine gemeinsame Herausforderung.* Berlin: Christoph Links Verlag.

Straughn, Jeremy B. 2009. "Culture, Memory, and Structural Change: Explaining Support for 'Socialism' in a Post-Socialist Society," *Theory and Society* 38(5): 485–525.

Strecker, Ivo, and Stephen Tyler (eds.). 2012a. *Culture and Rhetoric.* New York and Oxford: Berghahn Books.

———. 2012b. "Introduction," in I. Strecker and S. Tyler (eds.), *Culture and Rhetoric.* New York and Oxford: Berghahn Books.

Sühl, Klaus. 1994. *Vergangenheitsbewältigung 1945 und 1989: Ein unmöglicher Vergleich?* Berlin: Brandenburgische Landeszentrale für politische Bildung.

Ten Dyke, Elizabeth A. 2001. "Tulips in December: Space, Time and Consumption before and after the End of German Socialism," *German History* 19(2): 253–76.

Terdiman, Richard. 1993. *Present Past: Modernity and the Memory Crisis.* Ithaca, NY: Cornell University Press.

Thelen, Tatjana. 2009. "Social Security, Life Course and Religious Norms: Ambivalent Layers of Support in an eastern German Protestant Network," in T. Thelen, C. Leutloff-Grandits, and A. Peleikis (eds.), *Social Security in Religious Networks.* New York and Oxford: Berghahn Books.

———. 2011. "Shortage, Fuzzy Property and Other Dead Ends in the Anthropological Analysis of (Post)Socialism," *Critique of Anthropology* 31(1): 43–61.

———. 2012. "Economic Concepts, Common Grounds and 'New' Diversity in the Anthropology of Post-Socialism: Reply to Dunn and Verdery," *Critique of Anthropology* 32(1): 87–90.

Todorova, Maria, and Zsuzsa Gille (eds.). 2010. *Post-Communist Nostalgia.* New York and Oxford: Berghahn Books.

Veen, Hans-Joachim. 2001. "Einheit, Einheit über alles: Das Gerede vom nötigen Zusammenwachsen Ost- und Westdeutschlands führt in die Irre," *Die Zeit*, 13 July.

Verdery, Katherine. 1996. *What Was Socialism and What Comes Next?* Princeton, NJ: Princeton University Press.

———. 1998. *The Political Lives of Dead Bodies: Reburial and Postsocialist Change.* New York: Columbia University Press.

Verdery, Katherine. 2003. *The Vanishing Hectare: Property and Value in Postsocialist Transylvania.* Ithaca, NY: Cornell University Press.

———. 2012. *Secrets and Truths: Ethnography in the Archives of Romania's Secret Police.* Budapest and New York: Central European University Press.

Wagner, Ringo. 2007. *Der vergessene Sportverband der DDR.* Aachen: Meyer & Meyer Sport.

Wagner, Wolf. 1999. *Kulturschock Deutschland: Der zweite Blick.* Hamburg: Rotbuch Verlag.

Wanner, Catherine. 1998. *Burden of Dreams: History and Identity in Post-Soviet Ukraine.* University Park: Pennsylvania State University Press.

Watson, Ruby S. (ed.). 1994. *Memory, History and Opposition under State Socialism.* Santa Fe, NM: School of American Research Press.

Weber, Hermann. 1997. "Rewriting the History of the German Democratic Republic: The Work of the Commission of Inquiry," in R. Alter and P. Monteath (eds.) *Rewriting the German Past.* Atlantic Highlands, NJ: Humanities Press.

Wende, Waltraud. 2000. "Einen Nullpunkt hat es nie gegeben: Schriftsteller zwischen Neuanfang und Restauration—oder: Kontinuitäten bildungsbürgerlicher Deutungsmuster in der unmittelbaren Nachkriegsära," in G. Bollenbeck (ed.), *Die janusköpfigen 50er Jahre.* Wiesbanden: Westdeutscher Verlag.

Williams, Paul. 2007. *Memorial Museums: The Global Rush to Commemorate Atrocities.* Oxford: Berg.

Wittlinger, Ruth. 2006. "Taboo or Tradition? The 'Germans as Victims' Theme in West Germany until the early 1990s," in B. Niven (ed.), *Germans as Victims.* Basingstoke: Palgrave Macmillan.

Wolle, Stefan. 1998. *Die heile Welt der Diktatur: Alltag und Herrschaft in der DDR 1971–1989.* Berlin: Christoph Links Verlag.

———. 2007. "Leben mit der Stasi: das Ministerium für Staatssicherheit im Alltag," in H. Schultz and H-J. Wagener (eds.), *Die DDR im Rückblick.* Berlin: Christoph Links Verlag.

Wolle, Stefan, and Armin Mitter. 1993. *Untergang auf Raten: Unbekannte Kapitel der DDR-Geschichte.* Munich: Bertelsmann.

Wuschig, Ilona. 2005. *Anspruch ohne Wirklichkeit. 15 Jahre Medien in Ostdeutschland.* Münster: Lit Verlag.

Yoder, Jennifer. 1999. "Truth without Reconciliation: An Appraisal of the Enquete Commission on the SED Dictatorship in Germany," *German Politics* 8(3): 59–80.

Zelizer, Barbie. 2008. "Why Memory's Work on Journalism Does Not Reflect Journalism's Work on Memory," *Memory Studies* 1(1): 79–87.

Zigon, Jarrett. 2010. *Making the New Post-Soviet Person: Moral Experience in Contemporary Moscow.* Leiden: Brill.

Films

Bauder, Marc, and Dörte Franke. 2006. *Jeder schweigt von etwas anderem.* Bauderfilm.

Becker, Wolfgang. 2003. *Good Bye, Lenin!* X-Filme Creative Pool.

Benigni, Roberto. 1997. *Life Is Beautiful (La Vita è Bella).* Miramax.

Egger, Urs. 2007. *An die Grenze.* Colonia Media Filmproduktions GmbH.

Haußmann, Leander. 1999. *Sonnenallee.* Communications AG.

INDEX

Note: 'n' denotes chapter notes; italics denote images.

www.ingramcontent.com/pod-product-compliance
Lightning Source LLC
Chambersburg PA
CBHW070921030426
42336CB00014BA/2484